Designing with
FPGAs and CPLDs

Prentice Hall Series in Innovative Technology

Dennis R. Allison, David J. Farber, and Bruce D. Shriver   *Series Advisors*

Bhasker	*A VHDL Primer*
Blachman	*Mathematica: A Practical Approach*
Chan and Mourad	*Digital Design Using Field Programmable Gate Arrays*
El-Rewini, Lewis, and Ali	*Task Scheduling in Parallel and Distributed Systems*
Jenkins	*Designing with FPGAs and CPLDs*
Johnson	*Superscalar Microprocessor Design*
Kane and Heinrich	*MIPS RISC Architecture, Second Edition*
Kehoe	*Zen and the Art of the Internet: A Beginner's Guide, Third Edition*
Lawson	*Parallel Processing in Industrial Real-Time Applications*
Nelson, ed.	*Systems Programming with Modula-3*
Nutt	*Open Systems*
Rose	*The Little Black Book: Mail-Bonding with OSI Directory Services*
Rose	*The Open Book: A Practical Perspective on OSI*
Rose	*The Simple Book: An Introduction to Management of TCP/IP-Based Internets*
Schröder-Preikschat	*The Logical Design of Parallel Operating Systems*
Shapiro	*A C++ Toolkit*
Slater	*Microprocessor-Based Design*
SPARC International, Inc.	*The SPARC Architecture Manual, Version 8*
SPARC International, Inc.	*The SPARC Architecture Manual, Version 9*
Strom, et al.	*Hermes: A Language for Distributed Computing*
Treseler	*Designing State Machine Controllers Using Programmable Logic*
Wirfs-Brock, Wilkerson and Wiener	*Designing Object-Oriented Software*

Designing with FPGAs and CPLDs

JESSE H. JENKINS

Manager, Strategic Marketing and Product Planning
Xilinx Corporation

PTR PRENTICE HALL, Upper Saddle River, New Jersey 07458

Library of Congress Cataloging-in-Publication Data

Jenkins, Jesse H.
    Designing with FPGAs and CPLDs / Jesse H. Jenkins.
        p. cm.—(Innovative technology series)
    Includes bibliographical references and index.
    ISBN 0-13-721549-5
    1. Field programmable gate arrays.   2. Programmable array logic.

I. Title.   II. Series.
TK7895.G36J46   1994   93-44063
621.39'5—dc20   CIP

Acquisitions editor: *Karen Gettman*
Editorial/production supervision: *Raeia Maes*
Cover design: *Wanda Lubelska*
Manufacturing manager: *Alexis R. Heydt*

Figures 6.3a, 6.3b, 6.5, 6.7, 6.10 reprinted with permission from ACTEL.
Figures 5.1, 5.2, 5.3, 5.4, 5.6, 5.7, 5.10, 5.11, 5.12, 5.13, 5.14 reprinted with permission from ALTERA.
Figures 9.5, 9.6, 9.7, 9.8 reprinted with permission from Concurrent Logic, Inc.
Figurs 9.12, 9.14, 9.15, 9.16, 9.17 reprinted with permission from Crosspoint Solutions, Inc.
Figures 8.2, 8.3, 8.4, 8.19 reprinted with permission from EXCELL Microelectronics.
Figures 9.9, 9.10, 9.11 reprinted with permission from Intel Corporation.
Figures 8.5, 8.6, 8.7, 8.9 reprinted with permission from International CMOS Technology, Inc.
Figures 8.13, 8.14, 8.15 reprinted with permission from PLUS Logic.
Figure 2.6b reprinted with permission from Prentice Hall.
Figures 9.1, 9.2, 9.3, 9.4 reprinted with permission from QuickLogic.
Figures 2.1, 3.1, 3.2, 3.3, 3.4, 3.5, 3.6, 3.19, 3.20, 4.9 reprinted with permission from Signetics Company.
Figures 4.1, 4.2, 4.3, 4.4, 4.5, 4.6, 4.7, 8.16, 8.17, 8.18, 8.19, 8.20 reprinted with permission from Xilinx
    Corporation.

Printed in the United States of America

10 9 8 7 6 5 4 3 2

ISBN 0-13-721549-5

PRENTICE-HALL INTERNATIONAL (UK) LIMITED, *London*
PRENTICE-HALL OF AUSTRALIA PTY. LIMITED, *Sydney*
PRENTICE-HALL CANADA INC., *Toronto*
PRENTICE-HALL HISPANOAMERICANA, S.A., *Mexico*
PRENTICE-HALL OF INDIA PRIVATE LIMITED, *New Delhi*
PRENTICE-HALL OF JAPAN, INC., *Tokyo*
SIMON & SCHUSTER ASIA PTE. LTD., *Singapore*
EDITORA PRENTICE-HALL DO BRASIL, LTDA., *Rio de Janeiro*

Contents

Preface

Digital system design has changed a great deal in the last ten years. Today's designers are confronted with many devices from which to choose and a corresponding set of design software to support the devices. To cut through the confusion, designers need a solid understanding of the basics for both devices and software. This book isolates the critical ideas necessary to understand Field Programmable Gate Arrays (FPGAs), Complex Programmable Logic Devices (CPLDs) and their supporting software.

Assuming only a knowledge of switching algebra and basic logic design, Chapter 1 builds up the properties necessary for any FPGA or CPLD to possess. Functionally complete cells, universal cells and routing architectures are introduced. These features, introduced in Chapter 1, motivate the needs that design software must satisfy.

The main ideas of cell placement, routing and simulation are presented in Chapter 2. The next four chapters explore commercial products (PML, LCA, MAX and ACT) in depth. The same format is used for Chapters 3 through 6, so readers can easily compare one architecture to another. Techniques for designing with each architecture are provided using the same small design.

To complement the material provided thus far, Chapter 7 presents a larger design. The design is detailed and cast onto each previous architecture so readers can assess the translation. Also included are simulation sections with general guidelines for simulating.

Chapters 8 and 9 present another eight architectures in less detail using a compressed format similar to that used in Chapters 3 through 6. Chapters 8 through 9 cover Crosspoint Solutions, QuickLogic, Concurrent Logic, ERA, ERASIC, PEEL and PlusLogic devices.

Chapter 10 presents the author's views on benchmarking, as well as an overview of the recent PREP benchmarks and some ideas on design metrics. The use of benchmarks and metrics is a prelude to the methods discussed in Chapter 11 on choosing an FPGA/CPLD. Chapter 11 gives a completely practical method for selecting the best possible device for a specific application.

Chapter 12 summarizes the process of migrating a design from an FPGA to another medium, such as a gate array or standard cell chip. Included are guidelines for successfully "retargetting" a design for higher performance and lower cost. A brief discussion of reconfigurable FPGAs is also given, highlighting the special needs that class of applications has, along with their benefits.

Many of the chapters include problems at the end, and readers are encouraged to do them. Some important design techniques (flip flop merging, one hot encoding, and others) are discussed in the problems so they should be read even if they are not completed.

Technical jargon is an efficient means of conveying information. Every effort was taken to introduce key terms in digital system design when first used. For convenience, a glossary is included at the back of the text. If the reader wishes to explore any ideas in more depth, a list of references is also included.

Any book, even by a single author, is the product of a team of capable and dedicated people. This book is no different in that respect. First, I have to thank my family, Patricia, Jesse and Jennifer. They got less of my attention than they deserved during the writing of this book. Second, there were several friends and associates at different companies who gave time and patience to explain ideas and review the text. Paul Sasaki, Khanh Le, and Bernd Schoning top the list. Khaled El-Ayat and Dennis McCarty of Actel and Peter Alfke of Xilinx also helped. Dennis Allison (HAL Computers) was my series advisor. Dennis helped reslant the book to be more user friendly and target a broader range of designers.

One class of Santa Clara University students suffered through an early manuscript in 1991, and two classes of University of California, Berkeley, extension students followed suit. Each time the material was presented, it improved due to their effort and ideas. Karen Gettman of Prentice Hall and Raeia Maes, the production editor, encouraged me and kept me honest.

Each of us is strongly influenced by our parents and we owe them a debt of gratitude that can never be repaid. Kathryn and Jesse, Sr. encouraged me continuously.

Some of us are fortunate to have other special people influence us. Dr. James A. Howard, my committee chairman at University of California, Santa Barbara, was such a person. Jim taught me at least 90 percent of everything I know about digital system design. Jim loved to teach and he trained thousands in the finer points of the art. I regret Jim did not live to see this text published, but I hope I have passed along some of his ideas and enthusiasm.

Jesse H. Jenkins

1

Anatomy of a Field Programmable Gate Array

1.0 INTRODUCTION

At a recent electronics show, three companies displayed disk controller cards for the new ultra high performance SXSI bus. All three systems fully complied with the current version of the unreleased SXSI specification. All three products were being launched simultaneously, and much money was spent on promotions, technical literature and seminars. One month later, the SXSI specification was released formally and it had changed. Two of the manufacturers had to withdraw their products and go back to the drawing board.

The first manufacturer, Company A, had targeted the extremely low end of the SXSI market, and committed to a gate array-based system. By carefully isolating only the key specifications, that could not possibly be changed in the SXSI specification, Company A's engineers put 90 percent of the design into a dense CMOS gate array and the other 10 percent into high current TTL bus interface logic. When the specification changed, both the gate array and the interface logic needed changing. The result: redesign the board.

The second manufacturer, Company B, had targeted the same low end (and, incidentally, high volume) market. Their strategy was similar, but they used a fast microprocessor and standard logic approach. The idea was that 90 percent of the design would be made with software, and the design sections that needed to be fast and have high current drive would be made from cheap standard logic parts. When the specification changed, the software could not be adapted to meet the speed needs of the specification change. The result: redesign the board.

The third manufacturer, Company C, had targeted the same low end market as Companies A and B. Their approach was to isolate much of the design into an inexpensive microcontroller, with the speed-sensitive protocol logic designed into a Field Programmable Gate Array (FPGA). Cost reduction would be done quickly by transitioning to a semicustom gate array if and when sales proved that the market was viable. The drive logic for the SXSI bus was still standard logic, but Company C carefully chose parts that were pin compatible with several different high current drivers. When the specification changed, Company C simply changed the contents of the FPGA to alter the protocol. Company C then shipped retrofit parts to customers that had already accepted delivery. The result: keep shipping the board, changing FPGAs only.

This story is typical of several success stories today. The bottom line is: FPGAs provide an effective means to get to market fast. Naturally, the story's conclusion would be quite different if all three companies used FPGAs.

Field Programmable Gate Arrays (FPGAs) are dense, programmable logic products that contain enough logic inside to be comparable to gate array products. They are also accompanied by modern design software to make that similarity persist through the whole design cycle. FPGAs, along with Programmable Logic Devices (PLDs), are quickly changing the way that system designers do their jobs.

In this world of cost reduction, it has been argued that FPGAs are too expensive to use for any designs except prototypes—with standard logic or gate array solutions being cheaper. This approach disregards the larger picture where very few systems reach manufacturing levels exceeding 10,000 boards. This number is below the accepted volume at which gate arrays make sense. Others might argue that if so few boards are manufactured, then standard logic makes the most sense. That view disregards the time and expense of redesigning incorrect printed circuit boards (PCBs). It also should be noted that one company's volume production is another company's prototype run.

For instance, a high volume personal computer maker might consider 5000 boards to be a prototype level, because a new system must be quickly sampled at dealers around the world. A manufacturer of integrated circuit testing ovens may never make more than 100 units worldwide. Large, scientific computer manufacturers also seldom produce more than a few hundred units for the highest end models.

Whether used for prototyping or high volume production, FPGAs are here and they are changing the way today's designers approach problems. This book is aimed at helping designers select and design with FPGAs and

Complex Programmable Logic Devices (CPLDs) and recommends useful design tool practices.

1.1 DESIGN FLOW: OLD AND NEW

First, examine the old style of system design. The usual way was to start with a specification, make a block diagram on a blueprint and begin. Sections of the diagram were isolated, then the detail was expanded on each piece until the correct level of logic design occurred. Next, the pieces were integrated. If there was any software to be developed to handle the system, it was specified at this time—at least with a flow chart. Then, a prototype was bread-boarded and debugged with the software, making changes as needed. If this system was part of something bigger, it would be integrated with that system and software. Often, the prototype would not work at full speed and had to be reexamined for bottlenecks.

After the prototype operated satisfactorily, all design changes were made along with a batch of printed circuit boards. The existing prototype could be used to develop a testing program while the PCBs were being built. During PCB fabrication, additional changes were suggested often by the system integration, leading to changes in the already committed PCB. With a lot of luck, multiple PCB design passes were eliminated. However, multiple design passes were usually the norm, not the exception.

The overall design, prototyping and test development time took six to twelve months for designs needing 500 to 1500 ICs. This development phase was a huge portion of the time-to-market cycle. With multiple PCB passes, the cycle stretched two to three years from product concept to product delivery. If the system was to be cost-reduced using gate arrays, another year or more was taken.

Technology changes faster than that. Quick companies were able to get into new market niches, establish market dominance and defend themselves against successors. The design-development pattern shortened to a point where product cycles were now between three and nine months.

A new scenario goes more like this. First, an idea is converted into a specification. The system is then partitioned into large blocks (memories, microprocessors, programmable logic devices, FPGAs/CPLDs and interface logic). A high level description is next formulated, using schematic capture or an abstract design language. The whole system is simulated—replacing the old prototype phase. When simulations appear accurate, a system netlist is extracted and this is used to design a PCB. While the PCB is being manufactured, the simulation is refined. The initial batch of boards is constructed and debugged. Most, if not all, of the changes are made in the system software, the PLDs or the FPGAs. Test procedures are developed from the simulated model of the final board, while PCBs are being fabricated. If the design was formulated well, it could be recast using gate arrays, to maximize profits for high volume production. Much of the simulation and testing developed is used by the gate array version.

Heavy reliance on FPGAs is a valid path to system design. FPGAs permit very fast manufacturing procedures and even quicker design changes, provided they are properly used. The payoff in providing fast time to market is the key to the success of FPGAs. These ideas will be expanded further in this book, but it is first necessary to develop the underlying principles of FPGA operation in order to understand their operation and effective use. To address that task, a quick review of logic design basics is necessary to establish a familiar notation, brush up the basics and revisit some ideas often forgotten. This first chapter will finish with design of a simple FPGA.

1.2 LIGHTNING LOGIC DESIGN REVIEW

It is not the intention of this section to teach switching theory and low level logic design. The book assumes basic knowledge of these theories. This, therefore, is a refresher focusing on material needed to explain FPGAs later. A few general concepts will be reviewed, however.

1.2.1 Switching Algebra

Binary variables can assume one of two values, usually called one and zero. An algebra exists for handling binary variables called Boolean algebra. The real world actually presents continuous values, so it is important to remember that the algebra only holds for a special set of observation times.

Boolean algebra presents a series of standard operations on binary variables that can be performed by electronic logic gates. Figure 1.1 shows the basic logic gates—AND, OR, NAND, NOR, EXCLUSIVE-OR (EX-OR) and INVERT. Other gate functions exist, but may be constructed from the list just described. Each gate function is completely described by a truth table that provides the correct output for all possible binary inputs. Table 1.1 gives a summary of the basic logic functions. The notation "$*$" is used for logical AND, "$+$" for OR and "$/$" for INVERT.

By combining the logic functions, other logic functions are derived. For instance, a NAND function followed by an INVERTER yields the AND function. The EX-OR followed by the INVERT function makes the EXCLUSIVE-NOR (COINCIDENCE) function. This is thought of by having one gate's outputs drive other gates' inputs.

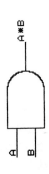

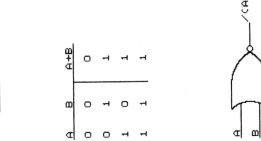

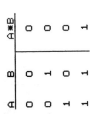
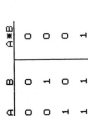

Figure 1.1 Basic logic gates.

TABLE 1.1   Basic Boolean Logic Properties

$$1. \ A * B = B * A$$
$$2. \ A + B = B + A$$
$$3. \ A * (B * C) = (A * B) * C$$
$$4. \ A + (B + C) = (A + B) + C$$
$$5. \ A * (B + C) = A * B + A * C$$
$$6. \ A + (B * C) = (A + B) * (A + C)$$
$$7. \ A * (A + B) = A$$
$$8. \ A + (A * B) = A$$
$$9. \ /(A * B * C) = /A + /B + /C \quad \text{(DeMorgan)}$$
$$10. \ /(A + B + C) = /A * /B * /C \quad \text{(DeMorgan)}$$
$$11. \ A * 0 = 0$$
$$12. \ A + 0 = A$$
$$13. \ A * 1 = A$$
$$14. \ A + 1 = 1$$
$$15. \ A * A = A$$
$$16. \ A + A = A$$
$$17. \ A * /A = 0$$
$$18. \ A + /A = 1$$

The following reviews building functions from primitives by example. Consider a function whose output is a logical one if the majority of its three inputs are logical one. First, construct a truth table that defines all combinations of input and output values (Table 1.2). Second, from the truth table, generate a logical one for each row of the truth table using an AND function and combine the AND function outputs with an OR function. Doing that with two input gates results in a logic diagram like Figure 1.2. Each cluster of two input ANDs decodes a truth table row by generating a logical one for that row alone. Each decoded row is summed with another row using an OR gate, and the overall partial results are logically ORed together. This method

TABLE 1.2   Majority Function Truth Table

A	B	C	F
0	0	0	0
0	0	1	0
0	1	0	0
0	1	1	1
1	0	0	0
1	0	1	1
1	1	0	1
1	1	1	1

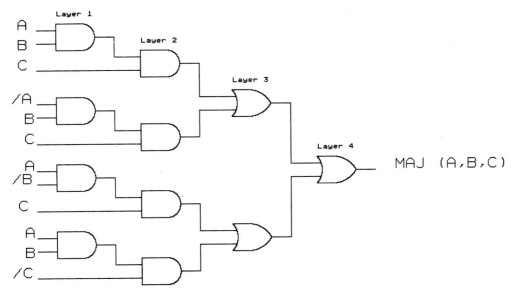

Figure 1.2 Majority function using two input gates.

uses a lot of gates, because the gates are restricted to having only two inputs (like Figure 1.1).

Extending the contents of Table 1.1 (basic Boolean properties) to include gates with more than two inputs is simple. The AND function generates a one only if all inputs are a one and zero otherwise. The NAND is the inverse of the AND. The OR function generates a logical zero only if all inputs are a logical zero and makes a one otherwise. The NOR is the inverse of the OR. Multiple input EX-OR gates are rarely made, but are possible using similar thinking.

The motivation for having wide input gates is one of speed and efficiency. The majority circuit of Figure 1.2 reduces in both gates and logic levels to that shown in Figure 1.3 by using multiple input gates. The new circuit uses less than half the gates and uses half the number of logic layers. A logic layer is the number of gates through which a signal propagates to arrive at the output. The number of layers in Figure 1.3 is two instead of four as in Figure 1.2. Time delay through gates directly affects operation speed, so multiple input gates are faster and more efficient than stacked few input gates. In standard logic families, the largest number of gate inputs was thirteen, so designers learned to stack gates or use PLD products to avoid this restriction. Gates with a large number of inputs are also called "wide gates."

In order to design systematically, a set of rules is needed for manipulating binary variables efficiently. Those rules are the assumptions, definitions,

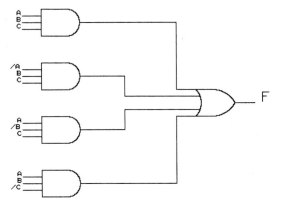

Figure 1.3 Majority function using three and four input gates.

axioms and theorems of Boolean algebra as summarized in Table 1.1. The basic rules are defined for one and two input values, but easily extend to multiple inputs, for wide gates.

Any combinational function can be described by a truth table, then expressed as a Boolean function. The most common function form is the logical sum of products (SOP), as was just shown for the majority function. Another method is to form the logical product of sums (POS). In this method, the function zero entries are made from the truth table, and the logical one entries occur automatically. Most designers excel at one method or the other. TTL and CMOS designers prefer sums of products, but ECL designers most often prefer POS. Because today's FPGAs are either CMOS or TTL oriented using the SOP method, the sum of products formulation is used in this book.

It will not be proven here that any function can be made as a sum of products, but it can be shown. Much of Boolean algebra is focused on manipulating logic functions to reduce the number of gates, number of gate inputs, and number of logic layers needed. Systematic methods exist for minimizing logic functions expressed as two level sums of products. These methods include Boolean Algebra, Karnaugh Maps (graphical), Quine-McCluskey (tabular) and Espresso (computer program). Several computer programs exist that are desirable because the size of logic functions (that is, the number of input variables and product terms) tends to be large. Functions above six variables present a real challenge for most designers to handle.

1.2.2 Functional Completeness

A concept key to understanding FPGAs is functional completeness. Functional completeness is based on accepting that any function can be made from a sum of products. If a single gate type is capable of forming a sum of products—using only that type of gate—it is called functionally complete.

This means any Boolean function can be made from one gate type only. It is particularly advantageous if you have a lot of that gate type.

   In the 1970s, much logic was made of discrete NAND gates, so it was important to build functions from NAND gates—just to debug designs from the scraps of remaining I.C. gates. As design methods changed to use MSI (medium scale integration) and LSI packages—often well underused—this practice occurred less. This will be demonstrated by first showing how the majority function can be built from NANDs. The majority circuit shown before can be logically described as:

$$F(A,B,C) = A*B*C + /A*B*C + A*/B*C + A*B*/C$$

Applying the double inversion rule:

$$F(A,B,C) = //(F(A,B,C))$$

Applying De Morgan's theorems (entries 9 and 10 in Table 1.1) we get:

$$F(A,B,C) = /(/(A*B*C)*/(/A*B*C)*/(A*/B*C)*/(A*B*/C))$$

This expression directly applies to Figure 1.4 which is a five gate, multiple input, all NAND version of Figure 1.2. For two level logic structures, it is usually assumed that variables and their' complements are available, as inputs.

   This example suggests that the NAND gate is functionally complete, because we are able to show that it can make a two level sum of products

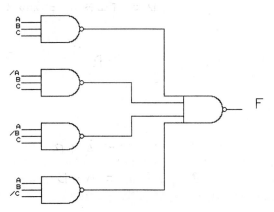

Figure 1.4 Majority function with NAND gates.

expression using only NAND gates. The key necessary qualities for functional completeness are that the gate can make the logical AND with a logical INVERT, or it can make a logical OR with a logical INVERT. Both AND plus OR are not required because De Morgan's theorem shows how these two functions can be made from each other using an additional INVERTER. It is interesting that the AND with OR together are not functionally complete because neither can make the INVERT function.

The usual verification for functional completeness permits tying gate inputs together, to logical zero, or one as needed. A simple demonstration for the NAND gate is to show the AND, OR and INVERT as in Figure 1.5. As an exercise, the reader should determine whether the EX-OR is functionally complete. All FPGAs are built from logic cells that are functionally complete.

1.2.3 Universal Functions

Universal functions or function generators are logic blocks that can be configured to make any logic function of the block inputs. There are several common ones, but the most standard ones are random access memories (RAMS), read only memories (ROMS), programmable read only memories (PROMS), erasable programmable memories (EPROMS), electrically erasable programmable memories (EEPROMS) and multiplexers. All of

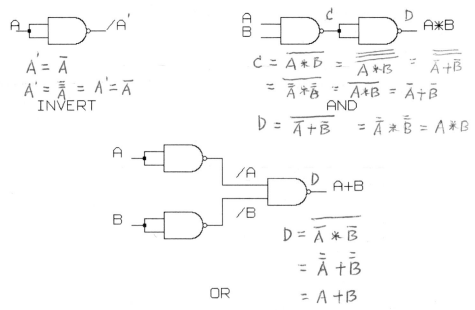

Figure 1.5 NAND is functionally complete.

these blocks can make functions by forming the function truth tables. FPGAs are often made from building blocks that are universal functions.

A multiplexer function can be used to make logic functions in the following way. Figure 1.6 gives a basic four input multiplexer. The truth table for the multiplexer is shown on the figure, but the equation is as follows:

```
DATAOUT = /S1*/S0*D0 + /S1*S0*D1 + S1*/S0*D2 + S1*S0*D3
```

By examining either the truth table or the equation, if we set D0 = D1 = D2 = 0 and D3 = 1, the DATAOUT function will be S1*S0, the logical AND function. Set D0 = 0 and D1 = D2 = D3 = 1, gives DATAOUT equal to S1 + S0, the logical OR. Set D0 = D2 = 1 with D1 = D3 = 0 and DATAOUT becomes /S0. This shows that the multiplexer is functionally complete. The multiplexer is universal because it can form any function of the two input variables S0 and S1 simply by setting the D values in the truth table to be either zero or one. As an exercise, define NAND, NOR, EX-OR and EX-NOR in the multiplexer function.

By similar argument, an eight input multiplexer can make any combinational function of three input variables, a sixteen input multiplexer can make any combinational function of four input variables, and so forth.

A functionally complete cell can form any combinational logic function

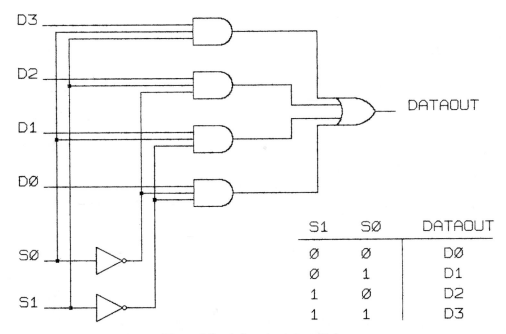

S1	S0	DATAOUT
0	0	D0
0	1	D1
1	0	D2
1	1	D3

Figure 1.6   A four-to-one multiplexer.

from one or more copies of that cell. A universal logic function can do the same, but may require fewer cells. This assumes that the universal cell has enough inputs to be efficient, which may not always be a good assumption, as will be shown later. Some FPGAs use universal cells and others use functionally complete cells as building blocks.

1.2.4 Bigger Blocks

One main element of effective logic design is using efficient logic blocks at a higher level. This approach is necessary to get designs done fast. Standard logic chips exist that select data (multiplex), generate a distinct combination selection (decode) and perform arithmetic (add, subtract, and multiply). Thinking in terms of these bigger blocks permits fast design to the point that most systems designers think in terms of larger blocks. Larger building blocks will be made from small FPGA cells as design techniques become more efficient. Additionally, some bigger blocks fit more naturally into particular FPGA architectures than do others. But, first, storage capabilities must be added to logic cells.

1.2.5 Flip Flops

The real power of logic circuits is greatly increased when memory elements are included with gates to make designs. This permits designs whose behavior changes in time. Most FPGAs include logic cells that combine functionally complete or universal cells with flip flops. Flip flops are memory storage elements, but most people think of RAM when they think of memory. Flip flops or latches store single bits, which can be independently set to store a logic one or cleared to store a logic zero.

There are many types of latches, but the most basic is the cross coupled NAND or NOR latch (Figure 1.7). Although flip flops may be built from gates as shown, they are often built from transistors so that separating out the individual gates among the transistors is hard. The two structures shown in Figure 1.7 are called asynchronous S-R (Set-Reset) latches. Their time behavior is described in the tables shown. The notation is that the S (or /S), R (or /R) are inputs; Q is the binary value of the current output and Q+ is the value that the output will become shortly after getting the current input. The next state of the flip flop, Q+, is a function of the current state (Q) and the current input (S, /S, R, /R). S is called Set and R is called Reset, because of their effect on the Q output.

For crossed NANDs, if /S goes to zero with /R held at one, Q will become one—it sets. If Q is one and /R goes to logic zero (with /S held at one) Q will become zero—it resets. The crossed NOR circuit is similar, but

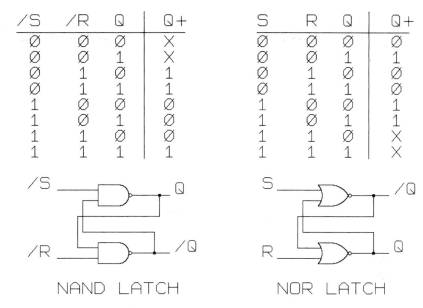

/S	/R	Q	Q+
∅	∅	∅	X
∅	∅	1	X
∅	1	∅	1
∅	1	1	1
1	∅	∅	∅
1	∅	1	∅
1	1	∅	∅
1	1	1	1

S	R	Q	Q+
∅	∅	∅	∅
∅	∅	1	1
∅	1	∅	∅
∅	1	1	∅
1	∅	∅	1
1	∅	1	1
1	1	∅	X
1	1	1	X

NAND LATCH   NOR LATCH

Figure 1.7   Basic set-reset latches.

Q becomes a one if S = 1 and R = 0 and Q becomes zero if S = 0 and R = 1.
Nonbinary behavior occurs for the crossed NAND circuit if /S = /R = 0.
Likewise, nonbinary operation occurs for the crossed NOR circuit if
S = R = 1. These conditions should be avoided.

Adding a synchronizing signal—called a clock—is useful. It permits
time controlled switching of the flip flops and latches, resulting in a systematic design method.

The next step in the flip flop evolution chain is the transparent D-latch.
Several versions of this type cell are shown in Figure 1.8, with corresponding
time-state tables. Note that the two versions with three gates and one
INVERTER all have static hazards shown. This means that it is possible for
the output to change briefly (glitch) to a logical zero when it should remain
a one during state transitions. The augmented design (Figure 1.8C) removes
this glitch by adding an additional gate.

The transparent latch is the simplest synchronized storage cell and is
used mostly to capture and hold data. The latch output tracks the input data
as long as the clock input is held at logic one. This creates problems when
designing sequential machines. For instance, consider three such cells cascaded as in Figure 1.9, forming a primitive shift register. When the clock goes
high, DATIN penetrates cell A landing at QA, enters cell B and finally enters
cell C. If the clock is sufficiently narrow, it may only penetrate A. A little
wider and it passes through to B. Wider still and it gets through C. What if
the clock lowers after data penetrates B but only halfway through C?

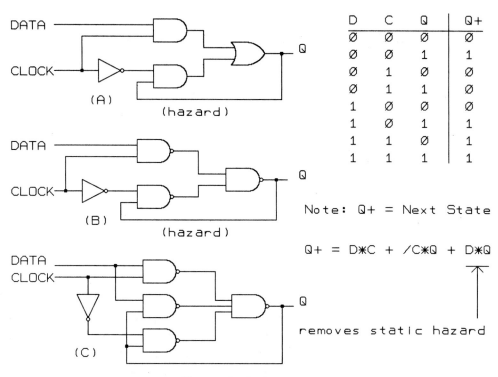

D	C	Q	Q+
Ø	Ø	Ø	Ø
Ø	Ø	1	1
Ø	1	Ø	Ø
Ø	1	1	Ø
1	Ø	Ø	Ø
1	Ø	1	1
1	1	Ø	1
1	1	1	1

Note: Q+ = Next State

$$Q+ = D*C + /C*Q + D*Q$$

removes static hazard

Figure 1.8 Basic D latches.

Inconsistent behavior occurs. To solve problems like this, edge triggering was developed.

Figure 1.10 shows an edge triggered D flip flop, the workhorse of sequential design. Extra gates are included that convert a sufficiently wide clock pulse into an internally controlled narrow pulse. This appears, from the outside world, to initiate state change on the rising edge of the clock, and is called edge triggered. Note the familiar cross coupled NAND gates at the flip flop output. The state table shown in Figure 1.8 gives the basic operation.

By using flip flops, designers have learned to create sequential machines that alter their behavior depending on sequences of applied inputs. Probably the simplest synchronous sequential machine is the shift register. Shift reg-

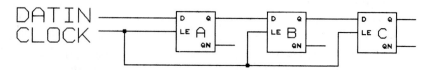

Figure 1.9 Shift register made from transparent latches.

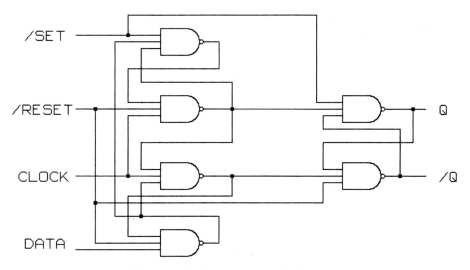

Figure 1.10   Edge triggered D flip flop.

isters are formed by chaining D flip flops together with the Q output of the first one feeding the D input of the next one in a chain that can stretch indefinitely. All flip flops must share the same clock, but a practical limit exists based on the clock skewing as the number of flip flops connected in cascade increases. The primary purpose of a shift register is to capture serial data. This is useful in sequence recognizers, waveform generators, disk controllers, local area networks and universal asynchronous receiver-transmitter (UAR/T) circuits.

Other sequential circuits using flip flops include handshaking interfaces, controllers, and counters. Counter design best illustrates the basic nature of sequential design, and will be developed in Chapters 3 and 4.

1.3 ANATOMY OF AN FPGA

So far, motives for having FPGAs have been discussed and a brief look at logic design has been given.

The operation of FPGAs will now be described. FPGAs are a misnomer—they should not be called "gate arrays" because they seldom are. In fact, the first commercially successful one—the Xilinx LCA—is still formally called the Logic Cell Array (LCA). The term LCA was not readily accepted, however, so the term Programmable Gate Array or Field Programmable Gate Array (FPGA) was coined. Designers then became more interested in these products for what they were—dense programmable products supported with gate array style software.

But what is an FPGA? An FPGA is a collection of functionally complete or universal logic elements placed in an interconnection framework. This has caused a split in the industry today. Some parts look like two dimensional cell arrays with little interconnection channels running horizontally and vertically between the cells. Other parts look more like stacked logic gates with programmable arrays, similar to regular PLDs. To distinguish them, some have called the channelled parts FPGAs and the programmable array parts Complex Programmable Logic Devices (CPLDs). Others have called them channeled and foldback architectures, by describing their interconnection as the distinguishing feature. Yet others have distinguished them using predictable or unpredictable timing as the key feature. This latter distinction occurs because the channelled part's timing is often hard to predict.

These categories are not as neat as might be hoped for, so both will be discussed in this book. They are both very useful, sometimes for very different reasons.

With all of that said, what would these devices look like? Assume a fictitious architecture created from the only universal logic cell discussed so far (in fact, similar to several that do exist). In theory, and possibly in the future, it will not matter what is inside the part—but for now, pack it full of eight-to-one multiplexers similar to the four-to-one muxes discussed earlier. The choice of eight-to-one is appropriate, because three input gates are more efficient than two input ones. The number of inputs to this cell is eleven because there must be three decode inputs selecting among the eight data inputs. This cell is shown in Figure 1.11A, but if the FPGA had only this kind of cell, flip flops would be difficult to make. Gates could only be built out of the multiplexer and then using the gates to make flip flops as shown in Figure 1.10. There would be freedom to make cross coupled latches, transparent D latches, or others, but the price of this freedom is inefficient usage of the multiplexers.

A common practice is to make the universal (or functionally complete) cell directly drive the D input of a regular edge triggered D flip flop, as in a hybrid cell including a D flip flop. This intermediate version is shown in Figure 1.11b, and it still has a problem. This forces all combinational functions to drive D flip flops. The usual way to solve this is to add another multiplexer to the larger cell, permitting the multiplexer to directly drive the D flip flop input, or bypass it and go to the outside world. Now, there is a reasonable building block—from many respects. It can form any combinational function of three input variables, and can form sequential functions that are built from D flip flops. Figure 1.11c shows the final cell, with Figure 1.11d giving a shorthand image. Note that the multiplexer data inputs of Figure 1.11d are not taken outside the cell. Only the clock and four select signals are inputs for forming logic functions, which greatly lessens the number of external connections needed to form logic functions.

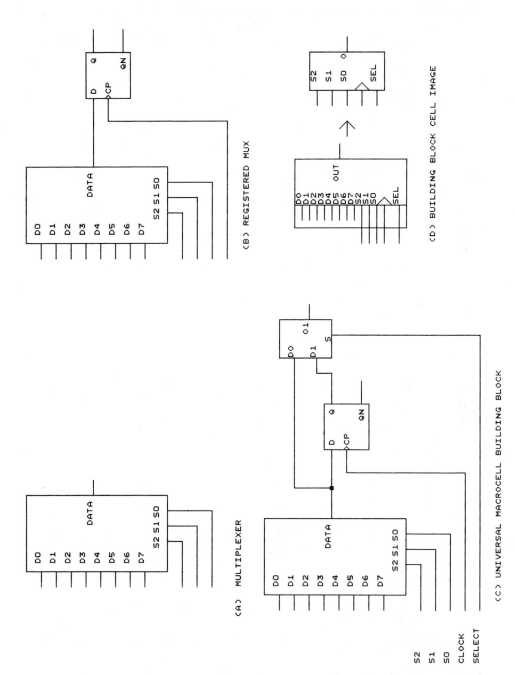

Figure 1.11 Steps in building block design.

(A) MULTIPLEXER

(B) REGISTERED MUX

(C) UNIVERSAL MACROCELL BUILDING BLOCK

(D) BUILDING BLOCK CELL IMAGE

Now, how can the multiplexing cells be connected? Following the above mentioned guidelines, they can be connected in one of two basic styles—by interconnect channels or programmable arrays. Figure 1.12 shows the cells connected with interconnect channels and Figure 1.13 shows them connected by a programmable foldback array. A quick look at how signals pass through will show the basic operation.

Signals enter the structure of Figure 1.12 on the input buffers, passing to the vertical and horizontal lines. Wherever a vertical line and a horizontal line cross, a connection can be made. How that is accomplished will be described in later chapters, but assume it can be done for now. Also assume that the contents of each mux cells data inputs are configured through some means not shown—called the programming circuitry. At this point, input signals can be applied to the select and clock inputs of the appropriate mux cells. The function of the mux cell is internally programmed and the output is presented to more vertical and horizontal lines, for connection to vertical and horizontal lines, and others. Signals from one mux cell output can propagate to the inputs of other mux cells and travel from the left side of Figure 1.12 to the right side. The horizontal lines between the mux cells are convenient paths for signals to skip over mux cells if needed and head to the right, toward the output buffers. When signals finally cross the inputs to the output buffers, they can be connected and exit the FPGA.

The CPLD architecture is shown in Figure 1.13. In this case, the outputs of all mux cells feedback to the inputs of all other mux cells as well as cross the input cells and the output cells. As signals arrive on the input buffers, they pass to the mux cell select and clock inputs, where they can be connected as needed. Again, assume that the contents of the multiplexer data inputs are configured by programming circuitry not shown. Functions of the inputs are formed in the mux cells and larger ones are formed by passing the mux cell outputs back to adjacent mux cell inputs. When the needed functions have been formed, they simply feedback into the array where they are connected to output cells. Figure 1.13 shows a fairly small number of cells in the foldback structure, but this is due to graphic limitations on paper. With today's technology, these cells can number in the hundreds.

Both of these architectures are simple, showing that FPGAs and CPLDs are made using an appropriate logic cell and an interconnect structure capable of forming a large number of different designs. Many critical details have been omitted, for the sake of simplicity. Obviously, there is the problem of how many input, output and bidirectional pins are needed. What about having specialized clock input pins? What is the correct number of vertical and horizontal lines to avoid signal congestion? Should the vertical and horizontal lines be broken into smaller sections to avoid blocking a large path?

The questions to be answered are many, and the most realistic way is

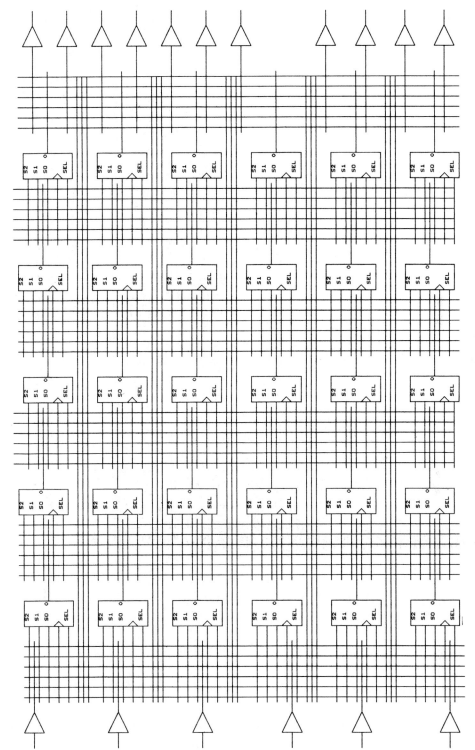

Figure 1.12 Channelled FPGA structure.

19

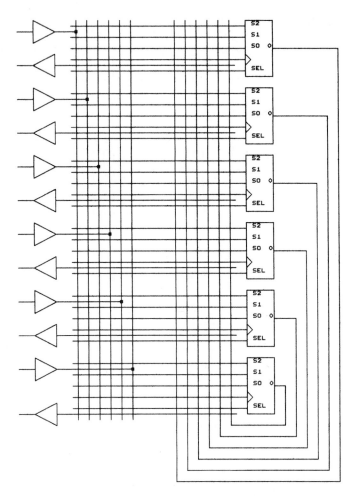

Figure 1.13 Foldback CPLD structure.

to examine some real devices in detail. Chapter 3 starts a series of chapters examining some commercially available parts. First, it is important to understand why design software is necessary to use FPGAs effectively, and this topic is addressed next.

PROBLEMS

1. Show whether or not the two input EXCLUSIVE-OR gate is functionally complete.

2. Show how to make a three input majority function from a four input multiplexer. Show how to make the three input majority from several three input multiplexers. Show how to make a three input majority function from several two input multiplexers.

3. Is the three input majority function functionally complete?

4. Build an eight-to-one multiplexer from the architecture of Figure 1.12.

5. Build a three-to-eight decoder using the architecture of Figure 1.12.

6. Build a four bit adder (that is, two-two bit operands) using the architecture of Figure 1.12. Do the same using Figure 1.13. Use as many parts as needed.

7. Show how to make a serial shift register using the architecture of Figure 1.12. Repeat it for Figure 1.13.

2

Design Software

2.0 INTRODUCTION

The architectures developed at the end of Chapter 1 included identical logic cells placed into a framework of possible connections. Using those architectures requires skillful translation of a designer's desired function into the exact cell and internal connections needed to form the final design. Working the problems at the end of Chapter 1 shows just how tedious that translation can be. This chapter discusses the needed capabilities of design software that automatically translates designs for FPGA architectures.

There are two primary functions FPGA software must perform. First, the software must convert the functions of the design into the functions (cells) supplied by the FPGA. Second, the design software should verify that the translated design is correct. The first function is called translation (sometimes compiling or fitting). The second function is called verification and can be done with design verification software and logic simulation. Both software functions deal with a version of the design called a netlist, which bears some investigation because it is a common circuit representation. Let's look first at the tasks of the translation problem, to assess the damage before proceeding to verification.

2.1 THE TRANSLATION PROBLEM

Figure 2.1 shows a circuit built from NAND gates. Its inputs and outputs are shown clearly. At this point, it is unclear what operation Figure 2.1 performs. It is the same dilemma the translation software would have. Suppose the task is to map the gates of Figure 2.1 onto the architecture of Figure 1.12. How would one proceed? What must be done first?

Unless other constraints are more pressing, assess the chance of the design fitting at the outset. First, count the number of input/output pins and compare the design needs to those pins provided by Figure 1.12. If it matches, or if Figure 2.1 has fewer pins, proceed. If not, ask if two or more parts are acceptable. Assuming it fits the I/O pins, the next concern is whether there are enough logic cells within Figure 1.12 to perform the functions of Figure 2.1. Care must be taken here, because an extravagant translation (or mapping) may not fit.

Looking deeper into the mapping process, a natural approach is to pack each mux cell of Figure 1.12 as full as possible. Remembering that the mux cell can make any logic function of three inputs, scan over Figure 2.1 to isolate groups of gates that fit the three input, one output criteria. Disregard flip flops, although latching circuitry occurs in Figure 2.1. In scanning, seek the biggest gate groups having only three inputs and one output. Bigger and smaller groups will be less efficient, so choosing as many three input groups first should reduce the number of mux cells needed.

An obvious, but frivolous, mapping is to place each gate into its own mux cell. This mapping uses the whole of Figure 1.12 very quickly and should be avoided. Some obvious gate groupings into single mux entries would be the following:

Gates G45 (INVERTER) and G46 (AND);

Gates G41 (NOR) and G40 (AND);

Gates G51 (inverter), G27 (NAND) and G24 (inverter);

Gates G33 (NAND) and G32 (NOR);

Gates that use single mux cells, having three inputs, include gates G37, G35, G10 and G2. Gates requiring at least two mux cells include gates G36, G8 and G9. These are some more obvious expected translations from gates to mux cells.

Gates having more than three inputs need at least two mux cells to form the function. For speed reasons, the best approach is to isolate inputs into the biggest groups of three inputs, then take the outputs of those cells to the inputs of the next mux cell. This approach reduces the number of layers

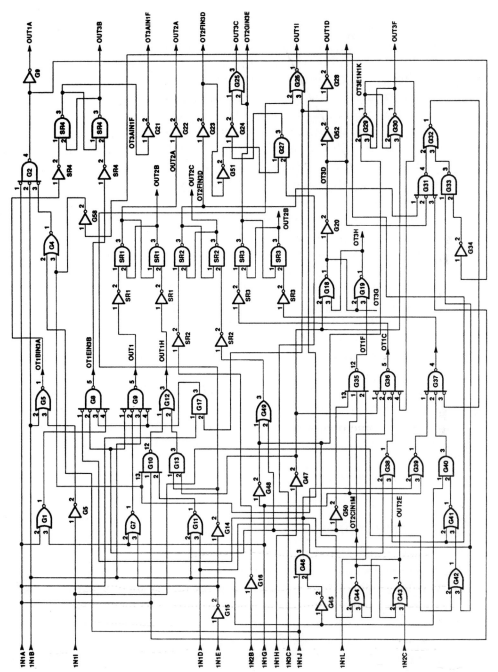

Figure 2.1 Example of a digital design.

25

needed to form the gate function. Speed is gained by reducing the number of mux layers.

By analyzing enough circuits, there will be readily recognizable gate patterns that will or won't fit a mux cell. Soon, it will be possible to develop a strategy of estimating whether a design fits, by dissecting the design into known three input patterns and adding up the pieces. Comparing this to the maximum number of cells tells whether the design will possibly fit the FPGA. This is exactly what the design software does.

The software that translates a target design for a specific FPGA uses a system of rules for function substitutions. At the simplest level, it needs a set of substitutions for the target design gates into equivalent FPGA cells (in this case, a set of mux cells). Then, it needs a strategy for best using the substitution rules.

The translation process is also called compiling. Compilers translate the design from an abstract version (schematic or equations) to a concrete version—a bitmap forming functions and connections. Other operations that are a part of the translation process are technology mapping, placement and routing. Technology mapping includes optimizing, but is basically translating the design into the cells provided by the FPGA. After technology mapping occurs, the cells are assigned to specific locations within the FPGA, and this is cell placement. Once the cells are assigned to specific locations, the signals are assigned to specific interconnect lines. The combination of the rules and the place and route strategy makes a heuristic design compiler, also called a fitter. A new jargon exists for the FPGA world, and the jargon may vary from vendor to vendor.

Once the translation software has scanned the target design and found the needed substitution patterns, it eliminates redundant circuitry. This makes sense, because many designs won't fit the FPGA unless the translation is as tight as possible. Collapsing the design increases the likelihood of a fit.

2.2 NETLIST OPTIMIZATION

Karnaugh maps and Boolean Algebra have traditionally been used to simplify logic designs. Today's software makes use of those techniques, but it also uses netlist optimization. Netlist optimization is design minimization after translating to a netlist.

A netlist is simply a text file showing logic functions and their input/output connections. Table 2.1 shows a simple piece of a netlist. Netlists can describe large functions such as adders, multiplexers, counters or microprocessors. Alternately, netlists can show small functions like flip flops, gates, inverters, switches or transistors. The same format can be used at several

TABLE 2-1 Example Netlist

```
*
NETSTART
*
OUT3 DFF I(OUT3_D,CLOCK) O(OUT3,N_OUT3)
OUT3_D AN2 I(A1,N20_1) O(OUT3_D)
B20_1 INV I(A2) O(N20_1)
OUT2_D OR2 I(N21_2,N21_4) O(OUT2_D)
OUT2 DFF I(OUT2_D,CLOCK) O(OUT2,N_OUT2)
B21_4 AN2 I(N21_3,A4) O(N21_4)
B21_2 AN2 I(N21_1,A2) O(N21_2)
B21_1 INV I(A1) O(N21_1)
B21_3 INV I(A3) O(N21_3)
OUT1 DFF I(OUT1_D,CLOCK) O(OUT1,N_OUT1)
B22_1 AN2 I(A1,A2) O(N22_1)
B22_2 AN2 I(A3,A4) O(N22_2)
OUT1_D OR2 I(N22_1,N22_2) O(OUT1_D)
*
NETEND
*
NETIN A1,A2,A3,A4,CLOCK
NETOUT OUT1,OUT2,OUT3
*
```

Note: DFF refers to a D flip flop; AN refers to the AND function; OR refers to the OR function.

different levels of description, so it is very flexible. A netlist with an embedded counter can be rewritten to have the component gates and flip flops comprising the counter, as an equivalent representation. This is called netlist expansion.

Because equivalent representations can be found, it is possible to apply a set of substitution rules to simplify netlists, eliminating redundant logic functions. The substitution rules and strategy are at the heart of today's netlist optimization software, which often include hundreds of substitution rules.

How a netlist minimizer might handle the decoder is shown in Figure 2.2(A). Note that the decoder has all input pins used, but only two of the eight output pins are used. The minimizer scans the decoder netlist first finding unused outputs (Figure 2.2B), then eliminates the gates that drive them. This permits a new netlist to be made, without the unneeded gates (Figure 2.2C). If there are now any new gates with unused outputs, these are eliminated and the process repeats until no more gates are eliminated. This is just a trivial example of netlist minimization, but simple application of small rules—like eliminate gates with unused outputs—can result in huge payoffs when larger designs are whittled.

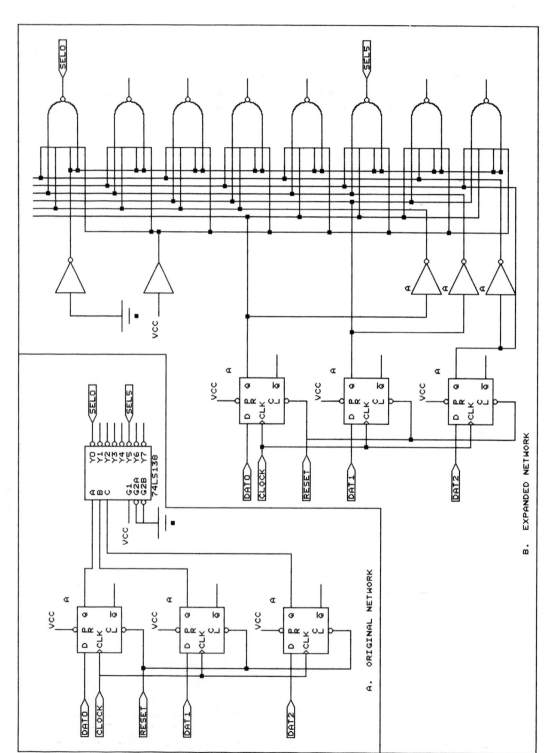

Figure 2.2 Netlist operations.

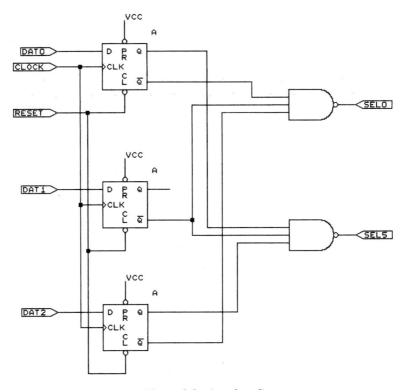

Figure 2.2   (continued)

Modern netlist minimization programs can eliminate unused gates, combine gates performing identical functions, eliminate flip flops, and merge logic functions right into the heart of a flip flop if needed. The rules used by this example are usually not as simple as shown, but they achieve big payoffs.

2.3 CELL PLACEMENT

Once a design has been minimized and translated, it needs to have its logic functions assigned to specific positions within the FPGA framework. This is the cell placement problem, and it is not trivial. If possible, it is preferable to have a computer program do this step because it requires iteration. Manual cell placement may be necessary, but is tedious and often requires several successive arrangements of the functions on the FPGA cells. Algorithms exist permitting pre-analysis of a design for best cell placement, depending upon the adjacency relationships existing among the design functions. In a two dimensional cell array, only a few necessary adjacent cell arrangements can be met, so other cell placements may be less than optimal.

The critical criteria for placement is that the needed connections to other logic cells can be made. Additional requirements are that minimum skew timing paths and other minimum time delays are achieved. There can be many constraints to meet, so several attempts are usually needed to achieve them.

2.4 CELL INTERCONNECTION

Assuming an appropriate placement of the cells occurred, the next step is to connect everything. This is called routing. When routing starts, the netlist is examined for interconnection information, and the placement is inspected. The interconnection software assigns signals from placed cell outputs to target cell inputs. In the example from Figure 1.12, connection occurs on the lines passing between the mux cells. For this simple FPGA, when a metal line has an output signal attached and the other end is tied to another mux cell's input, the metal line is used up. As the connection proceeds, the interconnect lines become occupied and congestion results. When congestion occurs, future connections are blocked and the routing software fails. Then, the software must replace the cells into another arrangement and try routing again.

The result of placement and routing is a design file describing the original design in terms of the FPGA cells. This file has cell position assignments and cell interconnections described for the channel or foldback network. The design file is finally translated to a bitmap that can then be passed to a device programmer to configure the FPGA.

At this point, it is easy to see that the connection architecture of the FPGA is an important consideration, to assess the potential for design connections. Clever software can aid a good connection architecture, but it cannot make connections where none exist. Bad routing software can waste even a good connection architecture. Good FPGA design software is vital.

2.5 CRITICAL PATHS

If any cell could be placed at any site and connected to any other site, the software task would be simpler, but not trivial. Adding to the complexity of finding an acceptable placement and connection is that certain timing relations must be met. Some signals have external requirements such that they must enter the FPGA, perform a logic function and immediately exit the part, to meet the need. This type of action is needed by microprocessor

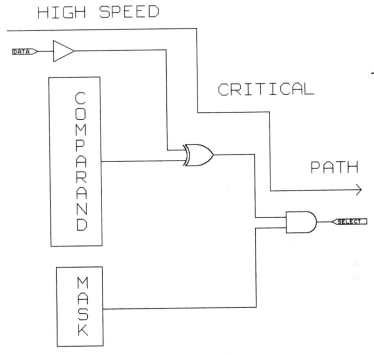

Figure 2.3 Typical critical path.

address decoders and fast comparators similar to Figure 2.3. Other times all of the flip flops in a shift register or counter must reside in adjacent cells within the FPGA, to guarantee near simultaneous clocking. Many timing restrictions can exist, and are called critical paths or critical nets.

Critical paths complicate the placement and routing of a design because they increase the number of additional constraints to meet. The usual handling of critical paths is to place cells on the critical path first, then place the rest of the design. Next, the cells of the critical path are connected to meet the timing needs, and then the rest of the circuit is connected. By placing the critical cells and connecting them first, there are now fewer options for placing and connecting the rest of the design. If too many critical paths are specified, very lengthy placement and routing sessions can be expected. It is best to keep critical paths to the absolute minimum.

2.6 DESIGN VERIFICATION

If the design was correctly translated, minimized, placed and routed, there is no real need for design verification. However, there are often bugs and quirks in the translation, minimization and connection process that must be identified and addressed. Design verification helps identify and resolve these.

The most common design verification tools are simply software that examines the transformed netlist and analyzes ordinary properties of the final design. For instance, a design rule checker can isolate the output of a cell and count the number of other cell inputs being driven from it. Each driven cell contributes to a cumulative load resulting in a time delay attached to the driving cell's output. Too many driven cells can give unacceptable time delays, so the designer may have to intervene and split a load among several identical driving cells. Another standard check is for unattached cell inputs which float and have noise problems. A third category is to identify cell outputs that are tied directly together, with no three-state capability. Many of these checks are incorporated into the translation packages, while other software includes design rule checking in the simulation section.

2.7 LOGIC SIMULATION

Logic simulation is the tool of choice for assessing the functionality and the timing performance of an FPGA design. In any type of simulation, a model of the logic network is created and it is driven by a model of the input signals—called stimuli—to create a model of the output signals—called responses. A key property of simulation is that it permits observation of internal logic responses when those responses may not be observable at the device pins. Debugging without simulation is akin to debugging a large digital system while only looking at the edge connector of a printed circuit board. Such debugging is possible, but difficult.

There are several kinds of logic simulation, and each offers important advantages. First, there is functional simulation that models the logic cells of the design and combines them with a model of the binary inputs (voltages) to make a relative response model (again voltages). The advantage of this kind of simulation is that it gives results back quickly, and simplistically. The disadvantage of this type of simulation is that it doesn't provide accurate, detailed timing—only relative relationships among signals. As suggested earlier, if the FPGA compiler places and connects the cells in interesting and mysterious ways, many timing changes occur that must be assessed. Functional simulation will not be much help here.

The second kind of simulation that is the most often used is digital timing simulation. In this kind of simulation, a model of the whole design is made by interconnecting cell models, but an additional element is associated with each cell model output—a time delay variable. Naturally, a real design model is made of hundreds or thousands of cell models, each with its own separate time delay.

The cell time delay is composed of three factors. The first factor is simply the time delay of the cell, without any external connections. This delay is actually two delays for most cells—a time delay as the cell output transitions from logic one to zero and a different delay when it transitions from zero to one. It is customary to specify these delay values in the FPGA data sheet. The second factor is the time delay associated with the routing capacitance of the metal connecting metal driving cell output to the driven cell inputs. The third factor is the sum of the driven cell input impedances. Some simulation models break this down even further, while others lump the last two time delay factors into a single value. During the simulation, each cell is assigned a time delay reflecting its interconnection context. The digital timing simulator is much more complex than the functional simulator.

The third category of simulator is the fault simulator. In this simulator, special techniques are used to provide a score (called a fault grade) for the design and the applied stimuli. The goal of fault simulation is to help designers make simulations that test every aspect of a design, according to industry standard criteria. The approach here is to make artificial problems with the design (called faults) and see if the resulting simulation responses appear different from responses from the correct design. Basic fault simulation is done by simply holding various cell outputs low (stuck at zero) or high (stuck at one), while the stimuli are applied to the model. This process is not done for all nodes at once, but can be done for several at a time if they are sufficiently independent of each other.

Fault simulation requires multiple simulation runs to calculate a fault grade. Such a tedious series of repeated simulations takes much computer time. For this reason, a great deal of work has been done to make fault simulation efficient and fast.

The work horse of FPGA design is digital timing simulation, which will be explored in more detail in the next section. Because of their simplicity, smaller PLDs (Programmable Logic Devices) have been well served by functional simulation, which provides no exact timing information. Large ASIC (Application Specific Integrated Circuit) designs need fault simulation to guarantee that the input stimuli adequately test the design. Fault simulation is definitely worth learning, particularly if the intention is to migrate the FPGA design to an ASIC. Digital timing simulation will now be explored in more detail.

2.7.1 Digital Timing Simulation: A Close-up

Figure 2.4 is a flow chart for a digital simulation program. The simulator uses several modules that consecutively refine input data into output data, like most programs. The input data consists of two parts. First, there is a model of the design to be simulated, which is a variation of the previously men-

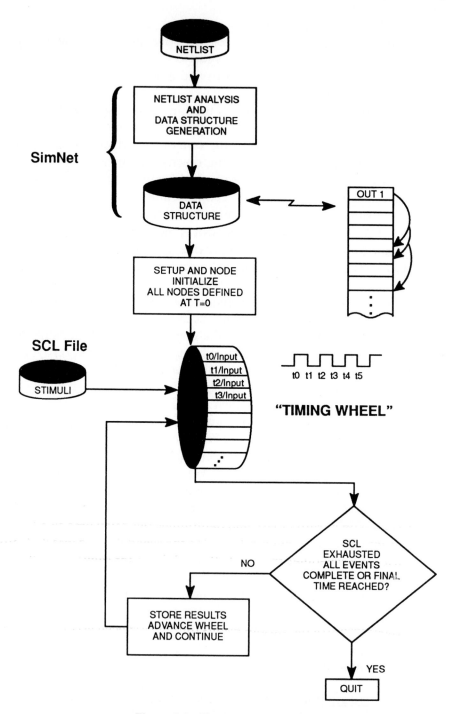

Figure 2.4   Simulation flow chart.

tioned netlist. Modifications are made to suit the needs of the simulator. Second, there is a model of the input stimuli. The stimuli model represents input voltage patterns versus time.

The simulator applies the stimuli to the model of the design. The job of the simulator is to make a model of the resulting outputs. Because the input stimuli are a sequence of binary numbers, they are called input vectors. Likewise, the output response sequence is called output vectors. Under certain conditions, the simulation input and output vectors can be used by an electronic tester, to test that the FPGA operation precisely mirrors the simulated behavior. When that occurs, the input and output vectors are called jointly "test vectors."

What the simulator does is straightforward. However, simulation requires much coordination, and several internal data structure lists. A primary portion of the simulator keeps a model of time and maintains a list showing when the next simulation event will occur. This module is called the scheduler. A simulation event is simply the occurrence of a netlist node making a binary change from one value to another. Nodes are internal gate outputs, flip flop outputs, primary inputs or primary outputs. If the node changes were simply binary, a transition would be from a logical one to a zero or vice versa. Real electronics is more complex than simple binary values can represent, so modern simulators model more realistic events than just binary transitions on the nodes. These will be discussed shortly.

2.7.2 Scheduling

The scheduler keeps a list of times and events, consecutively dispatching events for evaluation when their time comes. The recipient of the dispatched event is an evaluation module that assesses the logic conditions for the selected event. The evaluation module generates new values for the node (based on a truth table), and determines the delay time to accomplish a new event. The new event is returned to the scheduler and inserted into the event list. The scheduler then sorts through its event sequence and finds the next event to dispatch. The process repeats until the input vectors are exhausted or some predetermined stop time (user defined) occurs.

The scheduler has classically been a module that handles the time relationship of the various events through a special list called a "time wheel." In the time wheel, events are inserted as needed and removed when dispatched. The wheel essentially rotates as time progresses. The time wheel approach is quite efficient.

An alternative approach to handling time is to increment a time variable and determine whether anything is scheduled to occur. If nothing occurs, time is incremented and the question is asked again. This is like a polling procedure and is called time driven simulation.

The time wheel permits "event driven" simulation, which is faster than time driven simulation. Events occur seldom, so much computation is saved by not querying repeatedly whether any events occurred. It is more efficient to evaluate logical operations and determine when one evaluation triggers another event. Sorting the time wheel determines what will happen next. An efficient time sorting algorithm is used, as well as a flexible data structure to store events in time order.

2.7.3 Evaluation

The evaluation module is also straightforward. The simulator has a library of functions and each entry in the library has a routine that evaluates a truth table. Unlike an ordinary truth table, the entries in a simulation truth table reflect more realistic electrical conditions. Examples of these conditions are three-state outputs, unknown states, and time persistence. Some simulators allow each node to exhibit more than twelve different node conditions. The more states represented, the more accurate the simulator is. Also, the more possibilities that exist, the longer the simulation runs.

Figure 2.5 shows a small, but adequate, truth table for a simple NAND function model of the five-state variety. A normal binary NAND gate truth table has only four table entries for a two input gate. This truth table has twenty-five entries because the inputs to the gate are allowed to have five

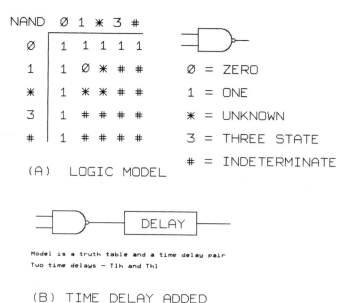

Figure 2.5   NAND gate simulation model.

possible values per input. In Figure 2.5, the inputs may be the usual binary one and zero values, but they also may be unknown, three-state or indeterminate. The unknown condition might arise in a real life situation if the gate input was coming from a flip flop whose output was not known—say at power-on time. The three-state input could occur if this NAND gate was driven by a high impedance previous gate output. The indeterminate input condition could occur if two three-state buffers were driving the same node with a wire AND node and one buffer is releasing its drive while the other asserts.

With just five states for a two input gate creating this much complexity, one can appreciate how a flip flop built from these gates might be interesting. The thing to remember is more states give greater accuracy, but take more evaluation time.

2.7.4 Modeling

Trends in simulation include highly efficient Behavioral Language Models (BLM). BLMs are simply evaluation modules that generate correct output responses to a given input stimulus. BLMs have no one-to-one relationship to a simple gate building block. A BLM is a procedure written to react correctly to a stimulus, but contains no particular gate model. The simplest BLM to consider is that of a D flip flop. The code listing shown in Figure 2.6a gives a D flip flop BLM. This code listing is a D flip flop model written in VHDL (VSIC Hardware Definition Language) which has been optimized for transportability among many computer design environments.

Details of the VHDL primitives used and their capabilities are beyond the scope of this text. The reader can see that the model is a code listing with a recognizable clock, clear, Q output and D input designator. For additional information, see the text by Armstrong referenced in the caption for Figure 2.6a.

Figure 2.6b shows a six gate version of the same flip flop, which will behave similarly, within the simulator. The gate version involves multiple successive evaluations of the NAND gate model at its truth table level.

Figure 2.6c shows a portion of an exotic BLM for a D flip flop written in a PASCAL type high level language. Added sophistication can check for race conditions, setup violations and oscillations.

The advantages and disadvantages of each approach are debatable. The BLM approach allows internal checking for setup and hold time violation within the routine evaluating the flip flop operation. The gate version requires an external function be attached to the model checking setup and hold time requirements. The BLM usually evaluates fast, but does not show the internal flip flop operation—remaining a black box. The gate version permits

```
EDGE_TRIGGERED_D: block (CLK = '1' and not CLK'STABLE
                                    or CLR = '1')
   begin
   Q <= guarded '0' when CLR = 1; else
   D when CLK = '1' and not CLK'STABLE else
   Q;
   end block EDGE_TRIGGERED_D;
```

Figure 2.6a   VHDL flip flop model.

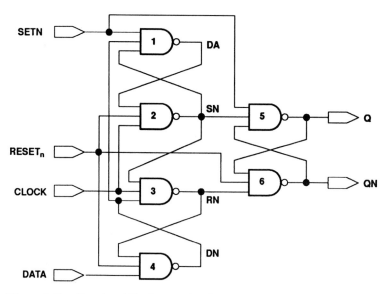

Figure 2.6b   Gate level flip flop model. (James R. Armstrong, *Chip-Level Modeling with VHDL,* © 1989, p. 50. Reprinted by permission of Prentice Hall, Englewood Cliffs, N.J.)

complete dissection of the module operation, requiring greater simulation time.

Each approach has its benefits. In particular, the gate level model permits thorough fault grading. Usually, large functions are modeled as BLMs, and smaller ones by gate structures.

2.7.5 Libraries and Convenience Features

To allow rapid simulation and minimize user interactions, simulator vendors provide libraries of simulation models with the building blocks needed to handle most designs. These libraries always include the basic gates, flip flops, inputs, outputs, transceivers and several additional functions.

It is mandatory to offer many convenience features. Convenience fea-

```
PROCEDURE d_ff_ck;
VAR clock_val,d_val : INTEGER16;
    rec_ptr        : ^rec_t;
BEGIN
  rec_ptr := qsim_instance_ptr^.user_data_area;
  WITH qsim_instance_ptr^:i, rec_ptr^:r DO
    BEGIN
    clock_val := qsim_con_value[i.d_ff_i_ck^^.bits[0];
    d_val := qsim_con_value[i.d_ff_i_d^^.bits[0]];
    IF clock_val = qsim_unknown THEN
      BEGIN
        qsim_drive_delay_output(i.d_ff_o_q,CHR(qsim_unknown));
        qsim_drive_delay_output(i.d_ff_o_q_,CHR(qsim_unknown));
      END;
    IF (clock_val = qsim_one) AND (r.old_clock = qsim_zero) THEN
      BEGIN
        qsim_drive_delay_output(i.d_ff_o_q,CHR(d_val));
        qsim_drive_delay_output(i.d_ff_o_q,CHR(4-d_val));
      end;
    r.old_clock := clock_val;
    end;
end;
```

Figure 2.6c Portion of a BLM flip flop model.

tures include the ability to alter the time delay of internal nodes, perform stimuli subroutines, catch glitches, flag race conditions, and permit incremental simulation. These features allow designers to operate efficiently and focus on details of design and debug.

2.7.6 Back Annotation

The process of altering the time delay of internal nodes is called back annotation. Back annotation is not a convenience, it is essential. The initial simulation model is simply the design netlist. Before the design is placed and routed, the time delays are unknown from one point on the FPGA to another. Once the design has been placed and routed, precise time delays become known. Design software calculates internal node time delays using circuit laws, metal lengths, dielectric constants and other parameters. This is the delay extraction process mentioned earlier.

Using the delay calculations, the software forms a node by node delay annotated netlist for the circuit, by altering the original netlist. This is back annotation. A subsequent simulation using this altered netlist is extremely accurate. This simulation can show trouble spots within the design that are not observable from the outside world. Back annotated simulation permits designers to literally "peel the onion" and step inside the silicon.

As an illustration of simulation and back annotation, the two diagrams shown in Fig 2.7 give a simple six NAND gate D flip flop. The top diagram shows the NANDs modeled with unit (1 nanosecond) time delays and the bottom diagram shows the same simulation with back annotation to include metal delays. The simulations are obviously not identical, but both may be suitable for a wide range of specifications. The most observable timing skew appears between corresponding SETN and Q signals.

This completes a quick look into the details of digital logic simulation. Whole textbooks have been written on this topic, but this book focuses only on the basics needed to understand FPGA and CPLD simulations.

2.8 AN FPGA FLOW

Figure 2.8 shows an elementary FPGA flow. The important steps are design capture, simulation and compiling. A natural sequence is to capture the design using schematics or equations with the software automatically extracting a netlist description of the design. The netlist passes then to the simulator for functional checking, to determine that the correct function was captured. Once this is determined, the design is compiled.

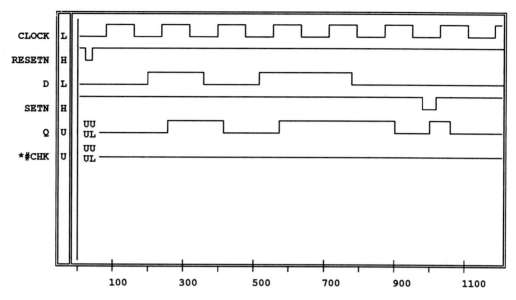

Figure 2.7a Flip flop simulation with unit time delays.

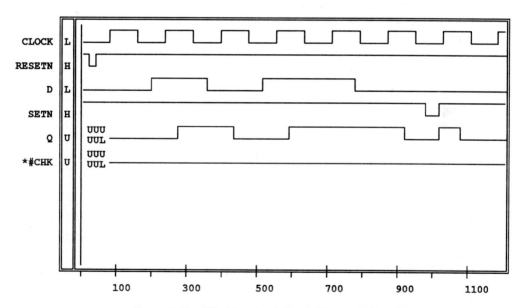

Figure 2.7b Flip flop simulation with actual time delays.

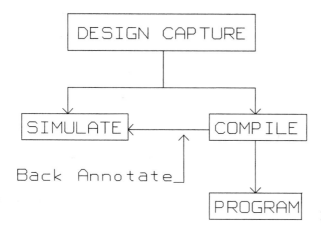

Figure 2.8 FPGA design flow.

The compilation process was mentioned before, and consists of placing and connecting cells to get the final FPGA configuration. Once the design has compiled, analysis software extracts the intercell connection time delays and back annotates the simulation netlist. If the annotated simulation operates to expectation, the design should work when the compiled design file is programmed into the FPGA. Unless serious bugs exist in the software, this flow works, and is at the heart of every FPGA flow discussed here.

2.9 SYSTEMATIC DESIGN FEASIBILITY ANALYSIS

At the beginning of this chapter, a logic diagram was examined (Figure 2.1) to determine whether it might fit into an FPGA or not. Analysis is usually done by partitioning the design into chunks that meet a desired pin count and capacity value. If the design must fit into one FPGA, then the input/output pins for the FPGA are simply those of the design. If the design can be put into several FPGAs (or even a few PLDs and logic chips), there are more tradeoffs to be made.

A single FPGA design can be advantageous from the viewpoint that only one chip must be purchased, tested and used. Several FPGAs may be desirable because it is possible to exploit specific characteristics of different FPGA families that are valuable and unique. No matter which approach is taken, after an initial partitioning and approximate pin assignment, an estimate of the design's capacity is needed.

Design capacity estimation is simply the process of tallying the design contents when its functional blocks are translated to equivalent FPGA cells. This is most often done using a table of equivalent cells at an MSI (medium scale integration) level. Table 2.2 is such a table for common logic functions such as gates, flip flops, counters, shift registers and decoders. These functions are the ones that most systems designers commonly use, and a similar table is provided in each succeeding technology chapter.

Manufacturer provided tables are interpreted using their cell libraries of equivalent functions. Care must be taken when using the tables from several viewpoints. First, the tables do not include full information about the function. An entry that states "four bit counter" may be a four bit synchronous up counter or a four bit ripple counter. Check these entries closely. Some manufacturers also give a four bit up/down counter while others may only give cell capacity for a four bit up counter. Similar comments can be made for decoders and multiplexers, where the data entering the function block may be inverted at the output for some manufacturers and uninverted for others.

Once the tables are understood, association of the target design to the tables must be done and an equivalent cell tally obtained. This is not conceptually difficult, but accuracy is important. The tables are never as complete as might be hoped, but common sense lets a tally proceed quickly. For instance, if the design needs a fourteen bit down counter, and the table has

TABLE 2.2 Mux Cell Equivalent Counts

Digital Function	# Mux Cells
1. Logic Gates (1–3 inputs)	1 cell
2. Logic Gates (4–5 inputs)	2 cells
3. Logic Gates (6–7 inputs)	3 cells
4. D Flip Flop	1 cell
5. D Latch	2 cells
6. JK Flip Flop	2 cells
7. Decoders	
2:4	4 cells
3:8	8 cells
8. Multiplexers	
2:1	1 cell
4:1	2 cells
9. Comparator (equality)	
2 bit	1 cell
4 bit	2 cells
10. Registers	
4 bit	4 cells
8 bit	8 cells
11. Counters	
2 bit	4 cells
4 bit	7 cells

entries for two and four bit up counters, an estimation can be made by tallying pieces and using tricks. Cells for three, four bit up counters cascaded with one, two bit up counter can be used. The assumption is that the /Q outputs of the up counters suffice to provide the down counting function. If a thirteen bit counter had been chosen, three, four bit counters cascaded with a flip flop and some gates would suffice.

In some design situations, an estimation of a design piece is obtained best from the design software. A bigger function is captured and the netlist optimizer collapses out unused pieces. This function is compiled giving the cell count that must be adjusted if the function has no I/O cells. This approach is seldom needed, and most designers are satisfied with a simple pencil and paper tally of the cells.

Once the cell capacity is tallied and the I/O pins are known, selection is based on other criteria—usually speed or price. It should be kept in mind that the tally is optimistic, because congestion can occur in a design, making it necessary to have more capacity available than will be used. Knowledge of the cell and interconnect architecture for the FPGA come into play at this point. Many manufacturers give guidelines such as: only target 80% or less cell usage. Some highly structured designs such as large shift registers or stacked parallel registers may not congest as easily and obtain nearly 100 percent utilization. Ordinary "glue logic" appears as if it were random, and may plug up the available connections very quickly. Again, only experience will help here.

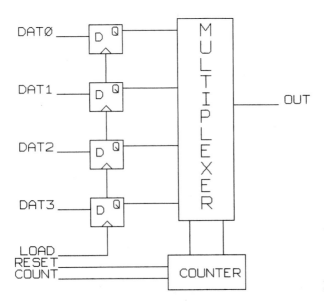

Figure 2.9   A small example.

PROBLEMS

1. Using Table 2.2, estimate the number of mux cells needed to design Figure 2.1.

2. Using Table 2.2, estimate the number of mux cells needed to design Figure 2.9.

3. Verify the comparator entries of Table 2.2. Show the needed mux cell configurations.

4. Verify the counter entries of Table 2.2. Show the needed mux cell configurations.

5. How many mux cells are needed to make a twelve input NAND gate?

3

Programmable Macro Logic

3.0 INTRODUCTION

This chapter describes Programmable Macro Logic, the first of several commercial products. Developed at Philips Semiconductors in the mid-1980s, PML was introduced to increase integration beyond the abilities of ordinary programmable logic devices. In addition to describing how this architecture operates, examples are shown of simulation, fault simulation, and design migration from one part to another. More detail on design estimation also is given. Many of these ideas will be used in later chapters for other architectures.

3.1 PROGRAMMABLE MACRO LOGIC

Programmable Macro Logic or PML™, is a family of programmable devices based on a foldback NAND gate building block. PML is offered in both bipolar and CMOS technologies. Bipolar PML uses a vertical AIM diode for programmed interconnect and CMOS PML uses an EPROM cell.

The foldback NAND structure is different from conventional PLD products which cascade logical AND gates into logical OR gates. In PML, every internal NAND gate can be connected to every other NAND gate

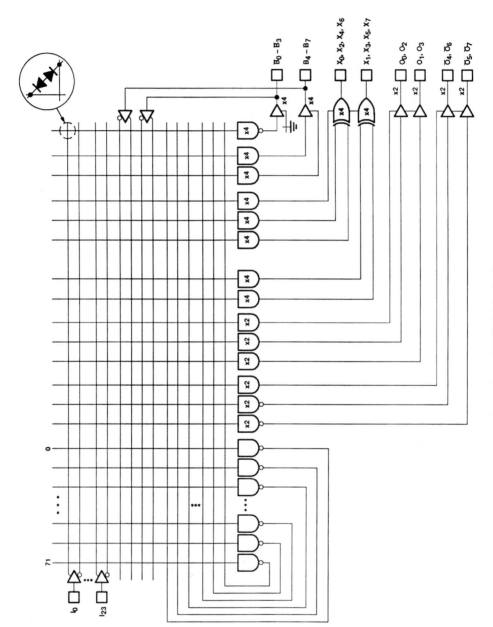

Figure 3.1 PLHS501 logic diagram.

48

within the programming array. High gate connection occurs because each NAND input has a possible connection to all other gate outputs. This results in an array of very wide NAND gates with complete connectivity. Functions may be nested within the structure before signals exit to the outside world through the package pins.

The choice of a NAND gate is appropriate because it is functionally complete and may be used to generate any Boolean logic function. The PML

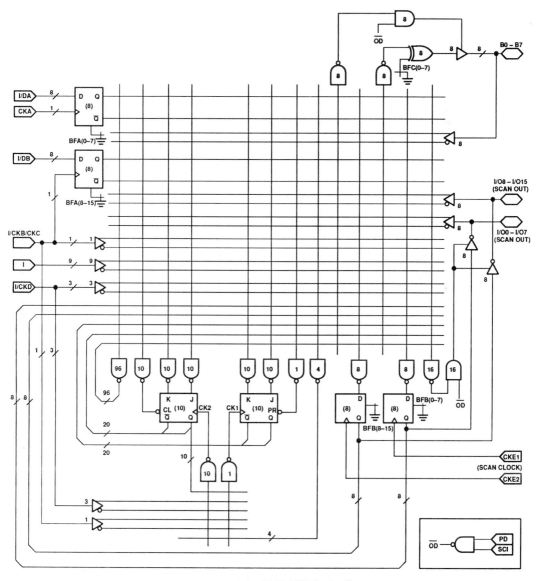

Figure 3.2   PML2552 logic diagram.

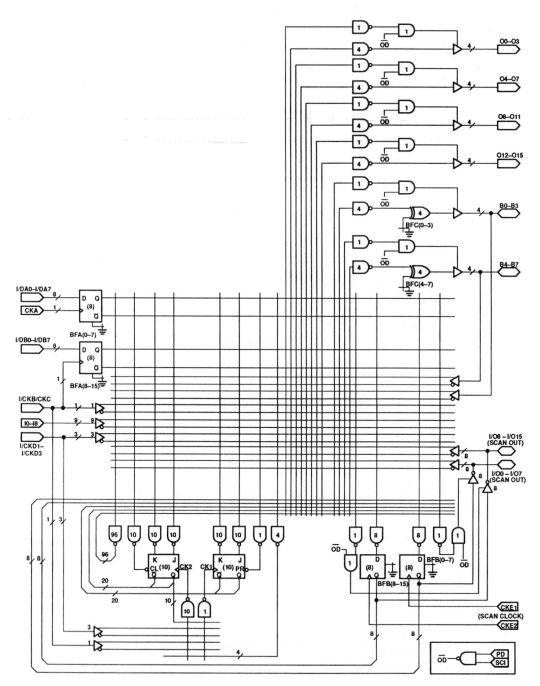

Figure 3.3   PML2852 logic diagram.

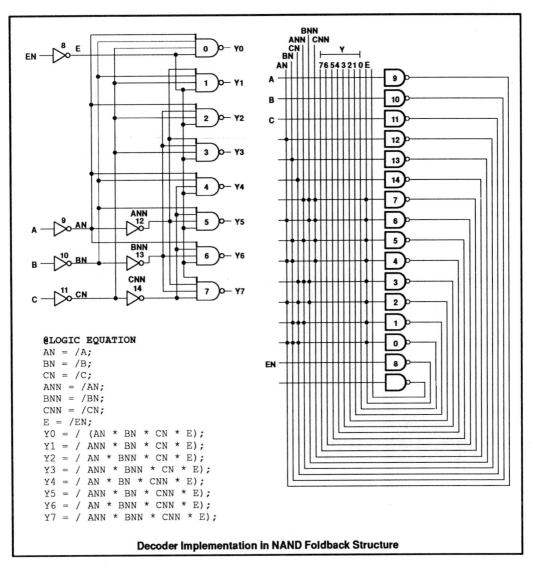

@LOGIC EQUATION
```
AN  = /A;
BN  = /B;
CN  = /C;
ANN = /AN;
BNN = /BN;
CNN = /CN;
E   = /EN;
Y0 = / (AN  * BN  * CN  * E);
Y1 = / ANN * BN  * CN  * E);
Y2 = / AN  * BNN * CN  * E);
Y3 = / ANN * BNN * CN  * E);
Y4 = / AN  * BN  * CNN * E);
Y5 = / ANN * BN  * CNN * E);
Y6 = / AN  * BNN * CNN * E);
Y7 = / ANN * BNN * CNN * E);
```

Decoder Implementation in NAND Foldback Structure

Figure 3.4   Foldback NAND gate decoder.

architecture permits very deep function nesting, but the very wide NAND gates permit efficient two level functions to be easily generated. The key to PML optimization is trading off width and depth of gating, as functions are formed.

Figure 3.1 depicts the PLHS501, which is a NAND only part. Figure 3.2 shows the PML2552, which is the first family member made from CMOS. Figure 3.3 shows the PML2852, the largest PML part. Each part is successively more dense in function, and the package pins expand from 52 to 68 to 84 going from the PLHS501 to the PML2552 and PML2852, respectively.

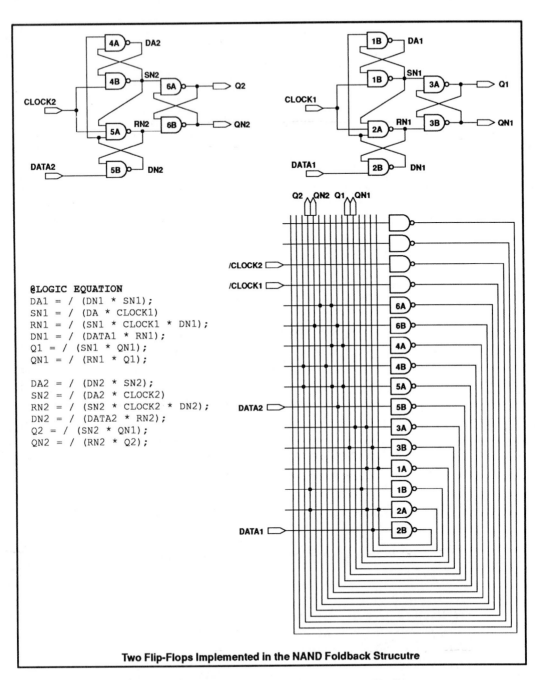

@LOGIC EQUATION
```
DA1 = / (DN1 * SN1);
SN1 = / (DA * CLOCK1)
RN1 = / (SN1 * CLOCK1 * DN1);
DN1 = / (DATA1 * RN1);
Q1  = / (SN1 * QN1);
QN1 = / (RN1 * Q1);

DA2 = / (DN2 * SN2);
SN2 = / (DA2 * CLOCK2);
RN2 = / (SN2 * CLOCK2 * DN2);
DN2 = / (DATA2 * RN2);
Q2  = / (SN2 * QN1);
QN2 = / (RN2 * Q2);
```

Two Flip-Flops Implemented in the NAND Foldback Strucutre

Figure 3.5 Foldback NAND gate D flip flops.

The basic design approach is that logic functions are made from the NAND gates. Cascaded connections are made in the foldback array. Signals arrive on the input pins, pass to the foldback array where logic occurs and finally exit at the output pins. Figure 3.4 shows how a three-to-eight decoder is formed in a piece of foldback NAND array, where input signals A,B,C and EN come into the array, and each of eight NAND gates decodes a distinct pattern. Each inverter and NAND gate is labeled, so the translation to NAND gates is clear. The equations for the decoder are also shown in the figure. Figure 3.5 shows how flip flops similarly can be built from the NAND gates in another piece of a foldback NAND array. Equations are also shown for the D flip flops, using SNAP notation, which will be discussed shortly. For the PML2552 and PML2852, flip flops are available, but additional ones may be made from the NAND gates, if needed.

3.2 A LOOK INTO THE NAND ARRAY

The basic NAND gate for PML parts is very wide, with all foldback gates having over a hundred inputs. The usable number of inputs can be derived from the logic diagrams, by tally. In Figure 3.1, the NAND gate contained within the foldback array has twenty-four inputs coming from the input pins. These, coupled with seventy-two inputs from neighboring NAND outputs, get tallied along with the eight possible inputs from the bidirectional pins. This totals to 104 inputs on each internal NAND gate (Figure 3.6). Figure 3.2 shows the similar arrangement for the PML2552, with a few more foldback NANDs, and additional flip flop outputs folded back. The PML2552 NAND gates have 258 inputs. The NANDs in the PML2852 array have over 258 inputs. These wide input gates are logically efficient and can take full advantage of logic minimization methods.

While not all of the PML gate inputs are used, the potential to make only one or two level logic functions exists. Previous logic solutions required deep gate cascading, due to relatively few available gate inputs. PML can avoid deep nesting in most cases. As an example, PML can generate very wide adders in only two levels of logic—skipping the usual carry lookahead gate cascade. By making the truth table for the adder as a simple sum of logical products, the PML solution is fast. Conversely, the adder could be made by building a two or four gate macro with carry lookahead, to save gates. Either approach is possible. Obviously, wide input gates easily make large input multiplexers and high resolution address decoders.

As shown before, flip flops can be easily made with NAND gates, so the PLHS501, having no flip flops, can be thought of as a sequential device. Shifters, counters and other state machines are possible with lots of design

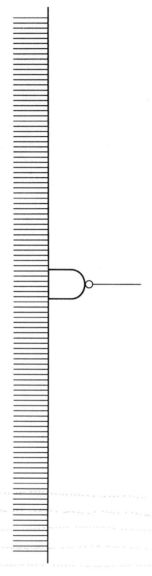

Figure 3.6 Smallest PML foldback NAND gate.

freedom. One interesting technique, discussed in the questions at the end of the chapter, is called flip flop merging, where state transition logic is built right into the flip flop.

Some designers prefer flip flop cells that are offered on the other parts. The flip flop cells can always be supplemented by adding flip flops made from NAND gates. From a D flip flop viewpoint, the PLHS501 can make twelve flip flops from its 72 gates. The PML2552 and PML2852 can build sixteen additional flip flops augmenting their internal 52 flip flop cells (remember, flip flops built from transistors are specialized hard cells). Additional flip flops can be built by wrapping external connections around the I/O cells of each device.

3.3 INTERCONNECTION

Interconnection occurs within the programming array by forming electrical connections through the AIM diodes in the bipolar PLHS501. AIM diodes were an early form of metal connected antifuses. The connection mechanism involves driving enough current in the reverse direction through a diode, so that metal melts and migrates right through a diode junction, shorting it out. Conversely, Wire AND-INVERT logic is formed in the EPROM CMOS PML2552 and PML2852. Because the architecture has full connectivity, the place and route problem is negligible. The design software simply maps the first available NAND gate or flip flop to the requirements of the netlist, and proceeds until all cells are used.

The PML family is called Programmable Macro Logic because embedded functions can be made and used recursively. Macros are connections of low level cells to form higher level functions, and in general are either soft or hard. Hard macros keep the relative placement of each logic cell and maintain a characterized timing. Soft macros are simply the higher level functions assembled from lower level cells, without maintaining cell placement. The timing characteristics of soft macros may vary from one version to another. It will be seen that flip flops built from gates (soft macros) behave differently than hard cell flip flops within PML.

Because of deep function nesting within the PML2552 and PML2852, care has been taken to include a special testability mode. The internal 36 flip flops (Figures 3.2 and 3.3) are configured automatically into a shift register when the scan mode (SM) pin is asserted. In scan mode, the embedded flip flops interconnect through special internal multiplexing. This shift register (called a scan register) is clocked by a special scan clock (SC) pin. Data is applied on the scan data in (SDI) pin. Through the scan register operation, the internal state of the thirty-six flip flops is directly controlled. The procedure can be automated on integrated circuit testers and other computer based equipment.

3.4 INPUT/OUTPUT

As shown in Figures 3.1, 3.2 and 3.3, several versions of I/O cells are offered. Each part has dedicated input, output and bidirectional pins. The PLHS501 offers outputs that are buffered, inverted, or Exclusive-Ored. Some are three-state controlled from the programming array, or tristated by fuse. The Exclusive-Or outputs are particularly useful for efficient generation of parity, CRC functions and additions. The PML2552 and PML2852 use output Exclusive-Or cells to invert the sense of an output signal by programming.

3.5 DESIGN SOFTWARE—SNAP!

The PML design software is given the acronym SNAP standing for Synthesis, Netlist, Analysis and Programming software. SNAP is a design framework that makes a netlist, performs a series of connection transformations on the netlist and finally makes a fusemap. The fusemap can then be programmed into a PML device.

Figure 3.7 shows the basic SNAP flow chart. The SNAP flowchart shows several optional design capture methods at the top, a gate array simulator on the lower left and a device compiler on the lower right.

The compiler block includes a device selection module, the pin assignment module, and the actual fusemap compiler. Designers are permitted to design independent of the final target device. The design may be migrated among the various PML parts, as needed. Migration occurs by making the capture and simulation phase be independent of the final compilation. Without knowledge of the final device at the outset, initial simulation time delays

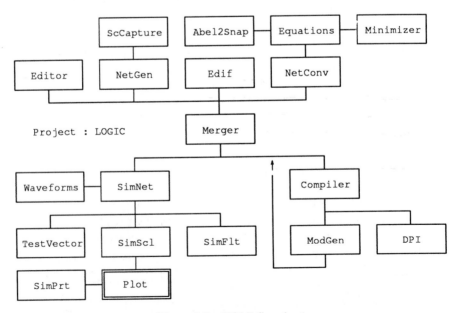

Figure 3.7   SNAP flowchart.

are set nominally to gate delays of one nanosecond. Once the design compiles, the exact internal time delays are known. An accurate simulation model is extracted from the fusemap and netlist back annotation occurs.

3.5.1 Design Entry

At the top portion of Figure 3.7, design entry occurs by any of four methods. First, schematic capture may be used. Schematic capture uses commercially available PC-based software (purchased separately). Alternately, Boolean equations or state equations may be written. Equations may be used by themselves, or combined with schematics. SNAP allows a design file made with DATAI/O's ABEL,™ to be directly entered, automatically translating it into SNAP equations. Also, a netlist may be entered describing the design.

SNAP supports design capture hierarchy. Any single method may be used, or any combination of the design entry methods may be used. Linkage of the hierarchical components occurs during the merger block of the SNAP flow. Ultimately, a flat (no hierarchy) netlist is produced with all modules interconnected.

After design entry, SNAP makes a netlist. SNAP also accepts and generates an EDIF (Electronic Data Interchange Format) compatible netlist. The EDIF netlist was chosen for compatibility with other simulators and schematic capture software. The EDIF format is useful for transporting designs among other workstations, but doesn't guarantee transportability. The format going into the merger block is EDIF compatible, but the format coming out of the merger block is not.

The merger block output is a composite netlist that is either passed to the left for simulation, or to the right for compilation. Being composed in the C language, and incorporating an EDIF-based netlist description, SNAP is designed to be adaptable to engineering workstations using the UNIX operating system. The initial SNAP offering is aimed at the personal computer environment. Like all FPGA/CPLD design software, SNAP's feature list grows with each release.

3.5.2 Design Simulation

Simulation stimuli can be entered by one of two methods. First, the simplest uses the H and L keys to draw a picture of the necessary inputs on the screen. This approach is similar to the popular child's toy called "etch-a-sketch." The second method is more typical of today's simulators, and is simply writing a text file which describes signals (by name) and when they make transitions from logical one to zero, etc.

SNAP's simulator is at the gate level. The simulator is based on one developed by Philips in Europe to support CMOS gate arrays and standard cells. The version operating on a personal computer is a five-state simulator (see section 2.7.1).

The first simulation operation is to expand the netlist coming from the merger block into a simulation model of the design. The netlist model then passes to a block below where input stimuli are applied (see Chapter 2). Next, the simulation occurs. The output file is then saved for plotting on the computer screen by the succeeding module.

Included in the simulation block is the fault simulator. Fault simulation is done by systematically simulating the designers stimuli while successively tying internal nodes to a logic one or zero on the design model. The idea is to determine whether the stimuli can distinguish a faulty circuit (stuck at logical one or zero) from a good one. Determination is done by comparing the simulation results of a good netlist, to those of a faulty one.

Fault simulation is run in several modes. Exhaustive, serial simulation gives the highest quality test. Parallel mode, incremental mode and several other fast options may be used. A full report is generated, providing histograms of the fault coverage on a vector by vector display. The histogram can be used to isolate sections of the simulation stimuli that do not improve the fault coverage. Fault coverage is a figure of merit for the simulation vectors and can be calculated from the simulation results. The input vectors can be altered to more efficiently increase the fault coverage.

A special feature is included in the simulation section that automatically formats the test vectors. The formatted vectors comply with specifications established by the Joint Electron Device Engineering Council (JEDEC) on PLD specifications. The formatted vectors can be automatically appended to the fusemap (the final configuration file) for the design. The composite file may be loaded directly into a PLD programmer which programs and tests the PLD automatically. Many device programmers are able to apply vectors, but not all of them.

3.5.3 Compilation

The compilation step is on the right hand side of the SNAP flow. One module selects the target device. Another module permits pin name definition. The only other optional choice is whether to optimize or not. SNAP's compiler currently uses netlist optimization. This technique gives significant reduction of logic by making a series of prudent substitutions into the design while maintaining functionality. The substitutions are a series of Boolean equivalent rules chosen to exploit the width of the internal NAND gates, and reduce gate usage. While optimization occurs, technology mapping occurs also.

At this point in the SNAP flow, target device fit is assessed. SNAP presents a summary of used internal functions. Specific internal functions for each device are shown in Figures 3.1, 3.2 and 3.3 as cell names by the gates and flip flops. If all resources are less than or equal to 100 percent utilization, the compilation proceeds. When the compilation completes, SNAP makes a fusemap.

PML interconnection capability is shown here. By virtue of each NAND being connectible to all other NAND gates there is no placement and routing problem. The NAND gates are used in any order and SNAP assigns connections for the fusemap generation. A model, extracted from the fusemap, is passed to the simulation module for back annotation. Should the post fusemap compilation be correct, the fused device will meet the desired specification.

3.5.4 Additional SNAP Options

SNAP offers several additional capabilities that are automatic. First, the fusemap may be reverse compiled to logic equations. Second, the ESPRESSO PLA minimizing software is included as an additional optimization tool. ESPRESSO compresses logic equations into two level minimal versions. Third, SNAP permits a netlist to be converted into equations, which permits some additional minimization in conjunction with ESPRESSO.

Designers wishing to incorporate previously programmed PLDs can do so by assigning names to the PLD pins, inputting the fusemap and operating the equation extraction module. SNAP can convert the fusemap file and pin name file to an equation file. This is possible because SNAP supports compilation for all of Signetics PLD products. The product line includes industry standard PLA, sequencer and PAL,™ devices as well as PML. Equation extraction permits editing an equation file with other equation files to combine smaller PLDs into larger devices. By incremental compiling, designers can successively add the equations for more PLDs into one target PML part until it overflows—as seen in the SNAP resource summary. Then, functions are removed until the resulting design fits. Full resource utilization is possible.

Netlists brought into SNAP by schematic capture, also can take advantage of the ESPRESSO minimizer, because SNAP's merger module includes an option to convert a netlist back into equations, which are then input to ESPRESSO.

3.6 DESIGN ESTIMATION

Design estimation for PML is straightforward. The contents of Tables 3.1, 3.2, or 3.3 is used successively to generate a tally for a design. Many common MSI functions as well as gates and flip flops are included. The designer simply

TABLE 3.1   PLHS501 Functional Equivalents

Function Description	PLHS501 CELLS
1. Basic Logic Gates	1 NAND
2. D flip flop (edge triggered)	6 NANDs
3. D latch (transparent)	4 NANDs
4. J-K flip flop (edge trig.)	10 NANDs
5. Decoders	
a. 2 to 4	4 NANDs
b. 3 to 8	8 NANDs
c. 4 to 16	16 NANDs
6. Multiplexers	
a. 2 to 1	3 NANDs
b. 4 to 1	5 NANDs
c. 8 to 1	9 NANDs
d. 16 to 1	17 NANDs
7. Comparators (equality only)	
a. 2 bit	4 NANDs
b. 4 bit	9 NANDs
8. Registers (serial load)	
a. 4 bit	24 NANDs
b. 8 bit	48 NANDs
9. Counters	
a. 2 bit	15 NANDs
b. 4 bit	36 NANDs

TABLE 3.2   PML2552/2852 Functional Equivalents

Function Description	PML2552 Cells
1. Basic Logic Gates	1 NAND
2. D flip flop (edge triggered)	1 D flip flop
3. D latch (transparent)	4 NANDs or 1 latch
4. J-K flip flop (edge trig.)	10 NANDs or 1 JK
5. Decoders	
a. 2 to 4	4 NANDs
b. 3 to 8	8 NANDs
c. 4 to 16	16 NANDs
6. Multiplexers	
a. 2 to 1	3 NANDs
b. 4 to 1	5 NANDs
c. 8 to 1	9 NANDs
d. 16 to 1	17 NANDs
7. Comparators (equality only)	
a. 2 bit	4 NANDs
b. 4 bit	9 NANDs
8. Registers (serial load)	
a. 4 bit	4 D flip flops
b. 8 bit	8 D flip flops
9. Counters	
a. 2 bit	2D + 3 NANDs
b. 4 bit	4 JKFF + 8NANDs

TABLE 3.3 Basic PML Timing

Parameter	PLHS501	PML2552/2852
Tinput	4	4
Toutput	13	15
Tnand	7.5	15
Tsetup	N/A	15
Tckq	N/A	5

Note: All interconnect delay is included, typical time delays. Values shown are in nanoseconds, PML2552/2852 are the −35 speed versions.

isolates a piece of the design by comparing it to entries in the tables, finds the gate equivalent of the piece, records it and continues. When every function has been converted to a gate equivalent, the gate equivalent pieces are tallied. The final tally is compared to the capacity of the target device. The target is 100 percent capacity.

The designer should consider preoptimized versions of the design pieces, so accurate tallying occurs. For instance, should a three-to-eight decoder be chosen as a building block, with only five outputs used, the gate equivalent should be reduced to five gates rather than eight gates. Similarly, only the used counter or shifter bits should be included. This permits a realistic estimate. The tallied value of gates and flip flops should then be compared to the corresponding device budget.

To clarify the estimation process, target the PLHS501 for the design problem shown with Figure 2.9. The four input flip flops can be edge triggered or latched. Choosing transparent latches at four NANDs per latch, requires sixteen gates. Adding to that two D flip flops—for the counter—takes six NANDS per flip flop, with six gates of transition logic. This tallies to thirty-four gates. The MUX requires five gates, bringing the estimated total to thirty-nine gates. This approach is fairly accurate for calculating the number of logic cells needed for small designs, but is less accurate for large designs.

3.7 DESIGN TECHNIQUES

The design techniques focused on here are the efficient building of decoders, multiplexers, shift registers (shifters), and counters. These basic machines are at the root of most logic design. This approach also will be covered for the architectures in chapters to follow.

Decoder design in PML is trivial. If all of the decoder input variables have both the variable and complement available, then one NAND gate decodes a selection. A three-to-eight decoder takes eight NAND gates; a four-to-sixteen decoder takes sixteen NAND gates, and so on. For tight gate estimation, the number of outputs used dictates the tally. SNAP automatically eliminates unused decoder gates, from soft macro decoders, but estimation is done best by using the exact number of gates needed. If all decode variables do not have the input variable and complements available, they may have to be made from more NAND gates.

Multiplexer design in PML is also simple. A MUX needs to form the logical OR of several data input points. To form this structure takes two NAND gate levels. At the input level of the NAND gates, separate data lines are assigned to each NAND gate. Applied to the other NAND gate inputs are the combinations of decode variables to select that particular data. All of the NAND gate outputs converge to the input of the output NAND gate.

The output NAND gate logically ORs the input NAND gates outputs, giving the selected data out. Again, unused gates should be avoided. A rough guideline for gate count estimation is that a MUX uses as many NAND gates as there are input data lines, plus one more for the output gate. A few more gates may be needed if the MUX select signals don't include the signal and its complement. A small MUX will be seen in the example, later, but one was already seen in Figure 1.6.

Shifter design also is simple, but the strategy chosen depends on the part used. Shifters usually need edge triggered D flip flops in cascade. J-K flip flops are also easily used, but should be saved for more complex state machines like counters. It is possible to make shifters from cascaded transparent latches by phase inverting the clocks, but this is not efficient.

The PLHS501 has only one shifter strategy, because it has no flip flops. At six NAND gates per shift bit, the PLHS501 can make a twelve bit shifter using all seventy-two gates in the foldback NAND gate array. A few more flip flops can be made, by externally connecting I/O pin gates to form flip flops. The I/O gates are slower than the foldback gates and limit the shift speed of the whole chain. PLHS501 shifters can operate at 33 MHz.

The PML2552 and PML2852 present an interesting special case. The strategy is to use D flip flops first, then J-K flip flops and then make flip flops from gates. J-K flip flops are converted into D flip flops by applying the data signal to J and its complement to K on the flip flop. The speed of D flip flop PML2552/2852 shifters is 50 MHz. Making D flip flops from CMOS NAND gates will degrade the operation to about 25 MHz. SNAP automatically makes additional flip flops from the foldback NAND gates.

Should the PML2552 shifter length be less than or equal to 36 bits, the internal scan mode shift register may be usable. This is a restricted use because of internal isolation that happens to the flip flops during scan mode, but this use is very efficient, needing no additional NAND gates.

Counter design in PML is more sophisticated. Because the PML building blocks are NAND gates and flip flops, the counter design methods taught in college logic design courses are appropriate. Most college courses do not illustrate the nature of the counter transition logic as the counter length grows, but it will be shown that the logic pattern is predictable. The transition logic is the combinational logic that directly drives the flip flop inputs.

Starting from the least significant count bit position, the number of inputs grows incrementally in direct proportion to the counter length. This is because each successive bit depends on all lower order bits.

Figure 3.8 illustrates the Boolean equations for a 4 bit up counter made from J-K flip flops. The SNAP syntax is used with * for logical AND, / for invert and + for logical OR. Figure 3.9 shows the corresponding logic diagram for Figure 3.8. The pattern is obvious, from either the equations or the schematic. As higher position bits are added, an incremental cost of only one flip flop and one NAND gate is needed. The needed NAND gate compensates for the NAND gates on the J-K inputs of the PML flip flops. As shown, all J-K inputs are tied together. Also, note that the least significant bit uses no additional gates. Down counters follow a similar pattern.

The counter strategy for the PLHS501 is simple. There are no flip flops, so they must be made from NAND gates. For small counters of two or three bits, D flip flops use the minimum number of gates. Flip flop merging (see the questions at the chapter end) is appropriate to use here. Larger counters

```
A.J = 1;
A.K = 1;
B.J = A;
B.K = A;
C.J = A * B;
C.K = A * B;
D.J = A * B * C;
D.K = A * B * C;
A.RST = 1;
B.RST = 1;
C.RST = 1;
D.RST = 1;
A.CLK = CLOCK;
B.CLK = CLOCK;
C.CLK = CLOCK;
D.CLK = CLOCK;
```

Figure 3.8 SNAP Boolean equations for a four bit counter.

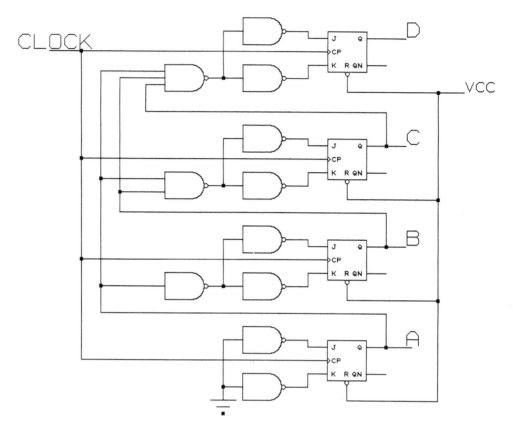

Figure 3.9   Counter schematic.

in the PLHS501 are inefficient and should be avoided. Small counters can operate as fast as 28 MHz. If a large counter is needed, a twelve bit ripple counter can be made from the gates, avoiding transition logic entirely.

The PML2552/2852 counter strategy is simpler. If counters are less than ten bits, they should be placed in the ten flip flop cluster of J-K flip flops, which have independent clocks. Ten bit and higher counters should first use the ten flip flop cluster with a common clock. Then, individual flip flops are added from the J-K group that has independent clocks. SNAP can be influenced to place specific flip flop functions into particular cell types, if needed.

For speed reasons, flip flops built from the foldback NAND gates in the PML2552/2852 should be avoided. Synchronous counters will fail to count above 36 MHz. Asynchronous (ripple counters) can operate as high as 50 MHz on the PML2552/2852.

3.8 A SMALL EXAMPLE

The simple latched MUX from Chapter 2 (Figure 2.9) will now be designed in detail showing how it fits into the PLHS501 and the PML2552. This example shows how a design is adapted to a particular architecture exploiting the available strengths. The example repeats on other parts, in successive chapters.

The design operation is straightforward. Data is latched in the four D latches by pulsing the load signal. Assuming the counter is initially reset to zero, the topmost latch bit is multiplexed to the pin labeled OUT. As the

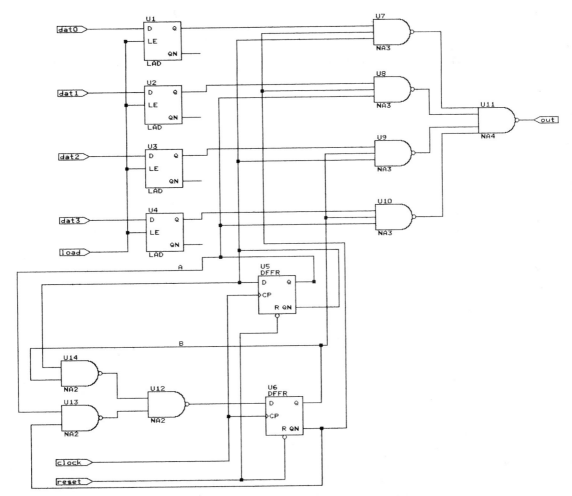

Figure 3.10 Small example logic diagram.

counter clocks, successive values control the MUX and consecutive data goes out. When this design translates to the PLHS501, SNAP expands the latches and counter flip flops into NAND gates. This occurs automatically, because the PLHS501 has no flip flops or latches. Figure 3.10 shows the design schematic. Figure 3.11 shows a simulation for the design using one nanosecond gate delays. The simulation reflects the ideal design before being compiled into a PLHS501. In Figure 3.11, the "U" signals on the OUT waveform are where the design had undefined states due to time delay before receipt of the RESET input signal. The small black patches are where oscillations or small glitches occurred in the timing.

Translation occurs automatically, with SNAP converting the schematic file into a first level netlist. This netlist shows the connection of the cells as drawn. Figure 3.12 shows the first netlist. Input latches (LAD cells) have data input (DAT0–DAT3) and a LOAD input. The latches generate signals which pass to the MUX gates of the netlist. The two edge triggered D flip flops have the cell designation DFFR. Figure 3.13 shows the corresponding macro netlist for a six NAND gate DFFR. The LAD (latch) cells are also built by SNAP from NAND gates. Full explanation of the netlist is not important, but it is similar to that discussed in Chapter 2. After the netlist is expanded into NAND gates during compile, SNAP maps the circuit to the PLHS501 fusemap.

The mapping process is different for the PML2552 because it contains hard cell flip flops. For the PML2552, SNAP automatically inserts hard cell

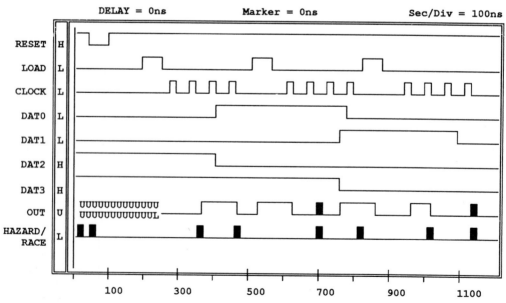

Figure 3.11 Small example pre-compile simulation.

```
**************************************************
*             Output of Netgene     Version Brv8o1   *
* Date:   2/ 7/1991                  Time: 23: 6:45 *
**************************************************
*                                                   *
* Input File Name    :      BOOK.EDF                *
* Netlist File Name  :      BOOK.MAC                *
*                                                   *
**************************************************
*
 MACRO
*
Z BOOK_SCH I(CLOCK,DAT0,DAT1,DAT2,DAT3,LOAD,RESET) O(OUT)
*
U1 LAD I(DAT0,LOAD) O(SN01,DM01)
U2 LAD I(DAT1,LOAD) O(SN05,DM02)
U3 LAD I(DAT2,LOAD) O(SN09,DM03)
U4 LAD I(SN10,LOAD) O(SN10,DM04)
U5 DFFR I(SN04,CLOCK,RESET) O(A,SN04)
U6 DFFR I(SN12,CLOCK,RESET) O(B,SN02)
U7 NA3 I(SN01,SN02,SN04) O(SN03)
U8 NA3 I(SN05,SN02,A) O(SN06)
U9 NA3 I(SN09,B,SN04) O(SN07)
U10 NA3 I(SN10,B,A) O(SN08)
U11 NA4 I(SN03,SN06,SN07,SN08) O(OUT)
U12 NA2 I(SN11,SN13) O(SN12)
U13 NA2 I(A,SN02) O(SN13)
U14 NA2 I(SN04,B) O(SN11)
*
 MEND
*
```

Figure 3.12 Small example netlist.

```
**************************************************
*           Output of Assembler  Version  1.85    *
* Date:   8/30/1993                Time: 22: 1: 0 *
**************************************************
*                                                 *
* Input File Name    :       DFF.N0               *
* Netlist File Name  :       DFF.N1               *
*                                                 *
**************************************************
*
 NETSTART
*
U1_G1 NAND I(U1_G2,U1_G4) O(U1_G1)
U1_G2 NAND I(U1_G1,CLEAR__E,CLOCK__E) O(U1_G2)
U1_G3 NAND I(U1_G2,U1_G4,CLOCK__E) O(U1_G3)
U1_G4 NAND I(U1_G3,CLEAR__E,INPUT__E) O(U1_G4)
U1_G5 NAND I(U1_G2,DM01) O(OUTPUT__D)
U1_G6 NAND I(U1_G3,CLEAR__E,OUTPUT__D) O(DM01)
*
*
CLEAR__H0 DIN501 I(CLEAR) O(CLEAR__E)
*
INPUT__H0 DIN501 I(INPUT) O(INPUT__E)
*
CLOCK__H0 DIN501 I(CLOCK) O(CLOCK__E)
*
OUTPUT__G0 NAND I(OUTPUT__D) O(OUTPUT__B)
OUTPUT__G1 NAND I(VCC) O(VCC_P19)
OUTPUT__G3 NOU501 I(OUTPUT__B,VCC_P19) O(OUTPUT)
*
 NETEND
*
 NETIN CLEAR,INPUT,CLOCK
 NETOUT OUTPUT
```

Figure 3.13 Six NAND gate D
flip flop netlist.

flip flops where possible. The PML2852 mapping is very similar to the
PML2552, but again, the mapping occurs automatically with SNAP.

After compilation, the PLHS501 time delays are folded into the simulation model resulting in Figure 3.14. The time delay differences are not
dramatic between Figures 3.11 and 3.14. Note the small amount of output
glitching on the precompilation (Figure 3.11) simulation. The glitching is
because gate delays are too fast, being one nanosecond per gate. After
compilation, the cell time delays (five to seven nanoseconds per gate) eliminate some of the timing glitches.

Figure 3.15 shows a portion of the fault simulation report generated for
this simulation. Fault simulation gives a measure of how well simulation
patterns test a design. A fault coverage of 100 percent is very good. The
simulation patterns never provide 100 percent fault coverage. The maximum
fault coverage achieved is only 90.6 percent, as seen in the histogram. More
explanation of fault simulation occurs in Appendix A.

Figure 3.16 shows the number of internal resources and pins used when
the design compiles into the PLHS501. The table breaks out the internal
resources according to device specific internal cells (shown in Figure 3.1), so
the user sees precise internal cell usage.

Sometimes, a logic function may be generated using an input cell or an
output cell in a way that the designer did not suspect. Note that from the
summary, this design only used thirty-eight gates when the estimate was
thirty-nine. This design uses up gates quickly when building the flip flops.

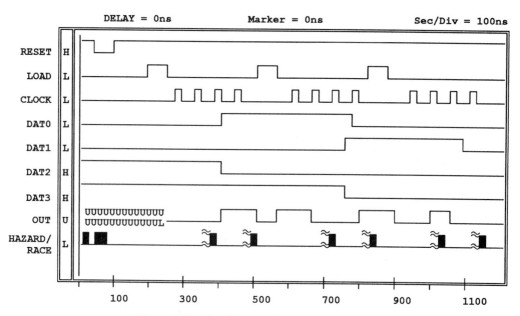

Figure 3.14 Small example post-compile simulation.

```
PATTERN#     %      0          20         40         60         80        100
-------------------+---------+---------+---------+---------+---------+
        1   0.0     .
        2   0.0     .
        3   0.0     .
        4   5.7     .***
        5   5.7     .***
        6  14.2     .*******
        7  14.2     .*******
        8  65.1     .********************************
        9  66.0     .********************************
       10  73.6     .***********************************
       11  73.6     .***********************************
       12  74.5     .***********************************
       13  74.5     .***********************************
       14  78.3     .*************************************
       15  79.2     .*************************************
       16  79.2     .*************************************
       17  79.2     .*************************************
       18  82.1     .*****************************************
       19  82.1     .*****************************************
       20  82.1     .*****************************************
       21  82.1     .*****************************************
       22  82.1     .*****************************************
       23  82.1     .*****************************************
       24  82.1     .*****************************************
       25  83.0     .*****************************************
       26  83.0     .*****************************************
       27  87.7     .********************************************
       28  87.7     .********************************************
       29  87.7     .********************************************
       30  87.7     .********************************************
       31  90.6     .**********************************************
       32  90.6     .**********************************************
       33  90.6     .**********************************************
       34  90.6     .**********************************************
       35  90.6     .**********************************************
-------------------+---------+---------+---------+---------+---------+
```

Figure 3.15 Small example fault simulation results.

```
======= SNAP Resources Summary =======
  Cell name    used/total      %
=============================================
    DIN501      7 /  32       21%
    NIN501      4 /  32       12%
    FBNAND     36 /  72       50%
     NAND       2 /  44        4%
    OUT501      0 /   4        0%
    NOU501      1 /   8       12%
    EXO501      0 /   8        0%
    TOU501      0 /   4        0%
Please hit any key to continue...
```

Figure 3.16 Small example
PLHS501 resource usage.

Actually, there are thirty-nine gates in the final netlist. The thirty-ninth NAND gate is disguised as the output cell NOU501 that performs a NAND function right at the output pad as the signal exits the device. The rest of the resource summary entries refer to the internal buffers, receivers and output cells.

Placing the design into the PML2552 is straightforward. A natural first association is to put the design's input data latches into the input D flip flops of the PML2552. This is done by simply assigning the input data pins to the pins which are connected to the input data latches, and drawing the latches or writing their equations. Note that using flip flops for latches may not always be an option in some situations.

The counter can be configured either from the groups of J-K flip flops, the D flip flops (combined with gates) or the gates alone. Flip flop selection depends upon the requirements of other functions, as this design is too small to fill an entire PML2552. The output multiplexer will be made from the foldback NAND gates.

Figure 3.17 shows the resource summary for the design when mapped onto the PML2552. Here, the input latches were pinned to land at the input data latch cells of the part. The counter clock was assigned to the clocking array for the part. By virtue of assigning the clock to a clock pin, the software must put the two bit counter into J-K flip flops that have access to the chosen clock. SNAP assigns flip flops in a direct fashion, connecting existing flip flops until it runs out of them, then SNAP uses the foldback NAND gate array to build any more flip flops needed.

To control where functions land in any of the PML parts, the designer must carefully assign pins to associate functions. Taking care with pin assign-

```
============ SNAP Resources Summary ============
   Cell name    used/total       %
=================================================
   CKDIN552      0  /    4       0%
   CKNIN552      0  /    4       0%
    FBNAND      25  /   96      26%
      NAND      10  /  104       9%
    DIN552       6  /   25      24%
    NIN552       5  /   25      20%
   CDIN552       0  /    4       0%
   CNIN552       0  /    4       0%
     CK552       0  /    4       0%
   IDFF552       0  /   16       0%
   BDIN552       0  /   24       0%
   BNIN552       0  /   24       0%
   JKCL552       2  /   10      20%
   JKPR552       0  /   10       0%
   EXOR552       0  /    8       0%
   TOUT552       1  /   24       4%
   ODFF552       1  /   16       6%
Please hit any key to continue...
```

Figure 3.17 Small example PML2552 resource usage.

ment is the single most critical aspect designers encounter when making PML designs. Additional control occurs through cell naming and by "path freezing."

The path freezing option in SNAP forces the compiler to not optimize specially tagged regions of a design, preserving precise connectivity. However, path freezing can defeat the optimization software, if misused. Lots of frozen paths make neighboring nets get "cold"—so they cannot be optimized. It is best to use freezing sparingly and let the netlist optimizer pack and flatten designs for maximum capacity.

3.9 PERFORMANCE

Programmable Macro Logic can be simply modeled per the diagram shown in Figure 3.18. The internal time delays must be broken out on a cell by cell basis and signals must be traced from input pins to corresponding output pins while tallying the delay totals. Each device data sheet shows the exact time

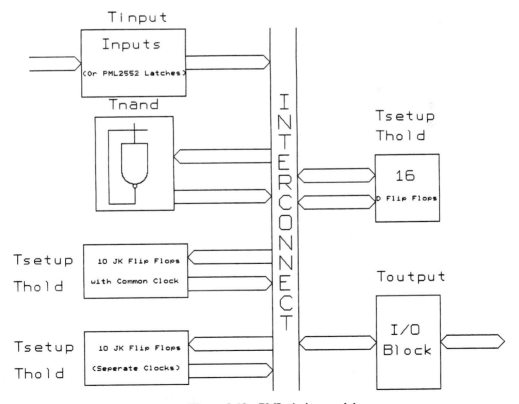

Figure 3.18   PML timing model.

delays for each cell type. Figure 3.19 shows several paths that a signal may pass through when going from the input pins to the output pins on a PLHS501. Values shown are maximum, worst case, so they are pessimistic. However, designers should not count on maximum worst case speeds, as these may be exceeded.

Table 3.3 (see page 60) briefly summarizes the cell performance for the PML family. The values shown are maximum time delays, and are the average of maximum low-to-high and maximum high-to-low values. The delays given are for the cells with full internal loading included, which means interconnect points are always present and essentially invariant. These numbers are unlike those of a gate array where the actual metal length varies. The parameters Tinput and Toutput are the time delays for the input and output cells. Tnand is the average value for the foldback NAND time delay.

Flip flop parameters are given from the input to the output of the cell. For instance, the D input on the PML2852 has an associated NAND gate that is permanently attached to the flip flop. The NAND gate time delay is included in the flip flop delay parameters. The chosen flip flop parameters are simply Tsetup and Tckq.

Using the setup (Tsetup) and clock to q time (Tckq), Fmax may be calculated. Fmax is the reciprocal of the sum of setup time plus Clock to Q time. This is the toggle frequency of the flip flop, without any additional logic added onto its data input. Adding additional logic increases the time delay for state transitions, and decreases the clocking frequency. If the additional time delay is known, it may simply be added into the sum just mentioned. Then, reciprocal of the sum gives the derated operating frequency. This is an important idea and will be used in later chapters.

The key to an accurate timing estimate is to count the loops made through the foldback NAND gates as the function is cascaded. Better accuracy is found if addition of low-to-high and high-to-low time delays (which are different) are used in the tally.

The time delay of an output cell can be a strong function of the capacitance it must drive. Exact loading conditions must be incorporated into the time delay equation for output cells. Loading dependence holds for both bipolar and CMOS, but more strongly affects CMOS.

3.10 POWER CONSIDERATIONS

The PLHS501 is a bipolar device and its power consumption is not a strong function of frequency. The power consumed is largely a function of I_{cc} and the applied supply voltage. The PML2552/2852 is another matter, because they are perceived to be CMOS devices.

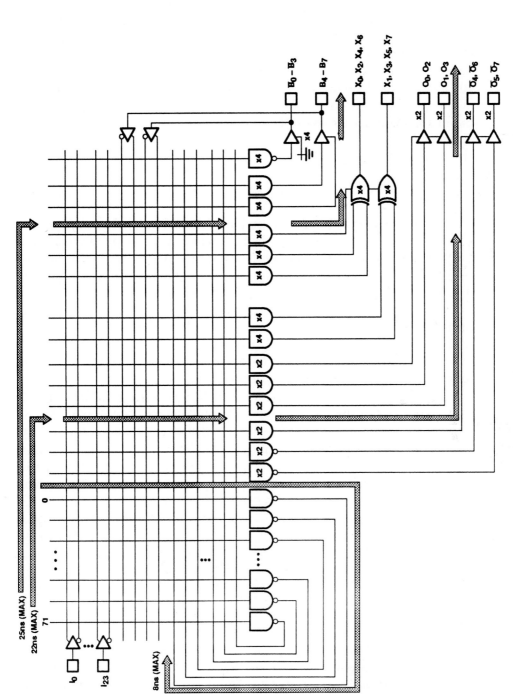

Figure 3.19 PLHS501 timing paths.

The PML2552/2852 have internal EPLD cells that are n-channel MOS-based. Hence, the transistors are always conducting current to some degree and exhibit some frequency dependence. To mimic a CMOS circuit in the static condition, a power blocking pin is available permitting the device to be put into a low power state. In the low power state, supply current is around 100 microamps. Under a conventional load, the device will pull about 160 milliamps of current when operating the flip flops at 15 MHz. The rest of the power dissipation must be described with a curve, relating frequency and consumed current.

3.11 CLOSING COMMENTS

Programmable Macro Logic has completed its first entry phase by providing a bipolar and two CMOS parts to the PLD marketplace. United States Patent 4703206 was granted to Napoleon Cavlan for the basic NAND gate architecture with Signetics corporation listed as the assignee. The most recent member of the PML family is the PML2852, shown in Figure 3.3. The PML2852 was designed as an extension of the PML2552 in an eighty-four pin package, including sixteen additional outputs. All design tips included for the PML2552 are applicable to the PML2852.

PML's chief strength is its potential connectivity of all internal cells. The price paid for this is largely that of functional density.

The nature of the PML architecture best suits it for application areas dominated by gate and flip flop random interconnect. Typical of those areas are bus handshaking controllers, disk controllers, graphics controllers and high speed state machines.

PROBLEMS

1. Estimate the number of NAND gates that will be needed to make the design from Figure 2.1 in a PLHS501.

2. Estimate the time delay for a signal applied to input pin DATO to get to the output pin OUT for Figure 3.10. Use the values for cells taken from Table 3.3 for the PLHS501. Repeat this for the PML2552. Assume the latch enable signal, LOAD, is asserted high for this calculation.

3. Flip flop merging is a useful design technique, that is often applied in gate array designs. Simply stated, the logic tied to the flip flop inputs is placed within the flip flop, as shown in Figure 3.20. The picture shows how this can be done, systematically. The advantage of this technique is that two layers of input logic essentially disappear, making the merged design as fast as if there was no input

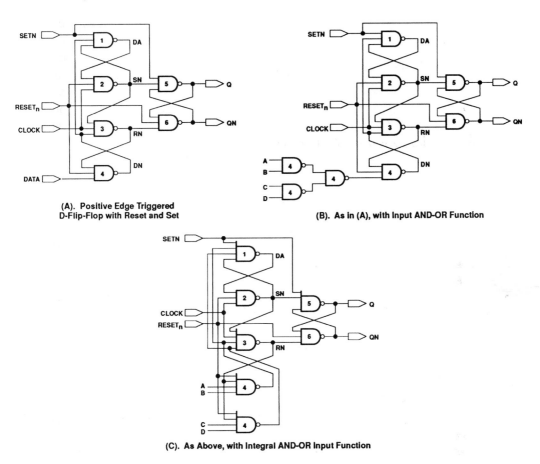

(A). Positive Edge Triggered
D-Flip-Flop with Reset and Set

(B). As in (A), with Input AND-OR Function

(C). As Above, with Integral AND-OR Input Function

Flip-Flop Merging

Figure 3.20   Flip flop merging.

logic. Two important properties of the FPGA cells are necessary: gate level granularity and arbitrarily wide input gates. Merged flip flops operate at the toggle rate of the flip flops. Design a three bit up/down counter, using merged D flip flops, built entirely from NAND gates. Show a schematic of the solution, and simulate its operation, if possible.

4. A similar procedure to flip flop merging can be used to gain speed advantages with transparent D latches. Show how a two to one multiplexer can be merged into the operation of a transparent D latch. Assume that one multiplexer input is input A, another B and the select input is S. S brings A to the multiplexer output when S is one and B to the multiplexer output when S is zero. The interest is not in the multiplexer output, but rather the Q output of the D latch, whose D input is attached to the multiplexer output. Show an all NAND gate version of the merged latch.

5. What is the biggest multiplexer that can be built using a PLHS501? Justify the answer.

6. Verify the four bit counter entry in Table 3.1.

4

Logic Cell Array

4.0 INTRODUCTION

The LCA family from Xilinx was the first device claimed to be an FPGA. Today, the LCA is the architecture most designers think of for the term FPGA. The LCA architecture has evolved through years of customer feedback. The goal of this chapter is to introduce the basic operation of the LCA and explore its strengths and limitations. The reader should gain a familiarity with LCA operation and appreciate how closely its design methods parallel those of a CMOS gate array. This chapter supplies additional techniques appropriate to LCA design. With this information one can begin to think in terms of this useful family and assess its ability to meet specific design needs.

4.1 LOGIC CELL ARRAY

The Logic Cell Array, or LCA™, is a CMOS family of programmable devices. LCAs provide fixed arrays of logical function cells connectible by a system of pass transistors driven by static RAM cells. The internal function cells are identical and may be configured. Each cell contains a combinational logic element, and one or more flip flops, as well as local multiplexing and interconnect paths. The central array is configured into a pattern of regularly spaced function cells interleaved with programmable connection.

Figure 4.1 illustrates the logical contents of one of these function cells called a configurable logic block (CLB). Figure 4.2 shows how an array of CLBs is arranged on the die. On Figure 4.2, the CLBs are rectangles, the I/O pad cells surround the periphery, and the small squares are switchpoint matrices. The little dots are places where metal lines can be connected to the CLBs, I/O cells and switchpoint matrices. More detail will be given, shortly.

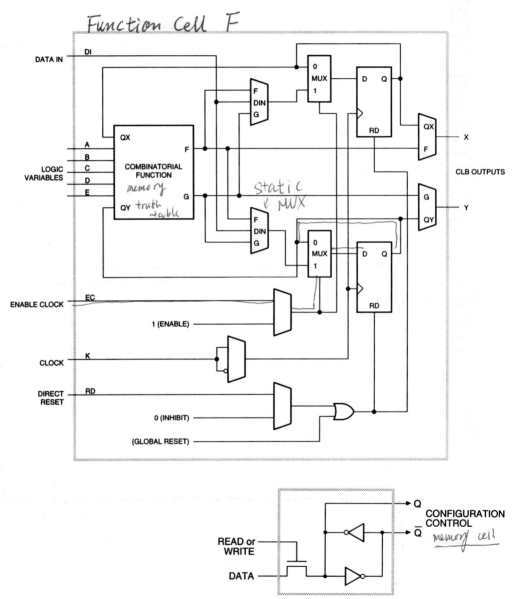

Figure 4.1 The 3000 family CLB.

Configurable logic block
(CLB)

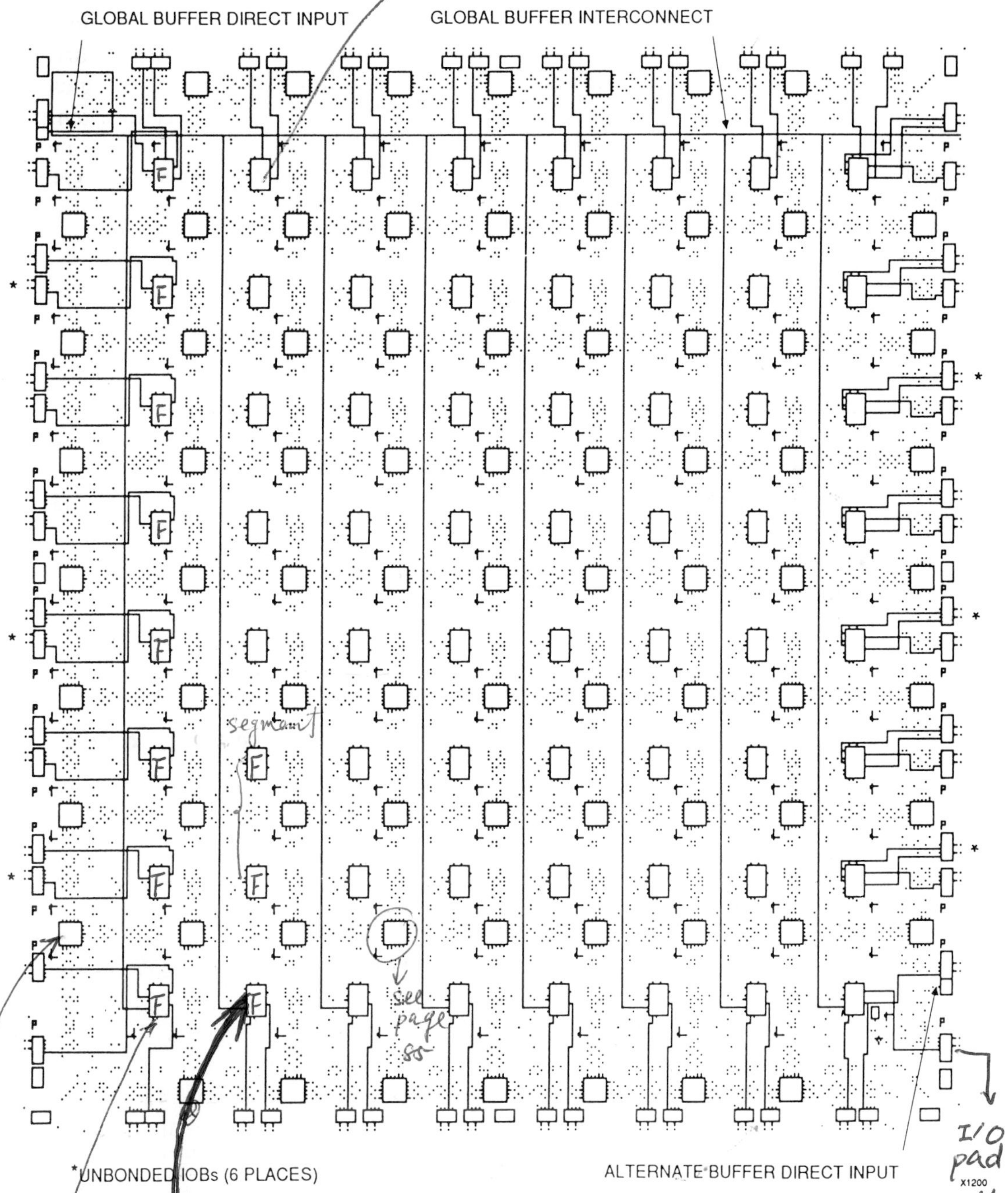

GLOBAL BUFFER DIRECT INPUT   GLOBAL BUFFER INTERCONNECT

segment

see page 80

I/O pad cell

X1200

*UNBONDED IOBs (6 PLACES)   ALTERNATE BUFFER DIRECT INPUT

Figure 4.2 The 3000 family architecture.

Function cell or configurable logic block

switchpoint matrices.

   The basic architecture comes in several variations, called the 2000, 3000 and 4000 series parts. The 2000 series was the first family and the 4000 the most recent. Each series has a regular array of identical CLBs, but the number of CLBs on a particular part within a series is different. Successive series members also have more I/O pins.

   Additional features within the CLBs have also improved since the original LCA product was released. Newer parts provide more flexibility and storage capacity within the logic array. There have also been technology refinements such as faster CMOS, internal wire ANDing, improved clock drivers, and more output current drive. The design software is essentially a standard gate array flow adapted for the LCA architecture.

4.2 A LOOK INSIDE THE CLB

The CLB shown in Figure 4.1 illustrates the core of the logic operator for the LCA. This version contains two flip flops, a combinational function box, and is used in the 3000 series LCA. The flip flops are connected to the combinational function box through multiplexers. The contents of the combinational function box is a static CMOS RAM, where one cell is shown in Figure 4.1. The function box RAM makes a truth table of any logic function of the input variables. The input variables are applied on the address lines of the RAM, and the RAM data outputs are the function outputs. The contents of the RAM binary row values are the logical ones and zeroes needed for the combinational function. The CLB fits the universal function model described in Chapter 1.

   Figure 4.1 illustrates a five input variable RAM. The seven inputs are multiplexed together to make a subset of five lines addressing the RAM. It is possible to generate any logic functions of five input variables with this RAM. If needed, the thirty-two entry RAM can be partitioned into two groups of sixteen entries, so the RAM also generates any two functions of four input variables. Other partitioning is possible permitting more options.

   Figure 4.3 shows the first LCA CLB from the 2000 series parts and Figure 4.4 shows the latest CLB used in the 4000 series parts. An evolutionary path for the CLB can be traced among the three figures. First, note that Figure 4.3 has only one flip flop, a small RAM and few signal paths into and out of the CLB. This arrangement caused some routing difficulties with the early software. Figure 4.1 can be viewed as an improvement, with two flip flops per CLB and additional RAM depth. Figure 4.4 is another improvement with more flexible RAM inputs, two flip flops, and several additional entry and exit points to the CLB. The 4000 series CLB literally opens up the cell so that more of the internal structure is directly available for outside

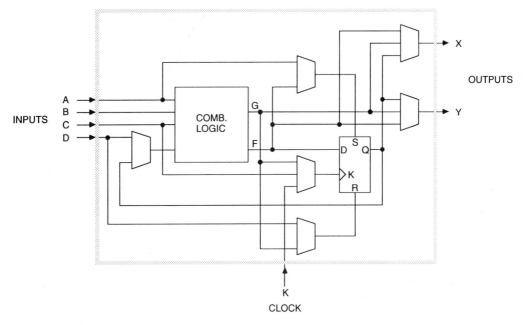

Figure 4.3 The 2000 family CLB.

connection. Other attributes (described later) exploit this added ability, but
the new flexibility improves both the density and the function packing for the
LCA 4000. In all CLBs, the trapezoidal muxes are statically controlled.

The LCA RAM (both CLB and interconnection) is volatile and must
be loaded prior to using it. Loading occurs during system reset, as a rule.
Xilinx has made loading the RAM possible in several ways. Loading can be
done automatically from a serial PROM, from a microprocessor, or from a
parallel PROM. The RAM can be reconfigured later to alter the functional
contents. Should that strategy be chosen, the LCA transforms its operation
"on the fly."

The CLB is a convenient structure for both combinational and sequential machines. The CLB RAM makes combinational transition logic for the
flip flops, or combinational functions bypassing the flip flops. Alternately,
the RAM may be bypassed, directly accessing the flip flops. A CLB limitation is the width of combinational functions formed with the RAM input
variables. This limitation occurs in all CLBs to varying degrees. Function
width is expanded by stacking CLBs or using three-state buffers external to
the CLBs. These buffers are associated with the long line interconnect paths,
meant for broadcasting important global signals.

Here is a review of how a RAM can make simple logic functions. The
truth table for an AND gate has all zero output values unless all inputs are
logic ones. This is shown in Table 4.1(a) where the inputs are called A,B,C

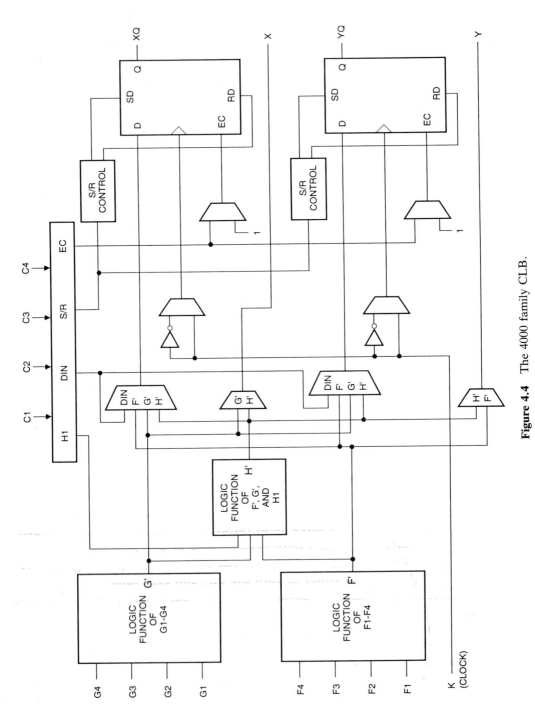

Figure 4.4 The 4000 family CLB.

TABLE 4.1 Some RAM Based Truth Table Functions

A	B	C	X	A	B	C	X
0	0	0	0	0	0	0	0
0	0	1	0	0	0	1	1
0	1	0	0	0	1	0	1
0	1	1	0	0	1	1	1
1	0	0	0	1	0	0	0
1	0	1	0	1	0	1	1
1	1	0	0	1	1	0	0
1	1	1	1	1	1	1	1
(a) AND Truth Table				(b) X = (/A * B) + C			

A	B	C	X	A	B	C	X
0	0	0	0	0	0	0	1
0	0	1	0	0	0	1	0
0	1	0	0	0	1	0	1
0	1	1	1	0	1	1	0
1	0	0	0	1	0	0	1
1	0	1	0	1	0	1	0
1	1	0	0	1	1	0	1
1	1	1	1	1	1	1	0
(c) X = B * C				(d) X = /C			

and the output is called X. Normally, a gate would perform this function. If an eight entry RAM with three address input lines were loaded with the values shown, it would respond the same as an AND gate. Any logic function of three input variables could be made this way.

As another example, consider the function X = (/A * B) + C. The truth table for this is shown in Table 4.1(b). This illustrates forming the sum of products function for three input variables. Here, the term C is a degenerate product, but it might have been A*B*C or B*C, as well.

A function of only two variables can be made by replicating the table contents (that is, the rows) in both the one and zero sense of the unused variable. A two variable function is shown in Table 4.1(c) for the function X = B * C, where the A variable goes unused. Notice that binary rows zero through three are identical to rows four through seven. This is illustrated for the simple function X = /C where both A and B are unused for the table in Figure 4.1(d).

The LCA 2000 function boxes can all have at most four input variables, so their logic functions are restricted to sums of products with at most four variables. The LCA 2000 CLB RAMs have sixteen data cell rows. The LCA

3000 and LCA 4000 family members have deeper RAMs, and more complex arrangements, but the principles are the same.

The expertise of the CLB is the class of functions requiring a few switching variables per flip flop. Small counters and sequence generators fit this class, and the LCA easily makes many of them in a single part. As will be seen shortly, another class which fits well are those sequential machines needing local interconnect. These machines include shift registers, linear sequential machines (that is, polynomial generators, random number generators, and encoding functions) and simple systolic logic arrays.

Independent of which LCA family is considered, all CLBs are large grain building blocks. Each CLB is usually "stripped down" to form the needed logic function, with some of the cell wasted. How efficiently the software packs the CLBs and maximizes their capacity is often the issue for mapping a design to the LCA architecture.

4.3 INTERCONNECTION

Interconnect within an LCA occurs in many ways. Much interconnect is accomplished within the part by an embedded RAM called the configuration memory. In the configuration memory, each bit is dedicated to the control of a specific internal switchpoint. The internal interconnect switchpoints are called Programmable Interconnect Points (PIPs). PIPs look like little dots on Figure 4.2. LCAs use the same five transistor RAM cell shown in Figure 4.1 for interconnect RAM. Some RAM cells control the interconnect multiplexers within each CLB, while others handle the routing of signals between CLBs, by connecting through the PIPs.

The most efficient interconnect is direct interconnect to north, south, east, and west CLB neighbors. The 2000 series direct interconnect permits the X output of each CLB to be connected to specific inputs on immediate north, south, east, and west neighbors. The Y output makes possible direct interconnect to its east neighbor. The 3000 series direct interconnect lets the X output connect to the east and west neighbors and the Y output to connect to the north and south neighbors. Direct interconnect is effective but it relies on appropriate function assignment to adjacent cells. Clearly, shift registers fit nicely. The direct interconnect method incurs little delay in passing signals from one cell to another through short electrical distance. Should direct interconnect be impossible, the LCA has alternatives—namely, general purpose and long line interconnect.

General purpose interconnect occurs through a grid of metal lines residing between the CLBs. These are short lengths of metal running vertically and horizontally in groups that intersect at a switching matrix. The switching matrix permits several distinct interconnect options. Figure 4.5 shows a switching matrix for the 3000 series parts. Relating back to Figure 4.2, the squares are the switching matrices and the rectangles are the CLBs.

The top row (1–5) in Figure 4.5 shows that top to bottom, top to left, and top to right connections are possible. Similarly, the next row shows right to top, left and bottom options. The next two rows show ten more options. If signals are assigned appropriately to the five metal lines, they can proceed in the general direction of the next target CLB. Multiple branches are permitted at the switch matrices.

The 2000 series and the 4000 series parts have different general purpose interconnect switch matrices than the 3000 series parts. The 4000 series switch matrix is shown in Figure 4.6. The dashed lines between solid segments represent pass transistors at each interconnect point on Figure 4.6. There must be a bit of RAM to control each pass transistor in Figure 4.6, so the transistor count goes up quickly per wire crossing. Note that the 4000

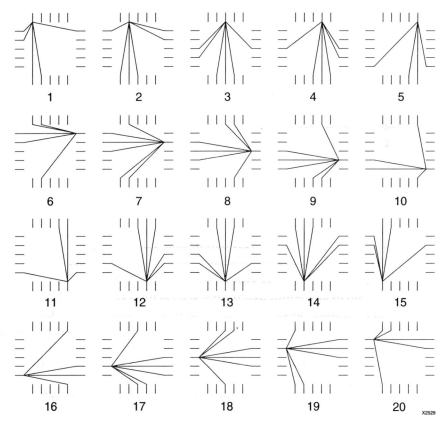

X2529

Figure 4.5 The 3000 family switching matrix.

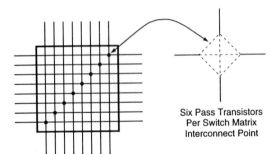

Six Pass Transistors
Per Switch Matrix
Interconnect Point

Figure 4.6 The 4000 family switching matrix.

family switch matrix permits fewer possible connections than the 3000 family. This limitation is compensated for by more versatility between single length connections and CLB inputs. Capacitive loading of the interconnections is lower in the 4000 family switch matrix than the 2000 or 3000 families, improving performance.

The general purpose interconnect lines correspond to the routing channels in a classic channelled gate array. It is possible for congestion to occur, requiring iterative layout of the logic functions. To reduce congestion, additional vertical and horizontal paths are included in all LCA families that do not intersect the switch matrices. These sparsely placed paths, called long line drivers, span the entire length or width of the die. In fact, on the 3000 series, three vertical long line paths are parallel and next to each general purpose interconnect column. As well, two horizontal long lines run parallel to each general purpose interconnect row. Long line paths are ideal for passing clocks to the CLBs minimizing skew. Skewing is reduced by using global buffers directly accessing the long line paths.

Next to each CLB is a pair of three-state buffers. These buffers access the long line paths and make bussed signals for multiplexing or wire ANDing CLB outputs.

4.4 INPUT/OUTPUT

One weakness of early gate array products was the specific I/O configurations allowed. These configurations were chosen to minimize the number of output drivers on a given die because output drivers take the most die area. However, guessing the exact requirements for most designers was impossible.

The LCA approach is to make most pins bidirectionals. This lets the user adapt the LCA to suit specific requirements. There is one limitation, in that the LCA permits only 4 mA of drive current in the 2000 and 3000 family parts. However, the LCAs drive pure CMOS environments well, never driving long communication lines, or heavily loaded busses.

Figure 4.7 shows the structure of the 3000 series I/O cell. Assuming the I/O cell is configured for input, the signal arrives at the pad, is received and sent to the D input of a flip flop or bypassed directly into the CLB array. The D flip flop at the input can be clocked from one of two different clock sources. When the pad is an output, a signal heading out first encounters an Exclusive-Or gate. One Exclusive-Or input controls the propagating signal to pass or invert the signal through the other input. The Exclusive-Or output signal then passes to the D input of a second flip flop or bipasses to a multiplexer. The Q output of the flip flop is multiplexed with the combinational output signal and drives an output buffer.

The output buffer has a separate three-state control that comes from the CLB array. The output buffer three-state control circuit also passes through an Exclusive-Or gate (for polarity control) before entering the three-state output buffer. The output of the three-state buffer is further controlled by another input that can be set for a high or low output slewing

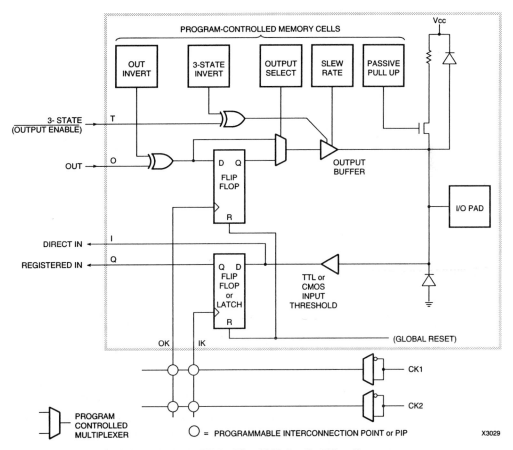

Figure 4.7   The 3000 family I/O cell.

rate. Low output slewing forces the signal to rise much slower than the high output slewing rate. The slew rate control also slows the falling rate of the signal, reducing ground bounce effects.

Finally, the output signal encounters a switchable passive output pull up resistance. Of course, there are clamp structures at the pad limiting current flow on undershoot and overshoot. In summary, one can see that a signal may be either latched on input, latched on output, purely combinational input, output, or bidirectional.

This I/O structure is nearly ideal. Two drawbacks are that it provides low current drive and the I/O cell flip flops are slower than the CLB flip flops. Drive level is important because performance is sacrificed if external capacitance needs more current. To date, none of the FPGA candidates can directly drive the 64 mA requirements of the data paths of most commercially used bus standards. Newer bus standards exceed 84 mA of current drive.

Of additional interest is the LCA 4000 boundary scan circuitry built into the I/O structure. In ordinary operation this circuitry is invisible to the designer. In test mode, it permits the I/O cells to be configured as a large shift register. Boundary scan improves the testability of the printed circuit board that uses it, and is discussed in more detail in Appendix A.

4.5 DESIGN SOFTWARE

The LCA design software is called XACT™. XACT has been engineered to accommodate a wide variety of user hardware and software configurations. Figure 4.8 shows the overall XACT operations partitioned into three categories: design entry, design implementation and design verification.

Design entry occurs by schematic capture, logical equations, or both. Xilinx supports the schematic software of popular engineering workstations or commercially available schematic entry running on personal computers. The XACT design netlist is called the XNF file. XNF is a variation of a standard netlist. The XNF file is passed to the placement and routing software or the simulation software. The placement and routing software operates automatically or manually.

If the designer chooses to place and route automatically, the software permits designer placement constraints and optimizes connections. One algorithm used for the automatic placement is modelled after a famous gate array algorithm called a simulated annealing algorithm. In this method, the designer varies the starting "simulated temperature" of the placement process by specifying that cells must remain adjacent to each other. Unspecified cells are allowed to remain unconstrained until their placement is dictated at some point along the simulated "cooling schedule." Simulated annealing

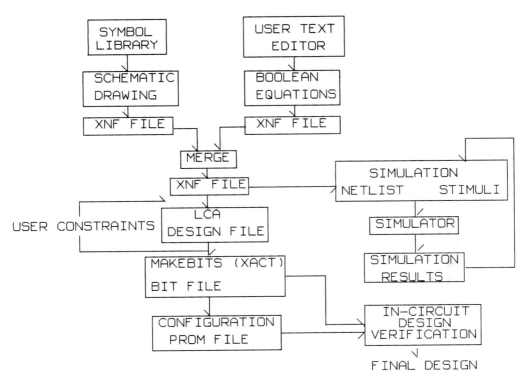

Figure 4.8   The LCA design software flow.

has been highly successful in the gate array world, but takes lots of time. Xilinx recommends that the software be allowed to perform its transformations over a lengthy period—literally overnight. Long time periods permit many different placements to be attempted so the best may be chosen. Should the designer wish, manual placement and interconnect is possible, and in many instances may be required for a tight fitting design. Improved algorithms are continually under development at Xilinx.

The LCA design method ultimately provides a final design file that becomes a PROM file. The PROM file is used to program an external PROM that in turn is loaded into the LCA configuration RAM when the LCA is initialized. The final design file can be used to back annotate the XNF file for design verification and simulation. Derating parameters, extracted from the placement file, permit more accurate simulation.

The design verification portion of XACT largely consists of simulation using a commercially available simulator running on a personal computer or workstation. Xilinx has constructed the design flow so that it can be run on workstations, using schematic capture and simulation. This approach permits designers to use the LCA methodology without having to learn many

new techniques. Xilinx simply provides the LCA specific compilation/trans-
formation software and libraries of cells. This software works with the
workstation schematic capture software and simulators. Naturally, each
specific configuration of software is tailored for the workstation environment
chosen.

When a design meets the designer's needs, it is stored in the configuration PROM, loaded into the LCA and tested in the target system. Another
interesting feature is the use of an in-circuit emulation unit that permits the
downloading of the configuration PROM file into the emulation tool. The
emulation tool permits the designer to observe the contents of specific CLB
cells, use breakpoints and perform elementary trace operations. Emulation
is not mandatory, because a good simulation usually suffices, but it is com-
forting to know that emulation is available. At least two emulation tool
makers have generalized this approach to make versatile gate array emulation systems.

4.6 DESIGN ESTIMATION

Now that the architecture and design methodology have been discussed, how
a design is done will be described. First, the designer should try and carefully
match the functional contents of the target design to the appropriate LCA
part. There are several parts from which to choose. For instance, there is a
series of LCAs that are comprised of CLBs having a single flip flop and four
input RAM CLBs. This family is the 2000 series of LCAs. The newest family,
the 4000 series, is also in production. The LCA family that has been focused
on is the 3000 series, consisting of CLB arrays with two flip flops and five
input functional RAMs. For the sake of an estimation example, choose the
3000 series.

Table 4.2 shows the number of CLBs required to make some typical
logic functions for the LCA 3000 family. All basic gates with one to five inputs
use a single CLB. For efficiency, two gates sharing the same four (or fewer)
inputs use just one CLB. This allows effective usage of the CLB by splitting
the functions across its five input RAM. Functions needing direct feed
flip flops should take advantage of the paths in the local CLB, avoiding
interconnect congestion. Functions of more than five inputs need multiple
CLBs or other design tricks. For instance, the logical AND is made for many
inputs from the long line three-state capability, by wire ANDing. Logical
NAND, AND and And-Or-Invert are made simply, with multiple parallel
five input CLBs. Functions needing more than two outputs (that is, decoders)
always require multiple CLBs. Functions of two levels using five or fewer
inputs can always be mapped into a single CLB.

TABLE 4.2   LCA 3000 Functional Equivalents

Function Description	LCA Resources
1. Basic Logic Gates	1 CLB (to 5 inp.)
2. D flip flop (edge triggered)	.5 CLB
3. D latch (transparent)	.5 CLB or 1 I/O
4. J-K flip flop (edge trig.)	1 CLB
5. Decoders	
a. 2 to 4	2 CLB
b. 3 to 8	4 CLB
c. 4 to 16	9 CLB
6. Multiplexers	
a. 2 to 1	1 CLB
b. 4 to 1	2 CLB
c. 8 to 1	4 CLB
d. 16 to 1	9 CLB
7. Comparators (equality only)	
a. 2 bit	1 CLB
b. 4 bit	1 CLB
8. Registers (serial load)	
a. 4 bit	2 CLB
b. 8 bit	4 CLB
9. Counters	
a. 2 bit	2 CLB
b. 4 bit	5 CLB

From a partitioning standpoint, simple latched static variables or variables that change seldom should be assigned to the I/O cells. Critical paths should not be assigned to CLBs residing deep within the LCA, if pin access is needed. To permit fast pin to pin reaction time, critical signals should be placed near LCA pins. Such placement permits shallow penetration and fast exit as quickly as possible near the entry points. This approach minimizes the interconnect capacitance of signals and assures signals do not encounter congestion. Routing congestion increases in the LCA central area.

Using Table 4.2, the designer assesses the number of CLBs needed for the design, by direct tallying. Then, the tally is compared to the available capacity on a given LCA (Table 4.3). The chosen LCA I/O structure must also match. The LCA architecture maximizes the number of bidirectional pins so only the number of signal pins is the primary concern, for I/O partitioning.

The designer may have to supplement Table 4.2 to add functions not shown. Additional entries should be tightly designed with optimal CLB placement in mind. For first-time designers, initial capacity targets should be 70 to 85 percent of the available CLBs. Manual intervention may still be necessary to achieve design connection even at these capacities. Judgement

TABLE 4.3   Capacity Chart for the LCA Families

Part Number	Number of CLBs	Number of I/O Pins
XC2064	64	58
XC2018	100	74
XC3020	64	64
XC3030	100	80
XC3042	144	96
XC3064	224	120
XC3090	320	144
XC4002	64	64
XC4003	100	80
XC4004	144	96
XC4005	196	112
XC4006	256	128
XC4008	324	144
XC4010	400	160
XC4013	576	192
XC4016	676	208
XC4020	900	240

will have to be used regarding the degree of randomness the target logic design has. Designs with regular structures of registers feeding registers will probably reach maximum capacity. Packed designs of completely independent combinational functions may not fare as well.

Once an LCA has been selected, one must consider the logic arrangement and select an appropriate pinout. This arrangement will evolve into a basic floorplan of the major functions. The floorplan helps at a later stage of the process, and correlates well with the block diagram of the target logic design. For best results, the I/O pin arrangement should not be too rigid, as this restricts the XACT software.

4.7 LCA DESIGN TECHNIQUES

Effective design with the LCA requires an understanding of the capabilities and limitations of the specific CLBs. Each CLB has limited function and storage capability, and it is critical to see just how those abilities can be used. Again, the focus is on the building blocks of decoders, multiplexers, shifters and counters.

Decoders are built by cascading the function RAMs of the CLBs while they are configured as either NAND or AND functions. The 2000 and 4000 series parts have only four input RAMs, so they must cascade sooner to expand input width. The 3000 series parts have five input RAMs, requiring shallower nesting of functions. To some degree, the three-state buffers can form wire ANDed functions for decoding, but this limits use for internal bussing. To make a standard three-to-eight decoder (that is, 74138) requires at least eight four input CLBs just to generate the distinct outputs for all eight combinations.

Multiplexers, like decoders, are built in the CLBs from gate equivalent RAM contents. Again, the limited number of RAM inputs requires expanding the number of CLBs to make wider gate functions. AND functions are expanded by taking the output of a four or five input AND into the input of another four or five input AND getting a seven or nine input cascaded equivalent. Likewise, wider OR functions can be made by cascading one OR function into another. The problem with this is that it consumes CLBs quickly and cuts into the function speed. Another problem is that the CLB flip flops go unused in many cases.

Shift registers are efficient in all three LCA series parts. By carefully assigning bits to adjacent CLBs, shifters need no global interconnect and do not block routing channels. The class of applications that use abundant shifters include communications equipment, pattern recognizers, polynomial generaters and data synchronizers. Just as decoders and multiplexers leave the flip flops unused, shifters usually waste CLB function boxes.

Counters present an interesting challenge in the LCA architecture. The classic textbook design methods (Chapter 3) only work for small counters. The transition logic for a counter grows very quickly in terms of the number of needed gate inputs as the high order counter bits are made. This approach is too limiting for the LCA, so Xilinx recommends an approach that is cascadeable and modular. This approach was commercially exploited in the 74F161 counter.

Figure 4.9 shows the 74F161 counter, where each flip flop cell has a similar gate cluster in front of it. The gate cluster accepts the state values of flip flops from lower order bits, as well as a special terminal count input. The counter looks across all bits in its grouping and generates a terminal count (TC in Figure 4.9) that is forwarded to the next group's input signal (CET). This approach is like generating a binary carry in adder equations. One group generates a carry out signal to another group's carry in input logic. The approach can be done over any number of bit groups that make sense.

Call a flip flop, with its input transition logic gates, a "count cell." The number of bits in the counter is equal to the number of count cells. Forming a reasonable count cell cluster size is important. Three bit clusters make sense for the 2000 family, four bit for the 3000 family and use of special carry inputs and outputs are appropriate for the 4000 family.

The primary penalty of this approach is speed, with the terminal count variable being the limiting item. Careful placement of cells within the bit groups minimizes terminal count propagation delays. This method is useful for other FPGA products seen in succeeding chapters.

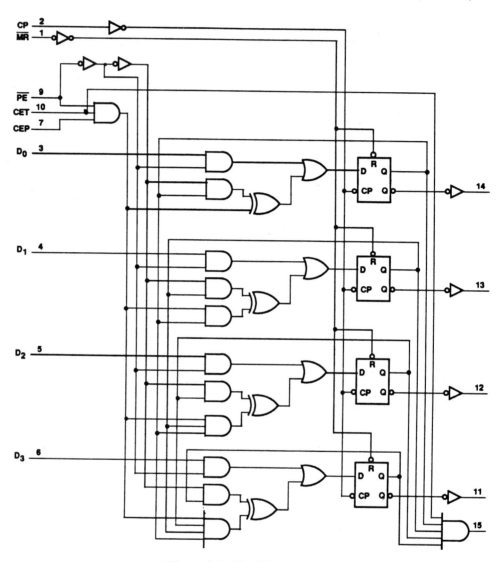

Figure 4.9 The 74F161 counter.

4.8 A SMALL EXAMPLE

As an example of the design process, configure the small example from
Chapter 2 for an LCA. This structure is shown in Figure 4.10. Four input
signals arrive in parallel and are stored with a single load pulse. The four bits
are latched at the input pins. The data bits then multiplex to a single output
line on consecutive clocks. The multiplexing is controlled by a small counter,
counting from binary zero to binary three. The counter resets itself and rolls

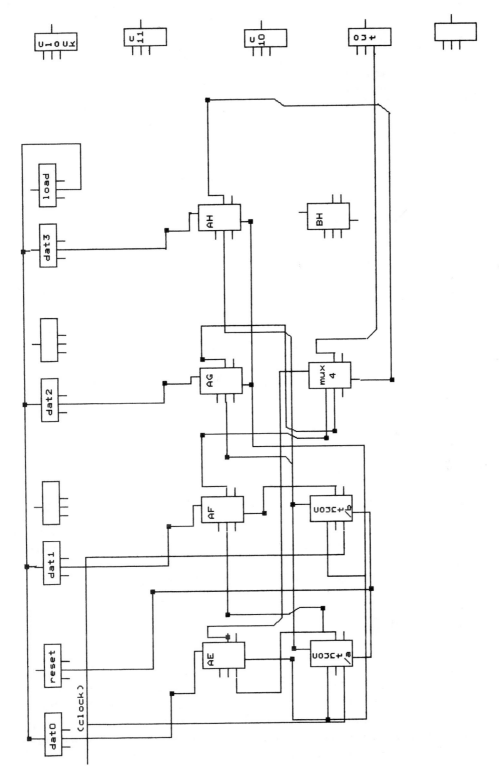

Figure 4.10 LCA partial world view of the example.

over from three to zero. The input clocking variable is separate from the output clocking variable, so each uses a distinct pin. The reset signal guarantees the counter starts from zero, and requires an input pin. Each input data bit requires a separate pin, as does the output bit. This tally sets the number of used pins at six.

The input data is stored in the I/O cells, and the outputs of each input flip flop connect to the CLBs. The CLBs are labeled AE, AF, AG, AH and MUX 4 in Figure 4.10. Inputs to the multiplexer are the four data lines as well as the selection signals. The selection signals are derived by decoding the two bit counter outputs (count/a, count/b). The two bit counter uses two CLBs. This design uses an LCA 2064 part that is smaller than the previously mentioned LCA 3000 parts.

Figure 4.10 is a partial "world view" of an LCA 2064. The world view shows cell placement and connecting metal. The function assignment is not aggressive and was hand placed using the XACT software. Cells BE and BF (that is, row B, column E) constitute the two bit counter, and cell BG is the core of the four input multiplexer. Cells AE, AF, AG, AH provide input to the multiplexer. Output occurs on the right hand side of the sheet. The clock comes in from the left top side of the sheet and forks to the two counter bits. The load signal enters and passes back to the input data latches where the input four bits are captured. The operation was described in Chapter 3. This particular design only uses seven out of sixty-four available CLBs and neatly exploits the I/O input latches.

4.9 PERFORMANCE CONSIDERATIONS

The LCA product line is manufactured in CMOS. This means that although the internal cell timing is fast, it is sensitive to capacitive loading. Loading is a strong function of cell placement on the LCA. The 3000 series parts are offered in four speed selections, −50, −70, −100 and −125 designated part. The dashed values show the upper clock toggle frequency (in MHz.) for internal flip flops. This sets the specified maximum limit on performance, because the toggle frequency is an upper bound for flip flop switching. LCA speeds will improve in the future with smaller feature CMOS processing.

Xilinx recommends some broad guidelines for estimating LCA performance across all families. Typically, a range of one-third to one-half of the maximum toggle rate is expected for ordinary designs. If the structure of the design is regular (such as a shift register) a designer can expect to operate closer to two-thirds the toggle rate. Under very careful placement of cells with all internal loading accounted for and logic minimized, higher speeds may occur.

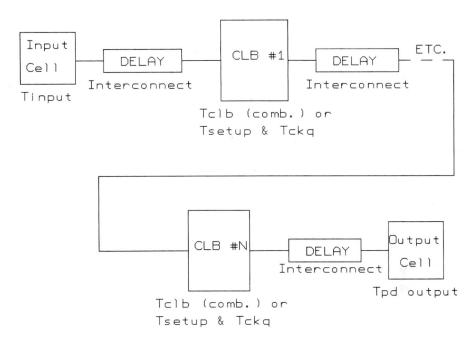

Figure 4.11   LCA timing model.

Figure 4.11 shows a simplified timing model for the LCA class of architectures. Table 4.4 shows approximate timing parameters for cells of the architecture. Values are given for the 2000, 3000 and 4000 series parts. It should be noted that the times given do not include the interconnect metal delays, but include only the internal cell times. The delay for output cells is shown for both the slow and fast slew rate controlled cells.

TABLE 4.4   Basic LCA Timing

Parameter	4000–7	3000–70	2000–70
Tpd clk buff	5	6	7
Tinput pad	4	7	6
Tin clock	7	3	6
Tpd output (fast)	7	10	9
Tpd output (slow)	10	25	9
Tclb (comb.)	7	9	10
Tsetup	2	5	7
Tckq	5	8	10

Note: Interconnection delays are not included, maximum values given. Values shown are in nanoseconds, 2000 and 3000 values from the Xilinx 1991 Data Book; 4000 values from the 1991 Preliminary 4000 Data Sheet.

4.10 POWER CONSIDERATIONS

The LCA is fairly pure CMOS. This means that the power saving abilities of CMOS are to be expected. When an LCA part goes static (no inputs wiggling), it draws only a few microamps of supply current. In real operation, its incremental power can be calculated with a knowledge of the design utilization, the system clock frequency and knowledge of the capacitive load. As well, there is a strong relationship with the input signal levels that may force the input receivers to pull Icc current if not completely switched off.

As with any large CMOS die, the estimation of the power dissipated is complex and a strong function of the environment into which the part is placed. Xilinx recommends the use of a power dissipation chart to assess power used.

4.11 CLOSING COMMENTS

United States Patent 4,706,215 was granted to Bill Carter, covering the basic CLB structure in the LCA. Although the LCA was the first entry into the FPGA marketplace and created the market, the competition has increased dramatically in a short time. The product with the most convenient features coupled with a superior architecture will be well positioned as the standard. Whether the LCA maintains this dominant position will be seen. It is certain that the LCA has had an impact on system designers that used it. Many have taken their products to market with a speed never before possible. It is certain that other manufacturers will continue to create similar products capitalizing on the momentum achieved by the LCA.

PROBLEMS

1. How many LCA 2000 CLBs will be needed to make the design shown in Figure 2.1? How many 3000 CLBs?

2. The LCA 3000 family has a CLB with two D flip flops. Each flip flop is edge triggered and has a single asynchronous input. This can create a problem for forming transparent D latches buried within the CLB array. Find a method of forming transparent latches within an LCA 3000, and show a solution to this problem. Hint: It should not require more than a single CLB and possibly some connections outside to do this.

3. J-K flip flops have been shown to be useful for other architectures. Show how to build a J-K flip flop from an edge triggered D flip flop, like that found in a

2000 series CLB. How would you build a J-K flip flop from an edge triggered D flip flop at a 2000 series I/O cell?

4. If one had to build counters like those shown for PML in Chapter 3, how quickly would the LCA 3000 cells be used up? Illustrate the point by finding a pattern in the logic and estimate the CLB usage as the counter grows to ten bits.

5. Estimate the number of CLBs needed to make a four bit adder using LCA 4000 series parts. Estimate the best case time delay for the highest order sum bit and carry out. Neglect interconnect delay, as this is a best case analysis.

6. Discuss the limits on upper count frequency for designs using a count cell approach similar to the 74F161 counter discussed in Chapter 4.

7. Discuss the efficiency of the LCA architecture in forming multiplexers and decoders. For starters, justify the contents of the cell usage tables in Chapter 4 and show the rate at which CLBs are used for larger decode and mux functions.

5

Multiple Array Matrix

5.0 INTRODUCTION

Planned families of parts with well-integrated tools are the current trend in FPGA and CPLD products. A model of this approach is the ALTERA MAX™. This chapter describes the MAX 5000 family, the MAX+PLUS™ software and gives appropriate design techniques. A small design example is used and similarities are shown with other FPGA families. A general discussion of performance, design estimation and technology mapping for this architecture are included, as well. An introduction to the new MAX 7000 family highlights its performance advantages and architectural advances.

5.1 MULTIPLE ARRAY MATRIX

The Multiple Array Matrix (MAX) combines elements of programmable array logic with the foldback NAND in a configuration using several interconnect matrices. MAX is made from CMOS EPLD technology allowing high density and the convenience of erasability. The architecture is shown in Figure 5.1. The MAX architecture consists of interspersed pockets of function and interconnect. The function blocks are called Logic Array Blocks (LAB) and the interconnection region is called the Programmable Intercon-

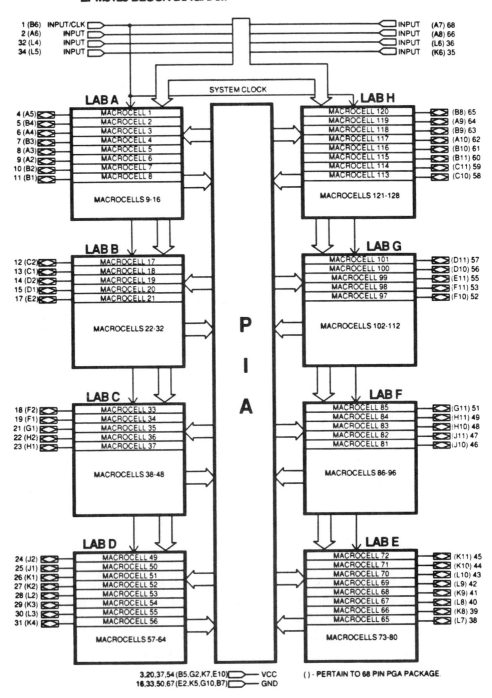

Figure 5.1 MAX architecture.

nect Array (PIA). For global interconnect, the PIA plays the role of the gate array routing channels.

One main feature of the MAX family is that it consists of small, medium and large pin count devices, starting with twenty pins on the low end and continuing to sixty-eight and eighty-four pins for the larger devices. With the recently announced MAX 7000, the MAX family continues to grow.

MAX support is an elaborate software environment called MAX+ PLUS. MAX+PLUS includes design capture, simulation and analysis in a user-friendly environment supported on personal computers and popular workstations.

5.2 INSIDE THE LAB

Figure 5.2 details the LAB. LABs typically contain sixteen macrocells and thirty-two expander gates. The number of macrocells and expanders per LAB varies some among MAX family members, but the ratio of expander gates to macrocells is 2:1. The expander gate is a foldback NAND gate. The macrocell (Figure 5.3) consists of a D flip flop with a logic function feeding its D input through the sum of three product terms. The logic function also passes through an Exclusive-Or function permitting easy reconfiguration of the D flip flop for efficient counting. Clearly, the macrocell is functionally complete, but not universal.

The macrocell flip flop can get its clock from a global clock source or from a logic array. The flip flop includes asynchronous presets and clears,

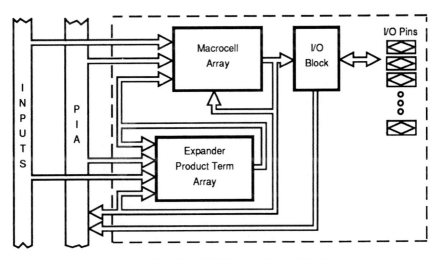

Figure 5.2   The MAX Logic Array Block.

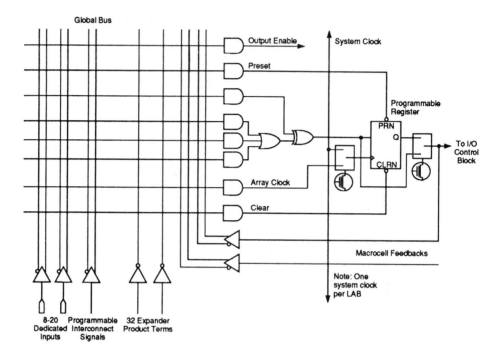

Figure 5.3   The MAX macrocell.

and drives a programmable multiplexer at its output. The flip flop output can pass to the macrocell output. Alternately, the output of the macrocell can be taken from the flip flop input logic giving a combinational function out. The macrocell output can then be routed either through a PIA or directly to an I/O control pad.

The macrocell flip flop can be structured to be a T flip flop by feeding the inverted Q output back to the flip flop D input. A J-K flip flop is configured using the product terms in front of the Exclusive-Or function at the D input. Clocking can be derived from a system clock, or taken from an array connection. Flexible clocking permits ripple and other independently clocked structures.

Also within the LAB are several expander gates shown in Figure 5.4. These gates permit the logical expansion of the macrocell combinational gates, like the foldback NAND gates described in Chapter 3. The expander gates can make combinational functions and flip flops. Remember, flip flops built from gates, may have a slight performance penalty.

The success of a design implementation hinges on the correct placement of functions inside the LABs. Correctly assigning functions to the macrocells and expanders is critical for effective LAB usage. The PIA must only be used for connecting one LAB to another, because there is a significant time delay penalty for connecting globally with the PIA, in the MAX 5000 family.

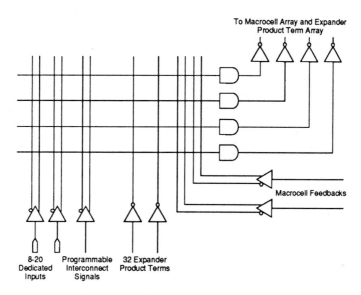

Figure 5.4   The MAX expander array.

The LAB, taken as a building block, is a very large grain function cell. Even taking the macrocells within the LAB, as the basic building block, the granularity is still quite large. Again, the design mapping involves stripping away unused functions to get what is needed from the cells. As usual, this process results in unused portions of the internal logic.

Configurations of the MAX macrocell can best be seen by examining Figure 5.5, a simplified view. By setting the flip flop asynchronous inputs A and F to logical ones, the cell entry points B, C, D, and E are the logical cell

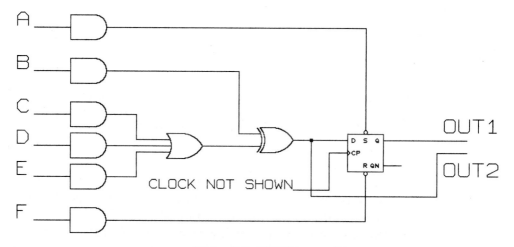

Figure 5.5   MAX macrocell.

inputs for combinational or sequential machines. For instance, setting B to a logical zero permits the sum of product terms formed at the C, D, and E inputs. Setting C, D and E to logical zero permits the Exclusive-OR to form the complement of the B signal. These functions can either be stored in the flip flop and passed through to OUT1 or they can bypass the flip flop to OUT2. Other functions exist.

5.3 INTERCONNECT

The interconnection occurs at two levels—locally, within the LAB and globally, using the PIA. As noted in Figure 5.3, the macrocell has seven product terms controlling flip flop behavior. The outputs of the macrocell also feed back into the LAB.

The PIA is a large vertical bus spanning the central length of the MAX die. The PIA is large enough to provide interconnect for the LAB inputs on each MAX part, which all have varying numbers of LABs. The width of the PIA varies among the MAX parts.

The PIA also accommodates all macrocell outputs and I/O pin feedback. For global interconnect, this includes all pins. From an electronic viewpoint, this requires strong internal PIA buffers to reduce signal skew and time delay when accessing this large bus. Smaller MAX parts do not provide a PIA because functions must map entirely into the single LAB on these parts.

As might be expected, overall speed strongly depends on how often a signal crosses the PIA. Functions contained wholly within LABs are fairly fast. These function speeds increased when MAX parts were made on a smaller feature CMOS process, with the MAX 7000 family. The MAX 7000 PIA is also significantly faster than that of the MAX 5000.

5.4 INPUT/OUTPUT

MAX parts use a mix of input as well as input/output cells (Figure 5.6). The input only cells are made available to all LABs. The input/output cells are associated with particular LABs because the macrocell outputs go to I/O blocks associated with specific pins. When configured for input, I/O signals go back to the PIA for broadcast to the entire part. By logically driving the pin output enable control, each I/O pin can be configured as input only, output only or a transceiver. Naturally, three-state busses can be made by sharing the same output control over multiple macrocells.

There are no flip flops at the I/O pins, as with the LCA. MAX flip flops reside in the LAB macrocells or are made with the expander NANDS, like

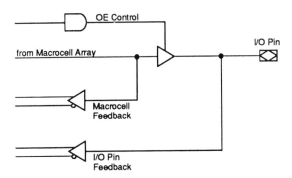

Figure 5.6   The MAX I/O cell.

PML. Output drivers have as high as 50 mA output current, but larger MAX parts have 25 mA specified. With more available outputs that can be driven, simultaneous drive of many cells can present a situation where the electrical ground rises in voltage. This means that a performance degradation occurs, so full current drive design restrictions exist, which are outlined in the data sheets.

5.5 DESIGN SOFTWARE

The MAX+PLUS flow is shown in Figure 5.7. MAX+PLUS is an environment where intermediate design netlists are common to multiple internal modules. The designer interacts with a high level software interface. Design entry is accomplished by schematic, logic equation, state, and truth table

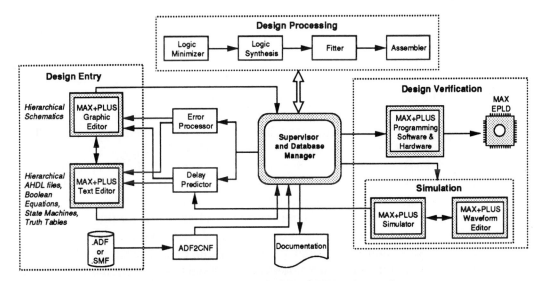

Figure 5.7   The MAX+PLUS software flow.

entry. The entry system supports hierarchy, as well. The successor software package, MAX+PLUS II maintains the philosophy of MAX+PLUS, but adds even more features.

Additional design input comes from netlists made by other PLD design software. This capability permits designs to be quickly changed from other design formats into the MAX+PLUS format. A macrofunction library is provided consisting of familiar 7400 series logic functions.

Compilation consists of a series of netlist transformations and final assembling to a program table interconnect file. The first transformations include extracting the interconnects from the schematics, equations or table formats. These files are formatted into a specific database for the "logic synthesizer." The logic synthesizer is a system of rules and pattern recognition algorithms that perform judicious substitutions to reduce the netlist logic. Chapter 2 showed some standard netlist optimization methods used by many FPGA software packages.

The next operation—the fitter—performs the equivalent of a function placement module, where specific logic functions are assigned to LAB macrocells or to the expanders. The fitted design is then connected, to give a final, placed netlist. The compilation process was outlined in Chapter 2.

In the MAX+PLUS technology mapper, the design is interpreted for the architecture by isolating and identifying where flip flops can land in a macrocell, or the expander—where logic can be assigned to the macrocell or the expander, and so forth. Finally, the designer extracts a netlist for simulation, using the MAX+PLUS simulator, to verify the translated design.

The simulator provides graphical input and output, with full time derating, to account for function placement within the design. The simulator permits conditional and incremental simulation and is event driven for efficiency. Timing resolution can be performed down to 100 picosecond intervals, if needed. Oscillation detection is available as well as flip flop setup and hold time checking. The MAX simulator graphical display has a zooming capability showing different levels of timing expansion, for convenience.

The assembler takes the finally compiled netlist and converts it into a program table for configuration with the MAX programming unit. The MAX programming unit then loads the design into a MAX part like any other PLD.

One key feature to consider is that MAX+PLUS presents the use of a closed design environment. A closed environment allows no direct external interface to other software packages. There are advantages and disadvantages to a closed environment. A major advantage is that when design errors are found, they may be isolated at one level and directly linked back to a different level for observation or correction. The linkage occurs automatically. As an example, consider encountering an error during compilation due to node loading. The exact node can be isolated and immediately referred to at the schematic level through a series of window references. The correction can be made and the direct results of the change observed immediately after recompilation. This is convenient.

The biggest disadvantage to a closed environment is that desirable commercial software may exist that cannot be tied in to the MAX+PLUS software. Specifically, other schematic capture packages and simulators will not be immediately compatible with MAX+PLUS. These packages will definitely not support the linkage that the closed environment provides. This situation can change in the future. The latest version of MAX+PLUS is called MAX+PLUS II and it can be linked to other commercially available software in some situations.

5.6 DESIGN ESTIMATION

Design estimation for the MAX product line is straightforward. Assuming the a.c. performance is appropriate, the next level of consideration is I/O partitioning and functional density. Basic I/O partitioning is simply selecting among the parts those that have enough of the correct kind of pins. First level functional estimation consists of tallying the relative flip flop and gate counts of the target design. Macrocell flip flops should be used if possible. It should be remembered that more flip flops can be built from gates, if needed. For designs needing many flip flops, the usual gate to flip flop conversion is taken as six expander NANDs equal one D flip flop. For gated D latches, this is taken as three or four gates per latch.

The target design must be broken down into a collection of the primitive building blocks corresponding to equivalent M.S.I. chips. For first level estimation, this approach identifies where the design fits into the MAX family parts.

A more direct approach is to capture the design using the MAX+ PLUS software and let the software eliminate unused logic. The designer then migrates the design from one MAX part to another until a fit is found. A simple method is to take the design, piece by piece, and tally the required number of gates and flip flops, comparing this to the target device capacity.

There are times when some item within a design is a compromise based on limited availability of existing M.S.I. functions. A classic example of this would be making a twenty-two input multiplexer from two sixteen-to-one muxes. Using flexible connections within a CPLD such as MAX, the designer gets the exact function needed from the raw building blocks. The design software often comes up with the same solution, but the designer gets precise design control. Many times, the designer builds up the design, rather than having the software strip away unneeded pieces.

Table 5.1 gives a listing of MAX family functional equivalents. This

TABLE 5.1   MAX Functional Equivalents

Function Description	MAX Resources
1. Basic Logic Gates	1 or 2 expander NANDs
2. D flip flop (edge triggered)	1 macrocell
3. D latch (transparent)	4 expander NANDs
4. J-K flip flop (edge trig.)	1 macrocell
5. Decoders	
a. 2 to 4	4 expander nands
b. 3 to 8	8 expander nands
c. 4 to 16	16 expander NANDs
6. Multiplexers	
a. 2 to 1	3 expander NANDs
b. 4 to 1	5 expander NANDs
c. 8 to 1	9 expander NANDs
d. 16 to 1	17 expander NANDs
7. Comparators (equality only)	
a. 2 bit	4 exp.NANDs/1macrocell
b. 4 bit	10 exp.NANDs
8. Registers (serial load)	
a. 4 bit	4 macrocells
b. 8 bit	8 macrocells
9. Counters	
a. 2 bit	2 macrocells
b. 4 bit	4 macrocells

table is similar to the cell tables described previously. Table 5.1 shows how many internal resources are used when various logic functions are made. As usual, bigger cells can be built up from smaller pieces using this table. A device selection table is still needed to target the design onto a specific MAX part after the tally is made. Table 5.2 gives this basic information, but package and capacities can easily become outdated, so for most recent information, contact ALTERA.

TABLE 5.2   Basic MAX Function Capacities

	EPM5016	EPM5032	EPM5064	EPM5128	EPM5192
MACROCELLS	16	32	64	128	192
PINS	20	28	44	68	84
Max FFs	21	42	84	168	252
NANDS	32	64	128	256	384

Note: FFs are edge triggered D type.

5.7 MAX DESIGN TECHNIQUES

The design techniques appropriate for MAX resemble both those of PML in Chapter 3 and the LCA in Chapter 4, as well as some that are specific to MAX. As usual, focus is on how to make standard decoding, multiplexing, shifting and counting blocks. However, the first concern is simply remembering that functions that remain completely within one LAB are faster than functions that span several LABs.

Decoders are straightforward. The most natural way to make a decoder is in the expander array. Signals entering the expander can be simply NANDed together to make the decoded variables needed. As usual, only those that are actually used, will be made and MAX+PLUS minimizes automatically. Designers can work at the symbolic level and let the software handle the function mapping, or designers can work at the lower primitive gate level. Because decoders do not use flip flops, as a rule, they will not be made in the macrocells. Using macrocells for decode, bypasses and wastes the flip flops.

Multiplexers are similar. The expanders are the best place for them to land. A small three-to-one multiplexer can be made in the macrocell section but also wastes the local flip flop. Sometimes multiplexers may require this for compacting them onto a particular LAB for speed. The expander is best suited for multiplexing.

Due to the small amount of transition logic on a macrocell D flip flop, shift registers are best configured from these. This permits strings of up to sixteen flip flop shifters to be made entirely within a single LAB. By using the thirty-two gate expander arrays as a flip flop source, five more bits may be added within a given LAB. Gate built flip flops are slower than the macrocell flip flops, but they may be faster than going through the PIA to an adjacent LAB to add more flip flops. The speed of each of these components will be evident in section 5.10.

Counters built from D flip flops present the usual problem—that is, too much transition logic driving the D inputs. This can be solved by using the count cell technique (that is, 74F161) that was described for the LCA in Chapter 4. Here, each D flip flop macrocell is configured into a small counter cell with its transition logic configured to accept and help generate the terminal count propagating signals previously described. Again, designers should be aware that, like carry look-ahead adders, there is a time penalty for this method. The time penalty has a corresponding capacity payoff. Very large counters can be built with the MAX architecture, by cascading within an LAB, and then cascading through the PIA from one LAB to another.

As expected, ALTERA provides a library of basic decoding, multiplexing, shifting, and counting cells and the software optimizes and places the cells automatically.

5.8 A SMALL EXAMPLE

The previously described example is now repeated in the MAX+PLUS environment. As mentioned before, it is quite small and is translated for a small MAX part, the EPM5032. The design can easily be moved to denser parts.

Figure 5.8 shows the design captured using MAX+PLUS soft macros, where the multiplexer is taken from the 7400 series library. It should be noted that unused functions in soft macros are automatically deleted when the design is translated for the part being used. Figure 5.9 shows the stripped down design translated to MAX primitives. Each internal buffer is shown in partial detail. In a full detail display, the propagation time for each cell is shown on the network attached to the output of that cell. The time delay for a path may be tallied if needed. A timing assessment is straightforward from such a display.

In the signal flow for Figure 5.9, the input data arrives at the pins. The data is received and routed directly to the D inputs of the LAB macrocell flip flops through the Exclusive-Or gates. The counter is generated from two D flip flop macrocells. The transition terms driving the counter flip flops fit within the three product terms at each cell, so expanders are not needed for the counter. The multiplexer can be made with additional macrocells, or with the expander NAND gates. This corresponds to the gating shown at the far right of Figure 5.9. The clock, load, and reset signals are handled similar to the previous versions of this example.

The macrocell and expander capacity estimates for this design are simple. The counter uses two macrocells, the multiplexer uses one, the input data latches use four macrocells. The pin requirements are eight, with one each for clock, load, reset, and data out, and four for data input. The whole design takes eight pins and seven macrocells. The entire design fits into a single LAB, so there is no need for a part using a PIA.

5.9 PERFORMANCE CONSIDERATIONS

The MAX timing model is shown in Fig. 5.10. Basic components of the MAX architecture are broken out so that paths are associated with their expected time delays. Performance estimation occurs by adding up the delays. Tracing a signal from the input pin to an output pin, gives all of the lumped time delays encountered.

In detail, a signal enters the part and incurs an input delay, Tin. It then forks to the expander (Texp), the logic array control (Tlac), the logic array (Tlad) or the clock (Tic). These paths may wrap around the expander,

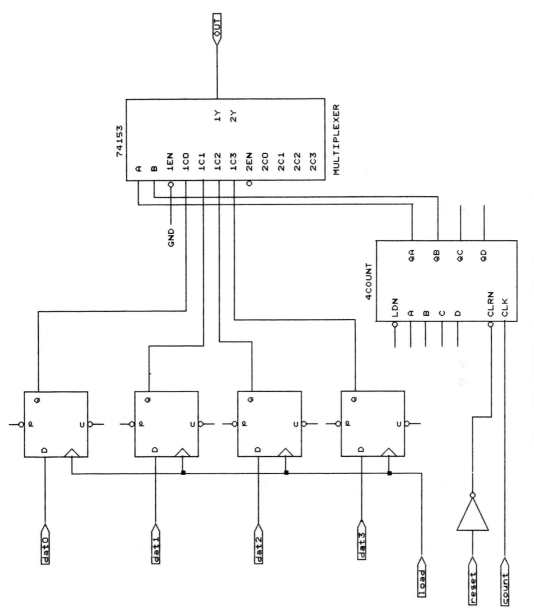

Figure 5.8 MAX version of the design example.

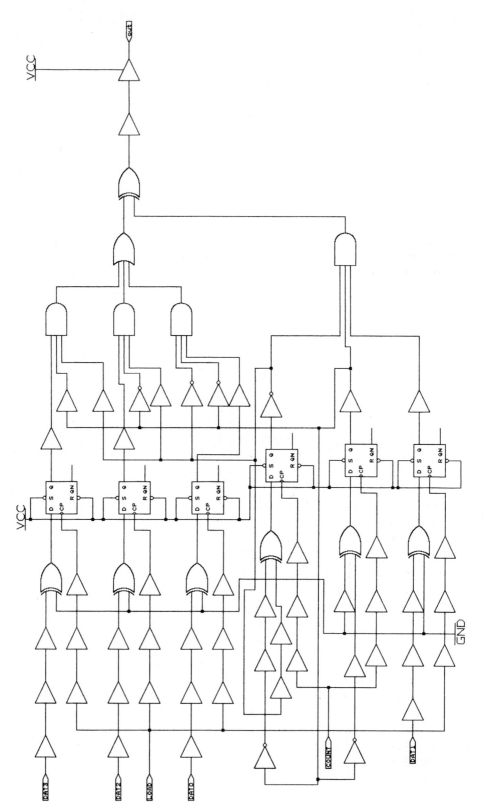

Figure 5.9 MAX example expanded.

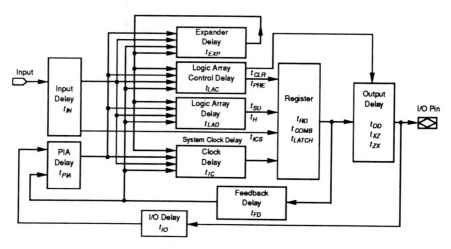

Figure 5.10   The MAX timing model.

proceed to the clear and preset of the macrocell register or bypass to the output. The signals may clock the flip flop or pass through the flip flop. Additional paths exist for feedback from the flip flop. As can be seen in Figure 5.10, even more paths exist, so the tally of additional increments is best done by the reader using Table 5.3 for the appropriate architecture.

To improve some of the timing and power specifications of the MAX 5000 family, ALTERA developed an enhanced architecture—the MAX 7000 family. Slated to be a large family of parts, Figure 5.11 shows the basic block diagram of a MAX 7000 part. In particular, note how I/O can occur directly with LABs or the PIA, which is different from the arrangement of the MAX 5000 shown in Figure 5.1.

Figure 5.12 shows the MAX 7000 macrocell, which contains D flip flops driven from product terms similar to the predecessor 5000 family and the familiar expander. The global clocks and the register bypass connections are the same on each, but the MAX 7000 has an optional global clear signal

TABLE 5.3   MAX Timing Parameters

Parameter	5128	−1	−2	5064	−1	−2	5032	−1	−2	5016	−1	−2
T inp	9	7	5	9	7	6	7	5	4	5	5	4
T out	6	5	5	6	5	4	5	5	4	5	4	4
T pia	20	16	14	20	16	13	—	—	—	—	—	—
T exp	20	14	12	20	14	12	15	10	8	10	8	5
T comb	4	4	3	4	4	3	3	1	1	1	1	1
T setup	10	8	6	8	8	6	8	5	5	8	5	2
T rd	2	2	1	2	2	1	1	1	1	1	1	1

Note: all times include local cell metal delays. See the delay for access to the PIA for interconnect through it. All values maximum in nanoseconds. Output delay includes 35 pf of load capacitance.

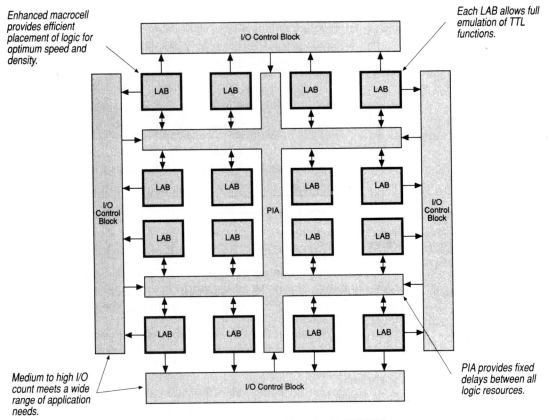

Figure 5.11 The MAX 7000.

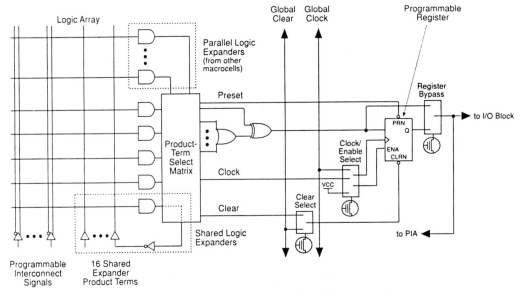

Figure 5.12 The MAX 7000 macrocell.

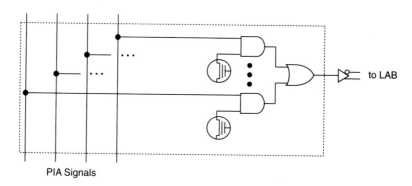

Figure 5.13   The MAX 7000 PIA.

absent on the MAX 5000. Rather than assigning three product terms per OR function, per the MAX 5000, the MAX 7000 has five product terms presented to a product term select matrix. The outputs of the product term select matrix can be assigned to the OR function, clock, preset, or clear, as needed. If the global clock and clear are used, the gates which would have been used to drive them can now be used to form product terms driving the OR function which feeds the Exclusive-OR gate. As usual, the Exclusive-OR can drive the D input or bypass to the I/O block and the PIA.

One of the most dramatic changes is in the design of the MAX 7000 PIA. Taken from the MAX 5000 delay of 14 nanoseconds down to a uniform value of 2 nanoseconds, the PIA structure is vastly improved. The design trick used for the new PIA is shown in Figure 5.13, where EPROM transistors are shown tied to an AND gate input leg. The transistors select the PIA signal

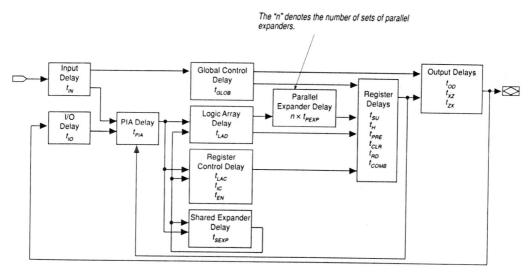

Figure 5.14   The MAX 7000 timing model.

TABLE 5.4   MAX 7000 Timing Parameters

Parameter	EPM7032-2	EPM7256-2
Tin	2	3
Tio	2	3
Tpia	1	3
Tglob	1	3
Tlad	5	8
Tlac	5	8
Tic	5	8
Ten	5	8
Tsexp	7	8
Tpexp	2	3
Tsu	3	4
Th	3	4
Tpre	3	4
Tclr	3	4
Trd	1	1
Tcomb	1	1
Tod	3	5
Txz	6	9
Tzx	6	9
Tlpa	5	8

Note: Tod is taken with output load capacitance of 35 pF. All values are maximum time delays in nanoseconds. Tlpa is the low power adder to Tlad, Tlac, Tic, Ten and Tsexp when in low power.

to pass into a LAB. The PIA signal does not pass through the EPROM cell as in the MAX 5000, creating a slow path. Instead, a static enabling value is applied to the non-signal-carrying leg, passing the signal through a fast gate. This approach is a form of multiplexing that speeds signal passage but reduces connectivity.

Because of these improvements and a smaller feature CMOS process used on the MAX 7000, different timing parameters are appropriate as well as a modified timing model. Figure 5.14 shows the new timing model and Table 5.4 includes values for the first two MAX 7000 members—the EPM7032 and the EPM7256.

5.10 POWER ESTIMATION

MAX is an EPLD based product. This means that the core is essentially an NMOS structure with CMOS I/O circuitry. Hence, the power dissipation is really not classic CMOS with respect to frequency. ALTERA suggests that the power be measured in the final design. The supply current is not a linear frequency function as ordinary CMOS exhibits, but does increase dissipation with frequency.

The MAX 7000 family includes the ability to lower the power on selected macrocells, by 50 percent or more. This is done at the expense of speed, but is handy for minimizing overall power consumption by assigning slow functions to macrocells which have their power lowered.

5.11 CLOSING COMMENTS

United States Patent 4,871,930 was awarded to Hartmann, Kopec, Wong and So for the basic MAX structure. The staged release of the MAX family is proceeding with both high-end and low-end family members available, at the time of this writing. Low-end parts contain no PIA and appear in small pin count packages. High-end parts come equipped with a PIA and medium to high pin count packages.

The MAX 5000 and MAX 7000 families are Complex Programmable Logic Devices—CPLDs. Because of their high degree of connectivity and density, the MAX parts are well suited for dense interface and high speed controller applications.

PROBLEMS

1. Estimate the number of macrocells needed to make the design shown in Figure 2.1. Should this design be done with macrocells or in the expanders?

2. Show how to make a J-K flip flop from a MAX 5000 macrocell.

3. Find a reasonable strategy for making simple up counters with the MAX 5000 cells. Does the strategy change any for the MAX 7000?

4. Can flip flop merging (discussed in Chapter 3 problems) be used with the MAX family? Explain how.

5. When various functions are formed, some resources are wasted. What gets wasted when multiplexers, decoders, shifters and counters are built from MAX cells?

6. Using expanders on the MAX 5000, show how many expander gates are needed to add one more SOP product to a macrocell. What is the setup time speed penalty to do this? How does the MAX 7000 improve this?

6

ACT

6.0 INTRODUCTION

ACTEL corporation chose a distinct path with its ACT products. Combining a fine grain building block, with an innovative programming cell, the resulting product is very similar to a CMOS gate array. This chapter shows the ACT family, its strengths and weaknesses and gives a context for evaluating it. As usual, the small example will again be shown and additional design techniques for the ACT architecture given.

6.1 ACT 1, 2 AND 3

The ACT™ programmable gate array product consists of a family of programmable parts that can be configured using an antifuse called PLICE (Programmable Low Impedance Circuit Element). The architecture provides rows of logic modules interleaved with horizontal and vertical antifuse connection regions. Unlike lateral surface fuses found in classic PLDs, the PLICE mechanism makes connections, not disconnections. Each logic module is an array of CMOS transistors with eight inputs taken from the interconnection region, and one output routed back to the connection region.

The logic module can be configured in several ways forming gates, latches, flip flops, and inverters. Some functions require several logic mod-

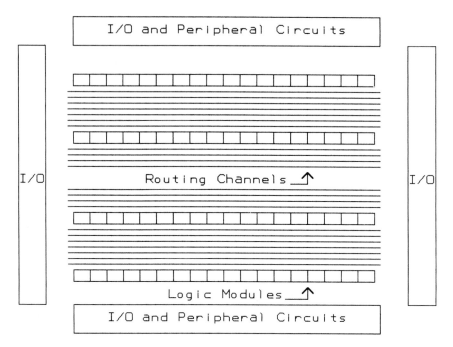

Figure 6.1   The ACT programmable gate array.

ules in cascade. The logic modules can be interconnected through routing channels to form the logic required to realize the designer's target design. Currently available technologies are 2 micron CMOS for ACT 1, 1.2 micron CMOS for ACT 2 and 0.8 micron CMOS for ACT 3. Figure 6.1 shows the ACT 1 arrangement. ACT 2 and ACT 3 are extensions of the ACT 1 idea.

6.2 INSIDE THE LOGIC MODULE

Figure 6.2 shows the logic module in detail. Because of its structure, the logic module is best suited for multiplexer based designs. Consequently, ACTEL directs designers to select functions that are most efficiently built from multiplexers. Simple sums of logical products and products of logical sums are strong candidates for efficient design.

From a partitioning viewpoint, designers are encouraged to map the most function possible into each logic module. A single gate dedicated to a single logic module is discouraged. Mapping at least two levels of logic into each logic module is encouraged. Naturally, the classic gate array trick of merging logic functions into flip flops is desirable and possible. By carefully applying these design methods, netlist compression occurs. Design conges-

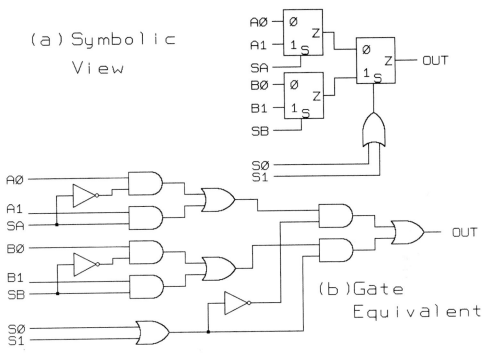

Figure 6.2   The ACT logic module.

tion is reduced by maximizing internal logic module connections. This creates fewer congested regions in the routing channels outside the logic modules. Netlist compression is simply minimizing external netlist connections by packing each module as much as possible.

It should be noted that the ACT 1 products do not contain any flip flops. Flip flops are built by cascading logic modules. The number of available logic modules varies from 295 in the smallest array to 1400 in the largest array for the ACT 1 family.

Figure 6.2a shows how the logic module appears from a macroscopic viewpoint. Figure 6.2b shows a gate equivalent of the internal cell structure. From a classic gate array viewpoint, the module has about eleven equivalent gates. Partial utilization is usually achieved because any configuration strips down the actual gates used.

To see how this flexible building block makes various functions, consider the equation:

```
Out = /(SO + S1)*(AO*/SA + A1*SA) + (SO + S1)*(BO*/SB + B1*SB)
```

By setting various inputs to logical ones or logical zeroes and connecting the same variable to different input pins, Out becomes one of several different logic functions. The ACTEL literature shows how to make more function connections, but the following examples show the basic approach.

Example 1:

Two input AND gate

```
set SO = 1, set BO = O apply inputs to SB and B1.
Output = (SB)*(B1)
```

Example 2:

INVERTER (this cell is discouraged by ACTEL)

```
set SO = 1, set B1 = O, set BO = 1, input on SB
Output = /SB
```

Example 3:

NOR gate

```
set A1 = SA = 1, set B1 = BO = O, input on SO and S1
Output = /(SO + S1)
```

The logic module is functionally complete and makes any logic function in cascade, by forming the AND with INVERT, NOR, etc. Table 6.1 shows the required inputs to generate more logic and storage functions with single logic modules. Multiple modules cascade to form larger functions, but designers should try to force as much function as possible into a single logic module. In particular, use of the available cell inversions make the generation of separate inverted intermediate variables unnecessary. This trick has a large design payoff.

The use of transparent latches, made from a single logic module, is also encouraged. Transparent latches are desirable because edge triggered flip flops require layout clustering (that is, adjacent logic modules) and contribute to design congestion. Transparent latches are often adequate and use few channel interconnects. This is also why the new ACT 2 and ACT 3 families include flip flop cells, providing speed and edge triggering without additional congestion.

TABLE 6.1 Additional Logic Module Configurations

Function								
	A0	A1	SA	B0	B1	SB	S0	S1
X*/Y + Z*Y	—-	—	—	X	Z	Y	1	0
X*Y + /Y*/X	1	0	X	0	1	X	Y	0
D - Latch	Q	D	EN	—	—	—	0	0
	(Output equals Q, which feeds back)							

Note: "-" entries denote don't cares.

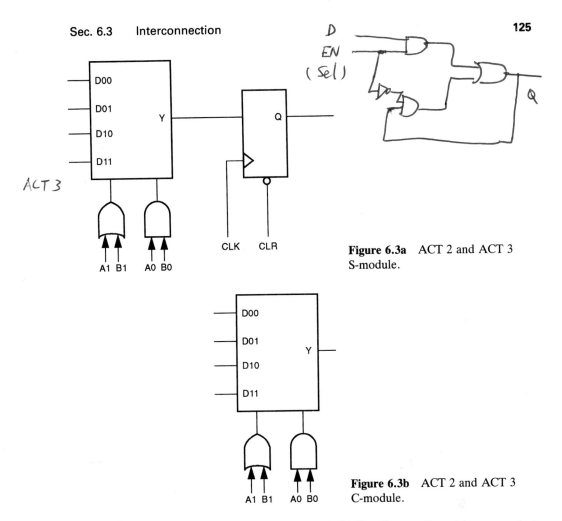

Figure 6.3a ACT 2 and ACT 3 S-module.

Figure 6.3b ACT 2 and ACT 3 C-module.

Figure 6.3a shows the ACT 2 and 3 flip flop cell, with expanded functionality on the logic module that drives the flip flop. Figure 6.3a is called the S-module, suggesting it is for sequential design. Figure 6.3b shows the ACT 2 and ACT 3 C-modules, which are enhanced over the ACT 1 cell. In particular, note the added gate inputs for the multiplexer control, which expands the number of inputs possible on many ACT 2 functions. The ACT 3 internal architecture is very similar to that of ACT 2.

6.3 INTERCONNECTION

PLICE interconnection occurs by a technique similar in idea to the AIM diode mentioned in Chapter 3. PLICE forms a short circuit made from polysilicon, giving a low impedance region. Figure 6.4 shows a cross section of the silicon arrangement. Via contacts are tiny vertical connection paths

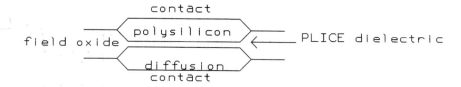

Note: PLICE dielectric is
Silicon Nitride sandwiched
between Silicon Dioxide

Figure 6.4 PLICE antifuse.

located in the polysilicon and diffusion silicon regions. Connection occurs by breaking down the dielectric sandwich (silicon nitride between layers of silicon dioxide) with a high voltage across the via. The dielectric breakdown permits a polysilicon whisker to migrate across the gap, forming a connection. Chapter 9 will discuss another antifuse approach, which only changes the silicon impedance. The impedance of PLICE interconnections—often below 200 ohms—contributes to signal time delay. The design software minimizes consecutive fuses encountered by signals, reducing time delay.

The eight inputs to each logic module are available in the routing channels, with four on each side. The output is available on both sides of the logic module for interconnect flexibility. When multiple modules are united to form a hard macro function, they are placed adjacent, and connected with identical metal patterns making predictable switching parameters.

Antifuse programming uses the interconnect paths themselves forming a coincident voltage selection point. When specific logic modules are placed, their programming order must be predetermined so innermost functions are programmed first. Successive functions—radiating outward from the die center—are programmed as the algorithm proceeds. The design software takes care of this automatically. There are both horizontal and vertical paths for antifuse interconnection. If only 85 percent of the logic module capacity is used, current software can place and route nearly 100 percent of the design.

Figure 6.5 illustrates the interconnect architecture where the rectangular blocks represent logic modules and the circled intersections are antifuse sites. For the ACT 1 family, there are twenty-two horizontal interconnect rows between the rows of logic modules. There are also three more metal rows with one for supply voltage, one for ground and one for test point observation. The ACT 2 family adds flip flops and expands the number of interconnect resources in a smaller feature CMOS process. The ACT 2 provides thirty-six horizontal routing channels and fifteen vertical ones. ACT 3 offers additional interconnect resources beyond those of ACT 2 and ACT 1.

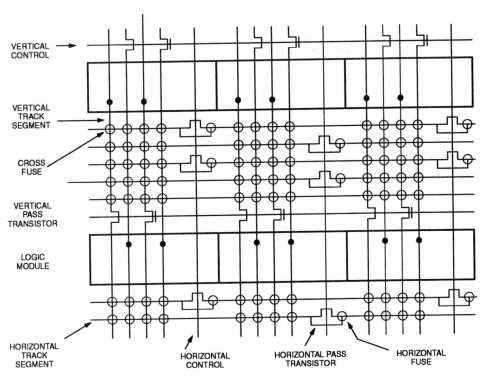

Figure 6.5   The ACT interconnect architecture.

6.4 INPUT/OUTPUT

The ACT 1 bidirectional I/O cell is shown in Figure 6.6. Each pin may be configured as an input, output, tri-stated output or transceiver. Configuration occurs by programming the two antifuses (F1 and F2) shown in the figure. The ACT 1 current drive is 4 milliamps, max. The ACT 2 current drive is 8 milliamps max, but ACT 3 raises this to 12 mA. The target current drive is for CMOS systems, but TTL levels are also possible.

I/O signal storage must occur in the logic modules on ACT 1 or ACT 2, or S cells on ACT 2. ACT 3 includes functionally enhanced I/O cells capable of capturing signals in either direction with edge triggered flip flops located near the chip I/O pads. These I/O cells are similar to those described in Chapter 4, for the LCA.

6.5 DESIGN SOFTWARE

The ACT design software (Figure 6.7) has many options. The only required steps are the design capture, the place and route and the programming. Additional options include preliminary timing simulation, prelayout critical

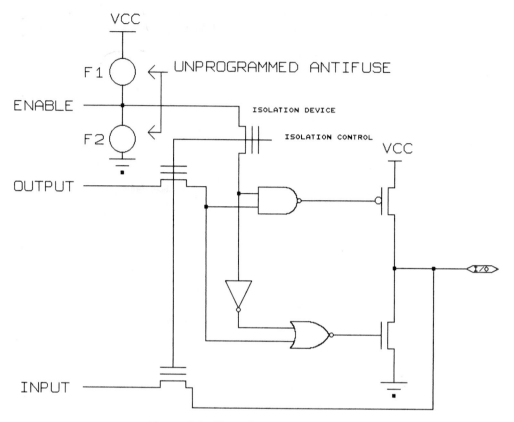

Figure 6.6 The ACT bidirectional I/O cell.

path timing analysis, postlayout timing analysis and simulation. Testing can be done with the Actionprobes and debugger, discussed shortly.

Design capture is usually schematic capture on a personal computer-based workstation. A library of SSI and MSI macros exists with the ability for user defined soft macros. When the design reaches an appropriate level of completion, a netlist can be extracted. The netlist is given the file extension .ADL, for ACT Design Language and is a fairly generic netlist. The ADL file may be directly placed and routed, but it is appropriate to check for design rule violations with the Design Validator.

The Validator checks for general electrical rule violations that include floating inputs, wire-ANDed outputs, output loading violations, and so on. Once a design passes the Validator, it is appropriate to generate a complete layout with the Configure program.

Automatic placement and routing occur with the Configure program. The Configure program input is the user defined pin assignment, the previously generated ADL netlist and any information influencing time critical nets. The output will be the exact placement, routing and a set of time delays

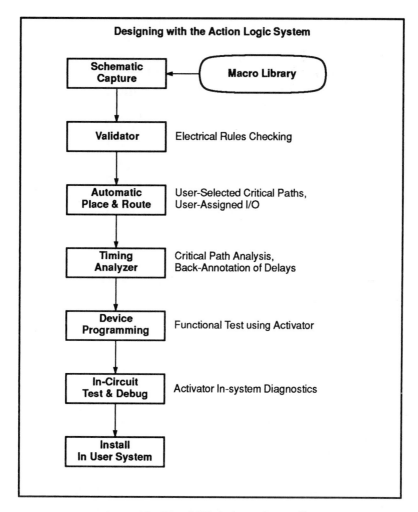

Figure 6.7   The ACT design software flow.

reflecting the capacitance for each net. If the design can be placed and routed, the net time delays are available for postlayout analysis. The design may be programmed at this point. It is appropriate to perform a postlayout simulation and critical path check using either the simulator or the Timer.

Timing analysis occurs using the Timer program. The Timer is simple, but powerful. The Timer reconstructs the netlist and associates both the intrinsic logic module delay and corresponding output metal delay. The association of pins that constitute a starting set and ending set for the signal paths is done. Next, the time delay tally between the pins is made, so the designer can examine the placement and routing results. The Timer can be used before design layout without metal delays. The more meaningful assessment occurs after layout, because the exact metal delays are then known.

Once design correctness is assured, a fusemap is made and loaded into the Activator, which programs a part. The Activator is a separate programming unit to handle the PLICE programming. Loading occurs over a serial port link from a computer. The Activator hardware translates the fusemap into a sequence of voltages that program the various PLICE coordinates.

The Debugger program may be used optionally and works with the Actionprobes. The Actionprobes are special I/O pins permitting access to user specified internal nodes. The Actionprobes capture signal transition information at the nodes, and pass it to the outside world, for testing. The output of each logic module has a three-state inverting buffer on it, making a large wire-ANDed node, which is taken to the external pin.

The selection of a single logic module output is done by decoding a serially loaded address targeting the desired logic module. Decoding also enables the logic module output for external observation. When the Action-probes are used for testing, they cannot be used as I/O pins also, so their assignment must be made carefully.

The Debugger makes a set of input vectors from a simulation file and applies these to the programmed part for analysis. The Debugger does not require the use of the Actionprobes, but the Actionprobes permit systematic access to the internal logic module nodes.

6.6 DESIGN ESTIMATION

Design estimation is straightforward. With the available set of hard macros and a library of soft macros, the designer simply tallies the design against the total budget for a particular ACTEL part. The guiding light is that the total capacity should not exceed about 85 percent of the available capacity. Beyond 85 percent may limit automatic placement and routing success. The use of a table similar to Table 6.2 is necessary, but this table is only a sampling of available functions.

At the outset, the designer must decide whether the appropriate ACT parts have enough logic modules and available I/O pins to meet the requirements. Careful assignment of functions, appropriate use of the special clock input pin and judicious partitioning are also required. Table 6.3 gives a capacity summary for the ACT 1 family parts. The ACT 2 and 3 logic modules are divided into two classes, S cells for sequential operations (Figure 6.3) and C cells for combinational operations. Assignment of S cells to counters, shifters and controllers is straightforward.

TABLE 6.2   ACT 1 Logic Module Functional Equivalents

Function Description	Logic Module Count
1. Basic Logic Gates	1 (up to 4 inputs)
2. D flip flop (edge triggered)	2 modules
3. D latch (transparent)	1 module
4. J-K flip flop (edge trig.)	2 modules
5. Decoders	
a. 2 to 4	4 modules
b. 3 to 8	8 modules
6. Multiplexers	
a. 2 to 1	1 module
b. 4 to 1	1 module
c. 8 to 1	3 modules
d. 16 to 1	5 modules
7. Comparators (equality only)	
a. 2 bit	1 module
b. 4 bit	5 modules
8. Registers (serial load)	
a. 4 bit	8 modules
b. 8 bit	16 modules
9. Counters	
a. 2 bit	5 modules
b. 4 bit	18 modules

TABLE 6.3(a)   ACT 1 and ACT 2 Capacity Table

	ACT1010	ACT1020	ACT1225	ACT1240	ACT1280
User I/Os	57	69	82	104	140
Logic Modules	295	546	430	684	1232
Max Flip Flops	147	273	363	565	998
Pins	68	84	100	132	176

TABLE 6.3(b)   ACT 3 Capacity Table

	ACT1415	ACT1425	ACT1440	ACT1460	ACT14100
User I/Os	80	100	140	168	228
Logic Modules	200	310	564	848	1377
Max Flip Flops	264	360	568	768	1153
Pins	100	133	177	207	257

Note: Max Flip Flops includes C modules configured as flip flops by cascading two modules to form an edge triggered D flip flop.

6.7 ACT DESIGN TECHNIQUES

As in previous chapters, this section focuses on the four basic building blocks of decoders, muxes, shifters and counters. The basic logic module is a double layered two level structure of combinational gates. Table 6.2 is the reference point.

Small Decoders tell the bad news. The logic module only has a single output variable. Decoders need as many outputs as there are distinct decode combinations. For the two-to-four or four-to-eight decoders, one logic module is used for decoding each variable—likewise for the four-to-sixteen decoder. Above four-to-sixteen, decode gets tricky because the largest basic gate built from a logic module has only four inputs. A five-to-thirty-two decoder needs thirty-two five input gates and these require additional logic modules pyramided to expand the number of inputs needed for decode. This is true for up to seven inputs and expands again for eight or more inputs.

Multiplexers are the expertise of the logic module. Two-to-one or four-to-one require a single logic module. An eight-to-one only takes three modules and a sixteen-to-one only takes five modules. This is because multiplexing is what the logic module does best—it literally is a multiplexer. Above sixteen inputs takes more than two levels of logic modules to form the final output and again, input limitations come into play.

Shifters present another interesting situation. For ACT 1, edge triggered D flip flops are made by cascading a master and slave transparent latch with one cell each operating off reversed clock phases. This approach was mentioned previously—it takes two logic modules per shifter bit. Shift registers require edge triggering to control shift position (Chapter 1). From an estimation standpoint, edge triggering forces adjacent logic module clustering for uniform performance. ACT 2 and 3 products offer concise solutions using the D flip flops. For the ACT 1, shifters use two modules per bit.

Counter design on ACT presents the classic problem seen with the LCA and MAX, namely, limited inputs. For small counters, the approach of D flip flops with transition logic makes sense. At four bits and higher, the method of the 74F161 count cell described in Chapter 4 makes sense. The count cell needs two logic modules for the flip flop and one or two modules for the transition logic. Remember, logic function can be merged into the flip flops on ACT 1. By using the count cell, long counters can be made at a uniform gate usage per count bit. Careful cell clustering is needed to minimize performance variation because of metal delays.

ACTEL provides a list of good design practices to get best results with their architecture. They also include a library of hard and soft macros for fast design entry. By using their tools, the designer will encounter fewer problems.

6.8 A SMALL EXAMPLE

Figure 6.8 shows the small example mapped into ACT 1 cells. The four data inputs, load, reset, clock and out signal require seven bidirectional pins configured as inputs and one as an output. Each four input latch is made with a single logic module. Latches were chosen for the input data because edge triggering was not required. The latch outputs are fed next to a four-to-one multiplexer made from five logic modules (AND3, 3A, 3B, NAND3A). The counter is made from an edge triggered D flip flop which has a built-in input multiplexer and an edge triggered D flip flop. Note that the counter uses the function merging capability of logic module flip flops, first shown in Chapter 3. Two additional gates make the input transition logic for the F1 mux.

The design uses only fifteen logic modules for this example, and easily fits in the smallest ACT part with about 90 percent remaining capacity. Figure 6.9 shows the corresponding output of the ViewLogic™ simulation as described previously, for other simulators.

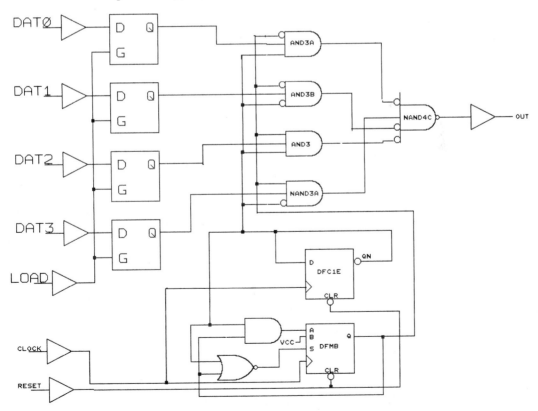

Figure 6.8   ACT example schematic.

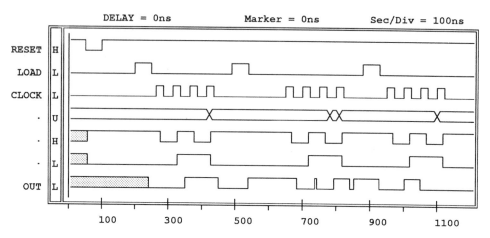

Figure 6.9   The small ACT example simulation.

6.9 PERFORMANCE CONSIDERATIONS

Time delay can be broken out into several components. Values discussed are for the ACT 1, 2 and 3 products currently available through ACTEL. Figure 6.10 presents a block diagram ACT1 and ACT2 timing model. Similar to those shown in previous chapters, the incremental time delay parameters are broken out to be added up for any particular design. Table 6.4 summarizes key timing parameters.

Key parameters are the delay of an input buffer, an output buffer and the internal delay of the logic modules when interconnected. The combinatorial logic delay is appropriate for the ACT 1 modules, and the sequential and combinatorial delay is needed for the ACT 2 and 3 modules.

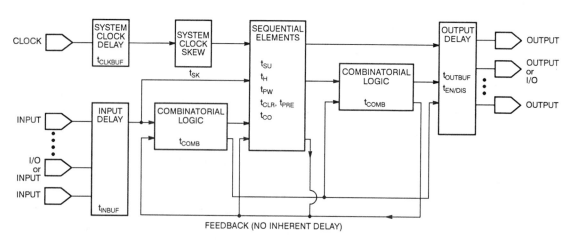

Figure 6.10   An ACT timing model.

TABLE 6.4 Key ACT 1, ACT 2 and ACT 3 Timing Parameters

Parameter	ACT 1	ACT 2	ACT 3
Tpd input	8.9	11.3	4.2
Tpd output	10.5	9.7	7.5
Tpd (C module, FO = 1)	9.7	7.4	4.3
Tpd (C module, FO = 8)	16.7	12.5	7.2
Tckq (flip flop)	7.4	6.2	3.0
Tsetup (flip flop)	5.0	1.0	0.8

Note: The fanout (FO) is one for all entries, except where noted. The output load capacitance is 50 pf for the output cell. All values are in nanoseconds.

Naturally, delay depends on whether the signal is rising or falling. For the output time delay, switching at 2.4 volts (TTL level) is assumed. Remember, the time delay of all CMOS outputs (indeed all CMOS logic) is very sensitive to capacitive loading, voltage and temperature as well as process variation.

The clock delay (using the Clock Buffer) is simply the time delay of an input buffer added to the delay of an internal buffer. One internal buffer is assigned to each routing channel, and all are driven from the single Clock Buffer. The total skew among the various channel clock lines is less than 3 nanoseconds.

Naturally, the Table 6.4 time values are technology dependent and may change in future versions of the product on different processes. ACT 3 time parameters are faster than those of ACT 2.

6.10 POWER CONSIDERATIONS

Other than the interconnect mechanism, the ACT product line is pure CMOS and obeys the classic CMOS power dissipation curve for digital circuits. That does not mean its power dissipation is easy to calculate.

It may be noted that the LCA power dissipation is similar in nature to that of the ACT families. There is a current component due to the I/O sections, an internal component and a parasitic leakage component. Neglecting the parasitic component, which is minimal, the dominating components are the output component and the internal component. The output current component depends on driven load capacitance external to the I.C. The internal component is a strong function of the switching frequency of internal transistors. If the part is driven from a CMOS source, the input component may be largely neglected, as well. The input current component may have to be considered if the part is driven from TTL because the voltage swing may not take the input transistors into their current blocking state.

The classic CMOS power dissipation equation is simply the sum of all of the mentioned components. The problems with using it are simple. The output load capacitance is seldom known, so the load capacitance is estimated from tables of capacitance for various lengths of printed circuit board capacitance values. These values are not controlled well in manufacture.

The internal component depends on frequency, which is fine for a simple inverter, but power dissipation for a flip flop is much harder to define, especially for a counter. For instance, the least significant bit of a counter switches at twice the rate of the next higher bit, and so forth. One might guess that each effectively operates at a different frequency. To be accurate, the exact switching of individual transistors within the flip flop gates should be assessed. This is a lot of work. On top of this, the number of programmed antifuses also affects the power dissipation.

The input current component is similar, because of the variable input signal switching rates. Because of these difficulties, most manufacturers provide curves of power dissipation versus frequency and load capacitance. This is the recommended approach.

6.11 CLOSING COMMENTS

United States Patent 4,758,745 was granted to A. El Gamal, Khaled El-Ayat and Amr Mohsen for a user programmable integrated circuit interconnect architecture and test method. The patent covers the PLICE, the ACT architecture and the internal testing structures. The architecture is scalable because it can be optically shrunk to achieve tighter geometries and higher performance for future products. The future for the ACT product line will include greater density and higher speed parts. Additional application-specific modules may be incorporated into the architecture as its similarity to both gate array and standard cell arrangements is striking. ACT 2 and 3 products already incorporate standard flip flops as well as a generous number of logic modules.

Since ACTEL's entry, other FPGA families have entered the world of small grain building blocks with CMOS antifuse interconnections. These other FPGAs will be discussed in a later chapter.

PROBLEMS

1. Estimate the number of logic modules that will be needed to make Figure 2.1 in the ACT 1 family.

2. Using ACT 1 time delays, estimate the best case delay from signal I1J to OUT2B on SR3 for Figure 2.1.

3. One Hot Encoding (OHE), sometimes called Bit Per State (BPS) encoding, is a design trick that trades off gate inputs for flip flops. If you have an FPGA that has lots of flip flops, but the number of gate inputs is lean, it is a valuable approach to consider. The idea is simple. Instead of encoding state variables to minimize flip flops, there is one flip flop per state in the design. For example, a four-state machine would have four flip flops. The assignment is one which sets a single flip flop to a value of one, with the rest set to zero. That is, on our four-state example, 0001, 0010, 0100 and 1000 would be the four valid states. The other unused states are don't cares, and permit minimization. However, because there is only a single one asserted for any valid state, we can neglect to check that the other values are zero in our state transition logic. This greatly reduces the number of inputs into the transition logic that must be examined. Using these ideas, complete the design shown in Table 6.5 using OHE. Minimize the design and solve it for both ACT 1 and ACT 2 architectures.

TABLE 6.5   Problem State Table

	N.S.		Output	
P.S.	X = 0	X = 1	X = 0	X = 1
A	A	B	0	0
B	A	C	0	0
C	A	D	0	0
D	A	E	0	0
E	A	F	0	0
F	A	F	0	1

Note: Input signal is X. Assume a clock also exists.

4. a. Design a three-to-eight decoder using ACT 1 cells.
   b. Design an edge triggered D flip flop using ACT 1 cells.
   c. Develop a "count cell" using ACT 2 cells, similar to the one developed in Chapter 4.

7

A Large Example

7.0 INTRODUCTION

To this point, several architectures have been examined and the basics of system design using FPGAs have been discussed. Examples covered the same small design, translated to each architecture considered. Larger examples are appropriate, to give an appreciation for some finer points of FPGA design. Too many designs are difficult to include, so one larger design created on several architectures will be studied. The design chosen is typical of a wide class of system designs, and it can be easily recast with small changes for other applications. In addition, a simulation will be examined in more detail and strategies discussed for simulating to prove the design is correct.

7.1 THE DESIGN

Figure 7.1 shows the design, which can be called a small logic analyzer. Figure 7.2 shows the analyzer as a three chip system, which can expand easily. The function is simple—data, coming from probes, passes through the FPGA to a fast SRAM (Static Random Access Memory). The data stores—in the SRAM at consecutive addresses. The SRAM addresses are formed inside the FPGA by a counter controlling the SRAM address lines. The

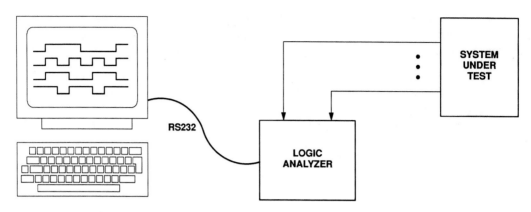

Figure 7.1   PC-based logic analyzer.

FPGA generates the read, write and chip enable signals for the SRAM. A free running clock that samples the data, drives a controller to make the SRAM write pulses, increment the address counter and update an internal timer.

The 8051 microcontroller turns the FPGA on and off and reads back the contents of the SRAM data. It is assumed that the 8051 passes the data serially to a personal computer for display. The 8051 also can be used to test the FPGA and the SRAM. An 8051 microcontroller was picked because it is cheap, moderately fast and well known. However, an 8051 cannot possibly capture and trigger on fast data samples, which is the goal of this design. For

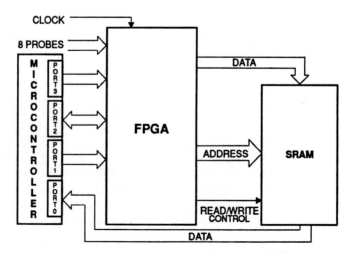

Figure 7.2   Three chip logic analyzer hardware.

these purposes, view the 8051 as a set of four eight bit ports used to transfer bytes to/from the FPGA or make strobe pulses controlling FPGA operations.

Each SRAM address holds an eight bit probe data value. At this point, the FPGA design could be a data acquisition circuit or, by adding an A/D converter, the design could be an inexpensive digital oscilloscope. As might be guessed, this design covers a large class of data moving systems. With more changes, the design could be a DMA port or a data channel.

Figure 7.3 shows the FPGA system blocks. They are: an address counter, a fast comparator, a control block, several registers and I/O ports. Control is a state machine enabled by a bit set from the 8051 and disabled by trigger circuitry (after a timeout). The control unit uses an external oscillator connected to the sampling clock input. The clock speed relates to the speed of the SRAM, and the FPGA control unit makes the SRAM write pulses from the clock pulses.

Samples taken at a speed faster than the SRAM write cycle are blurred by the analyzer. Samples taken at a rate slower than the probed signal transitions are also blurred (that is, the sampling theorem). A crude device can be made with a 40 MHz clock, sampling signals up to 20 MHz and capturing both transitions of probed signals. Faster signals will be ambiguously stored. Target a sample rate of 10 MHz, but that is not the upper limit of this design.

The SRAM is kept small, but can be expanded easily. The SRAM has only 256 locations, matching the eight bit counter being used, but the counter is expandable for bigger memories handling larger data frames.

To make the design a logic analyzer, it needs extra logic to stop data capture based on the probed data. This is the triggering feature and it is linked to a time delay function. The triggering operation is simple. The 8051 stores a binary pattern in the FPGA in an eight bit compare register. The register value is compared to the input data pattern from the probes. If there is a match, a timer is started. At the end of the timeout, control circuitry automatically halts additional data capture (that is, it quits writing into the SRAM). Triggering permits capturing samples before and after the trigger event, depending on the number of timer counts. Trigger capability is what makes this design different from a data acquisition unit.

The triggering comparator and timer must be hardware implemented to catch probe patterns in real time. However, an elaborate compare pattern is often hard to use, so the ability to disable the comparator must be included. The compare logic has an eight bit trigger enable register that forces an automatic compare over selected bits. The enable logic permits one or more bit compares to force the compare output to be a logic one, as if the corresponding probe value actually equalled its compare bit. This implements "don't care" compares. The compare operation will be more evident from the design equations, shown later.

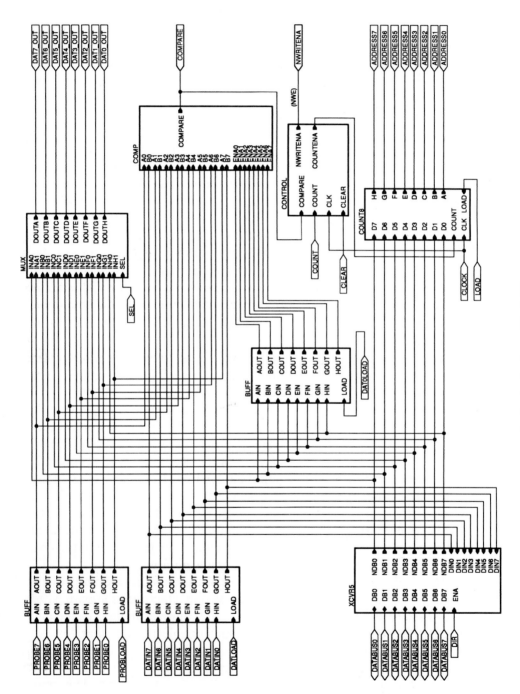

Figure 7.3 Logic Analyzer Block Diagram.

142

7.2 SOLUTION 1: PML 2852

Using SNAP (Synthesis Netlist Analysis and Program), Figure 7.2 mapped to the design of Figure 7.3. Most blocks were made by equation entry, but could have been made with netlists from SNAP library cells, or 7400 series soft macro entries. Other versions, made with other schematic library cells, will be discussed later.

Figure 7.4 gives the equation file for an eight bit buffer, used in three places. The first use is for capturing the probe data, clocked by PROB-LOAD in the block diagram. The second buffer use is for holding the eight bit compare data, clocked by the signal called COMPLOAD. Signals COMPINO-7 are provided by 8051 port three, and COMPLOAD comes from 8051 port one, which supplies control signals.

The third entry of the eight bit buffer is the enable register in the center of Figure 7.3. This register holds data coming through the transceivers from 8051 port two. The enable register is loaded by ENLOAD also coming from the 8051 port one.

By now a picture should have formed of how the 8051 is used. The 8051 uses one port attached to the bidirectional signals DATABUSO-7 (port two), another to COMPINO-7 (port three), and a third (port one) for control signals. COMPLOAD, ENLOAD, DIR, COUNT, SEL, CLEAR, ENABLE and COUNTSTRB all emanate from port one. The 8051 port transceivers (XCVRS) drive data heading to an eight bit counter (COUNT8), the data multiplexer (MUX) or the Compare Enable Buffer.

```
@PINLIST
AIN I;BIN I;CIN I;DIN I;EIN I;FIN I;GIN I;HIN I;LOAD I;
AOUT O;BOUT O;COUT O;DOUT O;EOUT O;FOUT O;GOUT O;HOUT O;
@LOGIC EQUATIONS
AOUT.D = AIN;
BOUT.D = BIN;
COUT.D = CIN;
DOUT.D = DIN;
EOUT.D = EIN;
FOUT.D = FIN;
GOUT.D = GIN;
HOUT.D = HIN;
AOUT.CLK = LOAD;
BOUT.CLK = LOAD;
COUT.CLK = LOAD;
DOUT.CLK = LOAD;
EOUT.CLK = LOAD;
FOUT.CLK = LOAD;
GOUT.CLK = LOAD;
HOUT.CLK = LOAD;
@INPUT VECTORS
@OUTPUT VECTORS
@STATE VECTORS
@TRANSITIONS
```

Figure 7.4   Eight bit buffer equations.

```
@PINLIST
INA0 I;INA1 I;INB0 I;INB1 I;INC0 I;INC1 I;IND0 I;IND1 I;
INE0 I;INE1 I;INF0 I;INF1 I;ING0 I;ING1 I;INH0 I;INH1 I;SEL I;
DOUTA O;DOUTB O;DOUTC O;DOUTD O;DOUTE O;DOUTF O;DOUTG O;DOUTH O;
@LOGIC EQUATIONS
DOUTA = /SEL*INA0 + SEL*INA1;
DOUTB = /SEL*INB0 + SEL*INB1;
DOUTC = /SEL*INC0 + SEL*INC1;
DOUTD = /SEL*IND0 + SEL*IND1;
DOUTE = /SEL*INE0 + SEL*INE1;
DOUTF = /SEL*INF0 + SEL*INF1;
DOUTG = /SEL*ING0 + SEL*ING1;
DOUTH = /SEL*INH0 + SEL*INH1;
@INPUT VECTORS
@OUTPUT VECTORS
@STATE VECTORS
@TRANSITIONS
```

Figure 7.5 Multiplexer equations.

Using port values, the 8051 enables the analyzer, loads the compare register, initializes the counter, or passes values through the data multiplexer. The data multiplexer ties directly to the eight bit RAM data input lines, and the signals ADRESS0-7 tie directly to the RAM address lines. For SRAM testing, the 8051 can load an address into the SRAM address counter, and output a value through the transceivers and MUX to the SRAM data lines. The value is then read back on 8051 port zero.

The multiplexer equation file is shown in Figure 7.5, the compare design file in Figure 7.6 and the COUNT8 design file in Figure 7.7. Each is a brute force solution to the basic function. Remember that SNAP's equation syntax is "+" for OR, "*" for AND, "/" for INVERT and ":+:" for EX-OR. The counter is made from J-K flip flops, using the method of Chapter 3, adding the capability to load the counter. Figure 7.8 gives the transceiver equations, and Figure 7.9 the control schematic. The operation of the control unit is described later, when its simulation is discussed.

```
@PINLIST
A0 I;B0 I;A1 I;B1 I;A2 I;B2 I;A3 I;B3 I;
A4 I;B4 I;A5 I;B5 I;A6 I;B6 I;A7 I;B7 I;
ENA0 I;ENA1 I;ENA2 I;ENA3 I;
ENA4 I;ENA5 I;ENA6 I;ENA7 I;
COMPARE O;
@LOGIC EQUATIONS
EQ0 = /(A0:+:B0)+ENA0;
EQ1 = /(A1:+:B1)+ENA1;
EQ2 = /(A2:+:B2)+ENA2;
EQ3 = /(A3:+:B3)+ENA3;
EQ4 = /(A4:+:B4)+ENA4;
EQ5 = /(A5:+:B5)+ENA5;
EQ6 = /(A6:+:B6)+ENA6;
EQ7 = /(A7:+:B7)+ENA7;
COMPARE = EQ0*EQ1*EQ2*EQ3*EQ4*EQ5*EQ6*EQ7;
@INPUT VECTORS
@OUTPUT VECTORS
@STATE VECTORS
@TRANSITIONS
```

Figure 7.6 Eight bit comparator equations.

```
@PINLIST
COUNT I; LOAD I;  D0 I;D1 I;D2 I;D3 I;D4 I;D5 I;D6 I;D7 I; CLK I;
A O;B O;  C O;  D O;  E O;  F O;  G O;  H O;
@LOGIC EQUATIONS
H.J = COUNT*A*B*C*D*E*F*G  + LOAD*D7;
H.K = COUNT*A*B*C*D*E*F*G  + LOAD*/D7;
G.J = COUNT*A*B*C*D*E*F    + LOAD*D6;
G.K = COUNT*A*B*C*D*E*F    + LOAD*/D6;
F.J = COUNT*A*B*C*D*E      + LOAD*D5;
F.K = COUNT*A*B*C*D*E      + LOAD*/D5;
E.J = COUNT*A*B*C*D        + LOAD*D4;
E.K = COUNT*A*B*C*D        + LOAD*/D4;
D.J = COUNT*A*B*C          + LOAD*D3;
D.K = COUNT*A*B*C          + LOAD*/D3;
C.J = COUNT*A*B            + LOAD*D2;
C.K = COUNT*A*B            + LOAD*/D2;
B.J = COUNT*A              + LOAD*D1;
B.K = COUNT*A              + LOAD*/D1;
A.J = COUNT                + LOAD*D0;
A.K = COUNT                + LOAD*/D0;
H.CLK = CLK;G.CLK = CLK;F.CLK = CLK;E.CLK = CLK;
D.CLK = CLK;C.CLK = CLK;B.CLK = CLK;A.CLK = CLK;
A.SET = 1;B.SET=1;C.SET=1;D.SET=1;E.SET=1;F.SET=1;G.SET=1;H.SET=1;
@INPUT VECTORS
@OUTPUT VECTORS
@STATE VECTORS
@TRANSITIONS
```

Figure 7.7   COUNT8 design equations.

```
@PINLIST
DB0 B;DB1 B;DB2 B;DB3 B;DB4 B;DB5 B;DB6 B;DB7 B;
NDB0 O;NDB1 O;NDB2 O;NDB3 O;NDB4 O;NDB5 O;NDB6 O;NDB7 O;
DIN0 I;DIN1 I;DIN2 I;DIN3 I;DIN4 I;DIN5 I;DIN6 I;DIN7 I;
ENA I;
@LOGIC EQUATIONS
DB0 = DIN0;
DB1 = DIN1;
DB2 = DIN2;
DB3 = DIN3;
DB4 = DIN4;
DB5 = DIN5;
DB6 = DIN6;
DB7 = DIN7;
DB0.OE = ENA;
DB1.OE = ENA;
DB2.OE = ENA;
DB3.OE = ENA;
DB4.OE = ENA;
DB5.OE = ENA;
DB6.OE = ENA;
DB7.OE = ENA;
NDB0 = DB0;
NDB1 = DB1;
NDB2 = DB2;
NDB3 = DB3;
NDB4 = DB4;
NDB5 = DB5;
NDB6 = DB6;
NDB7 = DB7;
@INPUT VECTORS
@OUTPUT VECTORS
@STATE VECTORS
@TRANSITIONS
```

Figure 7.8   Transceiver equations.

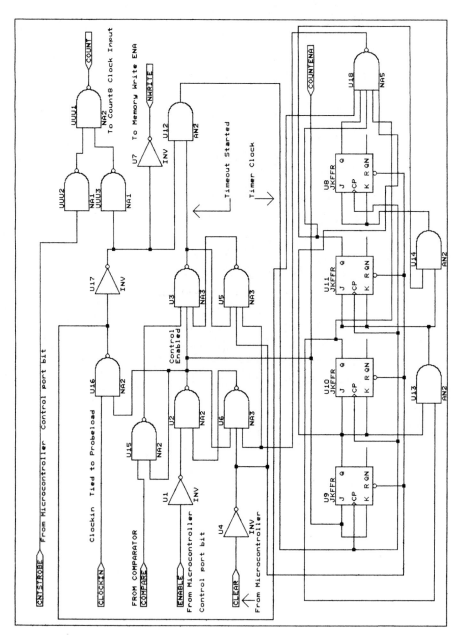

Figure 7.9 Control unit schematic.

The compare design file (Figure 7.6) may seem a little cryptic, at first, because it includes bits from the enable register. The enable bits are ORed to override probe miscompares on a bit by bit basis. Any probe not of interest does not affect the ones needed for forming an equality compare. All selected bits are ANDed for the final compare.

7.3 SIMULATING SOLUTION 1

When an FPGA arrives from the factory, it is assumed that the I.C. passed factory inspection, and was working when purchased. The simulation assumes one must only test whether the FPGA design is working when configured. That being the case, what would be a reasonable strategy to verify the operation of Figure 7.3? In general, the simulation must mimic the 8051 ports, and prove that the FPGA pins operate, as well as the buffers, comparator, counter, multiplexer, trigger, and control logic.

Starting with pin testing, the design can be tested like peeling an onion—from the outside inward. The approach taken is systematic testing of the design with stimuli modules.

To make an efficient simulation, it is vital that all of the registers are initialized early. Having known register values keeps the simulator from evaluating thousands of unknown values passing through the design, giving strange results.

It is also important to recognize which paths are independent and can be simultaneously simulated. For instance, the probe datapath is independent of the 8051 paths. The datapath across the top of Figure 7.3 is isolated from the address path along the bottom. Knowing this, apply datapath vectors in parallel with address path vectors, saving test time. This example will be kept even simpler, but one could use these facts to compress vectors at some later point.

A summary of the test strategy follows, and this approach applies to a large class of designs. Step one is extremely important:

1. Initialize all registers (that is, master clear and/or apply a sequence of data loads).

2. Isolate independent modules
   a. Datapaths
   b. Address Path
   c. Comparator.

3. Develop simulation tests for each module that drive logic variables to both values (one and zero).

4. Combine the independent pieces into a composite simulation, if possible.

Step one improves simulation efficiency, by eliminating useless evaluations of unknown conditions. Step two is a version of the old Roman strategy— Divide and Conquer. Step three is a direct application of the principles of observability and controllability, upon which most test simulation is based. Essentially, a test must force internal logic nodes to transition through all values that can occur. An added trick is to make the transitions be observable at the device pins, where a tester can see the results of the node changes. Step four is one of simple economics—do as much in parallel as possible (time is money).

More elaborate strategies yield high class tests, but this strategy is general enough to use in many cases.

7.3.1 Testing the Datapaths

First, test the PROBE0-7 pins, verifying the operation of the multiplexer and the DATOUT0-7 pins. A simulation showing this operation is shown in Figure 7.10. Each probe independently asserts to a logic one, then zero. While the PROBE pins are at logic one, PROBELOAD is asserted capturing the results in the input register. Then, the PROBES are driven to logic zero and clocked again. The corresponding DATAOUT pins respond. Note that SEL remains constant at logic one for this part of the simulation. This operation could be done with a few vectors by doing parallel data loads, but this shows the independence of each probe line.

Now, setting SEL to zero in Figure 7.11, data is applied to the DATBUS0-7 pins similarly. To pass the 8051 port DATBUS through the XCVRS, the control signal DIR must be zero. Again, the DATOUT pins respond correctly. Note that the widths of the DATOUT results track the DATBUS input signals. The signals are not loaded into a register as they were in Figure 7.10. The little glitches displayed at the left side of the waveforms for DATOUT0-7 show a time when the internal nodes are unstable at the beginning of the simulation.

7.3.2 Testing the Comparator

So far, the simulations show that the datapath is working in the only direction provided inside the FPGA, which is out to the RAM. Next, check the Compare logic. This is done using three eight bit values. First, it should be recognized that to be thorough will be tough. This comparator has two eight bit comparands (PROBE BUFF and DATIN BUFF) and each can assume

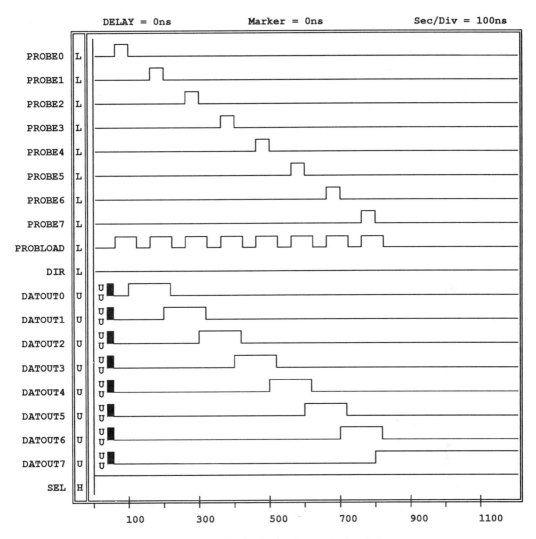

DELAY = 0ns   Marker = 0ns   Sec/Div = 100ns

Figure 7.10 Probe datapath simulation.

256 distinct values. In particular, for any value in the PROBE BUFF, there can be 256 values in the DATIN BUFF with 255 that don't compare and one that does. An exhaustive check of the comparator would take a lot more comparisons than can be shown here, so select a small subset of conditions to check.

Note that the compare signal is taken to the outside world, where it is not really used. This was done so that the comparator could be checked separately from the rest of the control unit. The compare signal is used internally to turn on a timer within the control unit. It is so important that

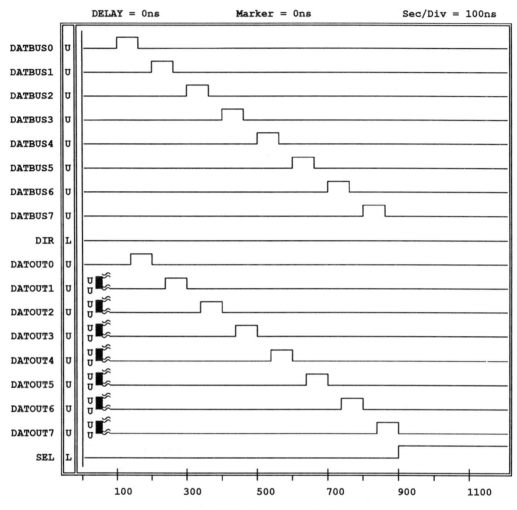

Figure 7.11 Port datapath simulation.

the compare correctly work, that the signal was dragged to an output pin just to prove its operation.

    With that noted, test that some standard patterns match and fail to match, and that separate enabling of patterns also works. Figure 7.12 shows loading of several patterns into the probe latch, the datin latch and the enable buffer. In the figure, see compare equal to one several times. SNAP's bus notation is used in Figure 7.12, where the COMPIN, DATBUS and PROBE buses show as double channels with a hexadecimal value for the current bus contents. The little integral signs designate that the bus is in transition from the previous value to the next value, shown to the right of the integral sign.

    In the upper left of Figure 7.12, a value of one is shown on the COMPIN bus. It is loaded into the compare register with the signal below it, COMP-

DELAY = 0ns   Marker = 0ns   Sec/Div = 100ns

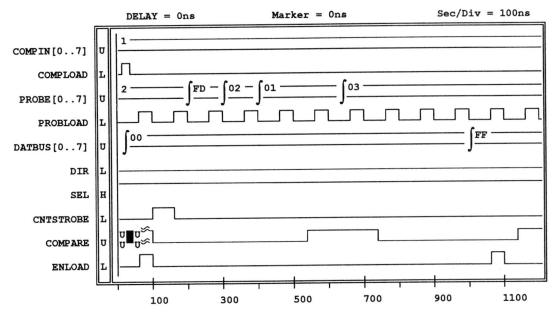

Figure 7.12   Comparator simulation.

LOAD. The one is loaded into bit position COMPIN0. Below COMPLOAD is the PROBE bus, with an initial value of two (PROBE1 = 1, and PROBE0, 2, 3, 4, 5, 6, 7 = 0). The PROBE bus is loaded into the input register with the PROBLOAD clock, and we can see several values (FD, 02, 01, 03) being applied to the PROBE bus later.

The DIR signal forces the DATBUS transceivers to accept data from the 8051 port, so a value can be loaded into the enable register. With all zeroes applied to the DATBUS and a pulse on ENLOAD, the enable register permits each compare bit to check its corresponding probe bit. The Compare signal asserts to a logic one when the PROBE values equal the COMPIN values, or when the enable register is loaded with all ones. Note the small undefined region at the left side of the COMPARE signal display. The undefined region is a result of the uninitialized enable register affecting the comparator operation. It settles down just after the ENLOAD signal asserts. CNTSTROBE and SEL are not used in this simulation, but are displayed nonetheless.

Initially, the COMPIN bus is looking for all zeroes with a one in bit position zero. When the comparator is enabled, the PROBE bus has all zeroes with a one in bit position one—hence, no compare. Then, the PROBE bus assumes hex values FD, 02 and finally 01 around time 400. Because the PROBE bus is driven into the register, its value will not be seen by the comparator until PROBLOAD latches it later. After that, there is about a 90 nanosecond time delay before COMPARE responds and becomes logical one. A couple of clocks later, the PROBE bus assumes the value 03 and COMPARE vanishes after appropriate clocking. Finally, the DATBUS is driven to FF and the ENLOAD signal asserts. This condition overrides every probe and compare value forcing the COMPARE signal to logic one at the end of the display.

7.3.3 Testing the Counter

The counter is an eight bit one. It has 256 distinct count patterns, and needs 256 clocks just to prove that it counts. First, the buffer should be checked by asserting a load to the counter through the transceiver (from the 8051 bus). Then, the counter can be checked, for its ability to count.

Checking the counter is done systematically, by loading a zero into the counter, and applying the clock. Now, the application of 255 more clocks occurs. A large loadable counter can be tested by loading bands of ones like 00011111, 00111111 or 01111111, and applying a clock to assure the count rolls over to the correct next value. If the design is expanded, this approach should be taken, to minimize the number of simulation vectors used.

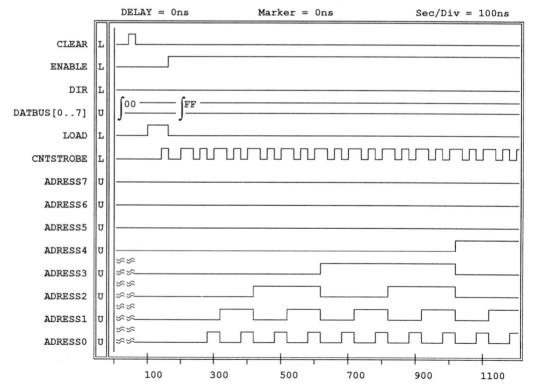

Figure 7.13   COUNT8 simulation.

Because the 255 clocks do not use the DATBUS transceivers, it makes sense that this time might be used profitably by testing the datapath signals and the comparator in parallel with testing the counter. Figure 7.13 shows a piece of the counter "count" simulation. The CLEAR, ENABLE and CNTSTROBE signals handle the Control unit, to permit the counter to be tested.

7.3.4 Testing the Control Unit

The Control Unit was designed as a separate schematic, making functional verification easy, for the module. Figure 7.14 shows how pulses applied to the Control Unit first clear it, and enable the first cross-coupled latch. Once the first latch enables, the second latch is set only if the compare signal pulses high. The pulse indicates a match occurred between the probed data and the comparand while the corresponding bits were enabled. When this occurs, the second latch sets permitting clocks to reach the timer.

The timer is a cascade of four J-K flip flops in a toggle pattern. The timer is initially reset by a clear pulse from the 8051 control port, which also initializes the two asynchronous latches. When fifteen pulses arrive after the compare signal enables the timer, the high order timer bit clears the enabling circuitry, as shown in Figure 7.14. Additional bits could be added to the J-K cascade, making a longer timer, but this is sufficient for the needs of this example.

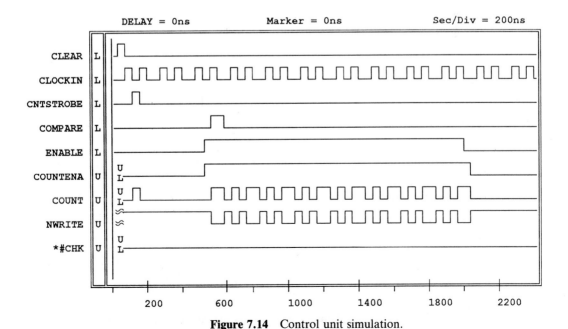

Figure 7.14 Control unit simulation.

7.4 THE COMPOSITE SIMULATION

Figure 7.15 shows many of the elements of the smaller simulations combined into a larger one. This is done with the noncompiled netlist version of the design, so it is unrealistically fast.

Figure 7.16 shows the cell usage of the logic analyzer when compiled into a PML 2852. These values can be used as a capacity reference for the design when it is compiled onto other architectures.

7.5 OTHER VERSIONS OF THE DESIGN

Figure 7.17 shows the logic analyzer schematic when captured on an ACT 1010. The higher level modules were captured as separate schematics, which are expanded by the ViewLogic™ software into a flattened netlist. The initial probability of placement and routing was estimated at 97 percent. When the design was mapped onto the architecture, it initially required 159 logic modules, but used only 157 after optimization. The ACT 1010 has 295 logic modules, so 157 is about 53 percent.

The ACTEL software provides a summary of nets that have distinguishing features. Of particular interest are the nets that have potentially long time delays associated with them. As might be expected, the signals "COMPARE" and "COUNTOUT" should be reexamined at simulation time to assess whether their operation is correct after placement and routing.

Figure 7.18 shows the design as schematic captured for the ALTERA MAX 5128. Again, the modules shown, were developed similarly to the PML design, with separate schematics. Usage for the MAX design included 59 macrocells and 30 expanders, giving a utilization of 46 percent as calculated by the MAX+PLUS II software. That utilization is somewhat misleading, because the assignment of functions within the design is between macrocells and expanders. For the 5128, 59 out of 128 macrocells were used (46 percent), but only 30 out of 256 expanders were used (11 percent).

The logic analyzer was also defined using PALASM, a design language developed at Advanced Micro Devices to support PAL-type devices. The PALASM language is widely supported, and this version of the logic analyzer was transported to the Xilinx XACT design system. Using XACT, the analyzer was compiled onto an LCA 3030. Figure 7.19 shows the cell placement image for the design when placed onto the LCA 3030 World View. Figure 7.20 shows the interconnections requiring routing channels and switch matrices. The final figure, Figure 7.21 shows the completed design with all connections made. Although Figure 7.21 appears very congested, in reality, only about half of the cells are used with this design. Figure 7.20, which uses

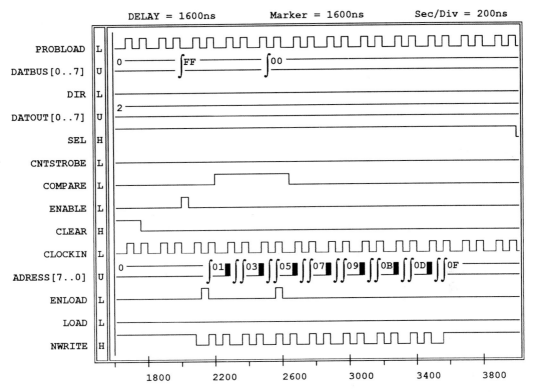

Figure 7.15 Partial composite simulation.

```
============ SNAP Resources Summary ============
     Cell name      used/total        %
=================================================
     CKDIN552        0 /   4         0%
     CKNIN552        0 /   4         0%
      FBNAND        95 /  96        98%
        NAND        72 / 104        69%
      DIN552         4 /  25        16%
      NIN552         4 /  25        16%
     CDIN552         1 /   4        25%
     CNIN552         0 /   4         0%
       CK552         3 /   4        75%
     IDFF552        16 /  16       100%
     BDIN552         8 /  24        33%
     BNIN552         8 /  24        33%
     JKCL552         4 /  10        40%
     JKPR552         8 /  10        80%
     EXOR552         8 /   8       100%
     TOUT552        16 /  24        66%
     ODFF552        16 /  16       100%
     TOUT852        10 /  16        62%
  Please hit any key to continue...
```

Figure 7.16 Logic analyzer cell usage.

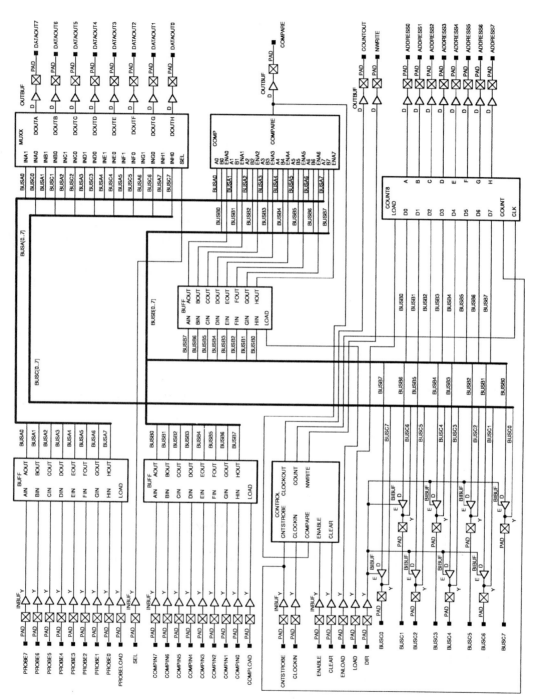

Figure 7.17 ACT 1010 logic analyzer.

156

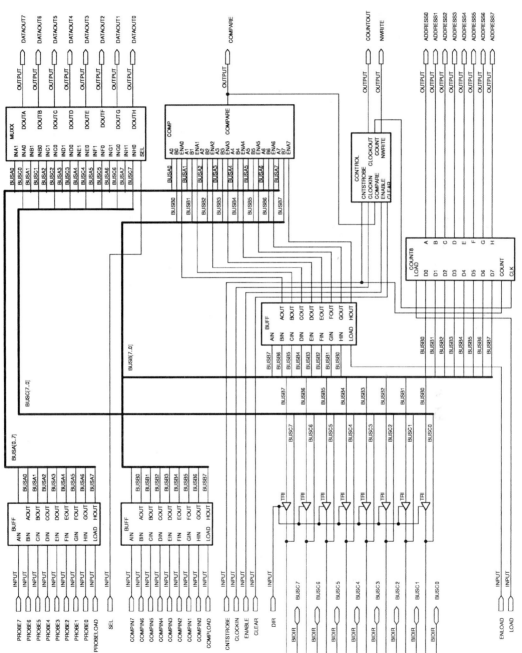

Figure 7.18 MAX 5128 logic analyzer.

157

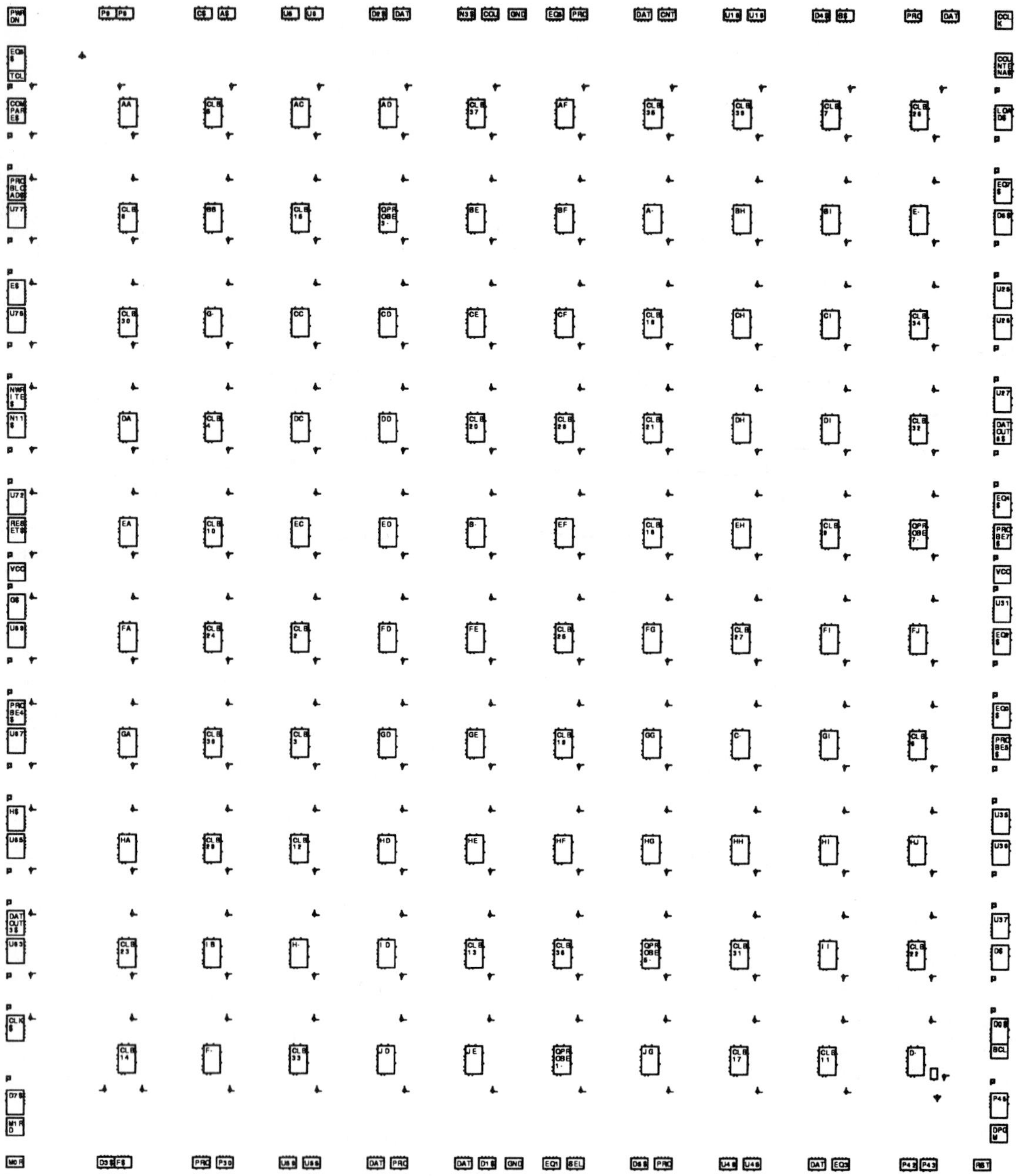

Figure 7.19   LCA 3030 cell placement.

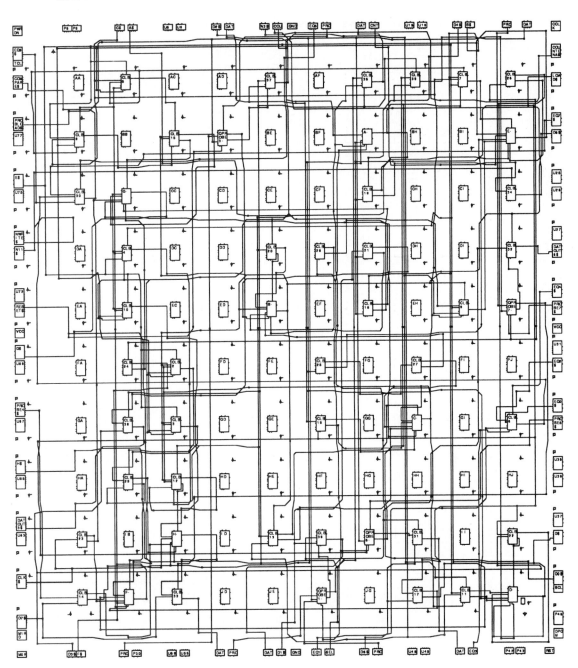

Figure 7.20   LCA 3030 with routed connections.

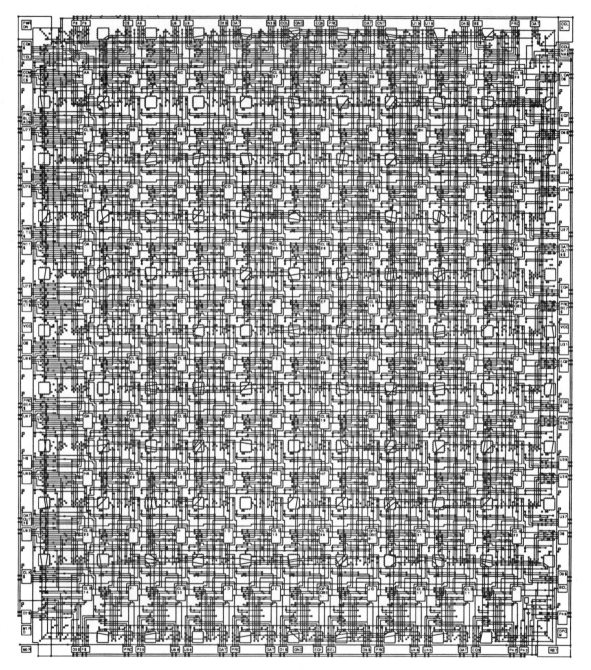

Figure 7.21   LCA 3030 complete world view.

the routing channels actually uses very few of them compared to Figure 7.21 which substantially uses free connections (nearest neighbor) and long lines.

7.6 CONCLUSIONS

The PML design had very nearly 100 percent usage of the device for this design, the ACTEL 1010 had 53 percent, the ALTERA MAX 5128 design had slightly over 46 percent and the LCA 3030 had about 45 percent. Comparing designs compiled onto different architectures is akin to comparing apples and oranges, but it is interesting to see the many ways in which a design can be mapped onto the various architectures. This problem will be addressed in more detail in the chapter on Benchmarks and Metrics.

PROBLEMS

1. How would one alter the design (Figure 7.1) to include the ability to read back the data without using a separate 8051 port?

2. How would one alter the design to make it expandable (that is, more data locations and a longer timer)? Are there any speed restrictions? Discuss them.

3. Alter the design to form a DMA controller. Use a word counter and an address counter.

4. Alter the design to make a simple digital oscilloscope.

5. Justify the cell usage for the ACTEL 1010 version of the logic analyzer design. Estimate within 10 percent.

8

Additional FPGAs and CPLDs

8.0 INTRODUCTION

Having examined four architectures in detail, many FPGA issues should be understood, at this point. To cover more products quickly, the following is a compressed approach to introduce additional FPGA parts. The same issues are covered more briefly for the ERASIC™, PEEL Array™, ERA™ and the FPGA™.

This chapter's products do not cover the rest of the available ones in today's market. The approach taken shows that it is possible to present more parts in less detail now that the basics of FPGA architectures and software have been presented.

The small example will not be presented for these parts, and much of the other detail is omitted. A basic capability summary and a quick overview of the FPGA software is given. With this information, the reader can decide whether to learn more about each of them.

8.1 ERASIC

Unlike previously discussed products, EXEL's ERASIC is made from a dense EEPROM (Electronically Erasable Programmable Read-Only Memory) technology. This important technology permits a configured logic device to be reconfigured by external application of programming signals rather than applying light—as opposed to EPLDs. The ERASIC is also nonvolatile.

The technology uses an NMOS (N-channel Metal Oxide Semiconductor) core with a CMOS periphery, but the EEPROM technology is still called CMOS (Complementary Metal Oxide Semiconductor).

Architecturally, the current ERASIC product, the XL78C800 (Figure 8.1), uses foldback NOR gates with configurable flip flops. The flip flops are contained in flexible I/O macrocells. The XL78C800 is in a twenty-four pin package with ten inputs, ten bidirectional signals, an optional output enable (or input pin) and an optional clock (or input pin). Eight of the inputs can be latched or treated as combinational inputs to the main programming array. As with the other foldback parts, an input signal connects to the main programming array passing through multiple logic layers. The NOR logic efficiently makes pyramided functions without using up pins.

The choice of the NOR function is appropriate because it is functionally complete, like the NAND function. The NOR can make any logic function when cascaded with other NORs. The ERASIC permits the direct generation of AND, OR, NAND and NOR functions when used with complementary input pins and available output options.

Figure 8.2 shows some interesting and useful variations the ERASIC provides. As shown in Figure 8.1, an input signal encounters a NOR function in the main foldback array, or a NOR while accessing the macrocells. At key points, small cells (diamond shapes) are inserted. These cells complement or pass input signals. This pass/complement option permits efficient generation of the functions shown in Figure 8.2.

The pass/complement functions are called PCEs (Polarity Control Elements). The PCEs are well placed at J and K inputs to flip flops, cell output points, and the global clear line. PCEs are also at the two transparent latch enable signals. By setting the PCEs appropriately, the J-K flip flops reconfigure as D, /D or toggle flip flops.

Figure 8.3 shows a close-up of the ERASIC I/O macrocell. There are eight possible macrocell configurations shown in Figure 8.4. Each macrocell configuration is distinguished by a unique combination of the corresponding configuration fuses assigned to it. Figure 8.4 details Figure 8.3, showing the macrocell options possible with the programmable combinations.

8.1.1 ERASIC Design Software

The ERASIC is configured using ABEL™ as a software development tool. The basic ABEL tool is extended with the additional capabilities of the EXEL Multimap and MultiSim modules. Multimap optimizes the design by efficiently sharing logic terms, removing redundant logic and translating logic to the cascaded NOR architecture. MultiSim permits internal node observation, tabular and waveform tracing and the use of simulation break-

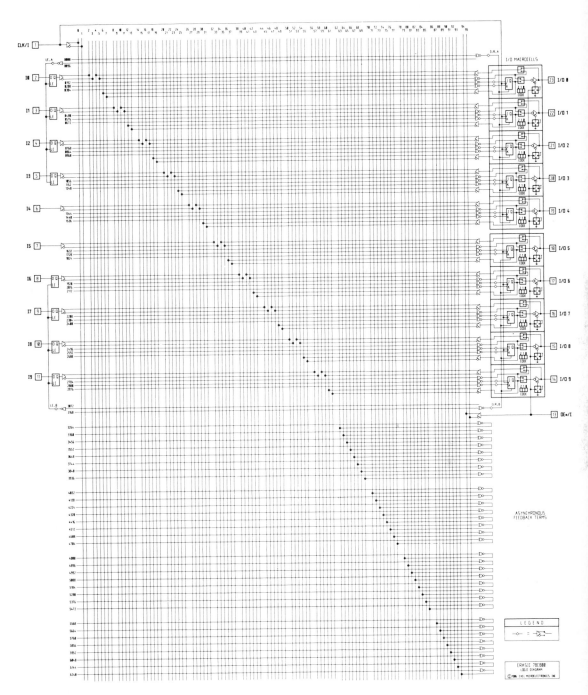

Figure 8.1   The ERASIC 78C800 logic diagram.

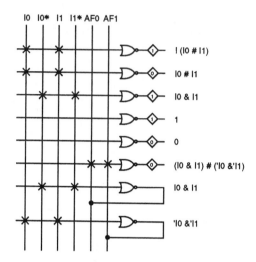

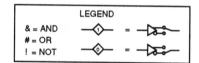

Figure 8.2 ERASIC logic functions.

points. As mentioned earlier, the availability of a gate array style simulator is crucial for effective design with deeply nested structures. The Multimap cell library presents a broad spectrum of soft macro TTL equivalents made from NOR gates. The Multimap software identifies unused portions of the TTL macros and optimizes accordingly.

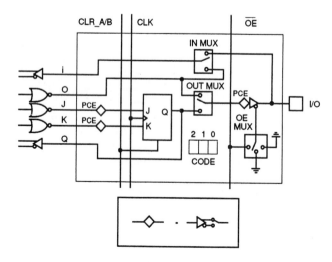

Figure 8.3 The ERASIC I/O macrocell.

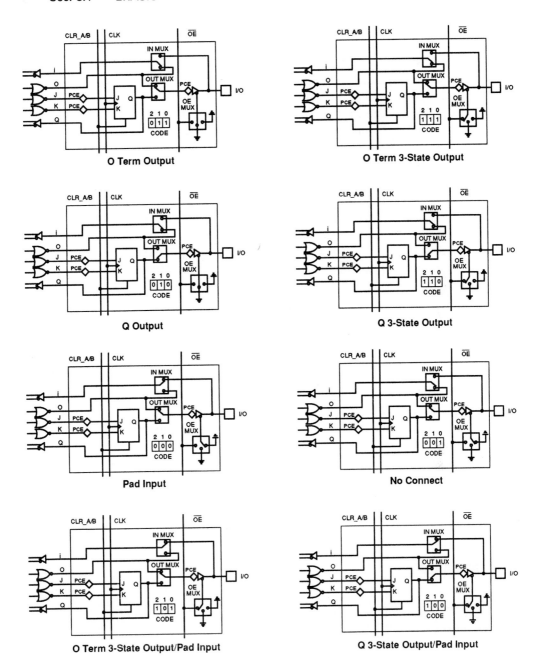

Figure 8.4   ERASIC I/O macrocell configurations.

8.1.2 ERASIC Performance

The ERASIC comes in two speed varieties, a 25 and 35 nanosecond Tpd version. The key parameters of interest are the I/O delays, the flip flop setup time, clock to Q propagation time and the internal gate delays. The toggle frequency is the inverse of the sum of setup time plus clock to Q time.

For the 25 nanosecond part, the input delay is 3 nanoseconds, the output delay is 7 nanoseconds, internal gate delay is 15 nanoseconds, setup time is 2 nanoseconds and the clock to Q time delay is 13 nanoseconds. The calculated toggle frequency is 66 MHz. These time values are typical values and include metal time delays.

Although the toggle frequency is 66 MHz, most designs will need to pass state variable signals through one or two levels of NOR gates for next state feedback. This feedback adds 15 nanoseconds per gate level. The added time is usually lumped into the setup time delay of the flip flop. For one extra NOR gate, the frequency derates to 33 MHz. For two NOR gates, it derates to about 20.2 MHz. You should refer to the manufacturer's specific literature to see if any enhancements have been made.

8.1.3 ERASIC Summary

The ERASIC has a lot of similarity to both MAX and PML, but it is unique in that it uses a foldback NOR gate. The ERASIC is fully connectible and has more symmetry than PML. It is hoped that this product line will persist, but the trend is toward faster, more dense parts. Being designed in CMOS, the ERASIC may be scalable to a smaller feature process, and expanded. Table 8.1 is an abbreviated capacity table for the ERASIC, showing cells needed to make functions. The table expands easily, and capacity estimation occurs in the usual way.

8.2 PEEL ARRAY

An additional dense architecture developed in the EEPROM technology is International CMOS Technology's PEEL Array. Unlike the channelled or foldback architectures, this product generates logical functions with a multiple AND array / OR array structure while using additional macrocells called Logic Control Cells (LCC). The basic architecture is shown in Figure 8.5 with a detailed drawing of the Logic Control Cell shown in Figure 8.6.

The PEEL Array is a family of several parts, each with a structure similar to that shown in Figure 8.5. Each family member has different numbers of Logic Control Cells and I/O pins. An additional global cell

TABLE 8.1 ERASIC Capacity Table

Function	Cells Used
4 input AND	1 gate
4 input NAND	1 gate
4 input NOR	1 gate
4 input OR	1 gate
4 to 1 Multiplexer	5 gates
4 bit Shifter	4 flip flops
4 bit Counter	4 flip flops and 4 gates

broadcasts internal clocks, presets, resets, etc. Signals enter the I/O pins, and go to an input bus running through the part. Signals then intersect with a horizontal AND bus, enter the Logic Control Cells (as needed) forming logical ORs. Signals then pass back to an input bus, or route to an I/O cell, or both.

As a ballpark speed indicator, a signal passes from an LCC output, crosses the logic interconnect array, and arrives at another LCC input in about 17 nanoseconds. Figure 8.7 shows the distributed logic array matrix of the standard PEEL Array products. Current PEEL Array family members include twenty-four, twenty-eight, forty and sixty-eight pin members. Expanded detail for the Global Cell and the basic I/O Cell are shown in Figures 8.8 and 8.9.

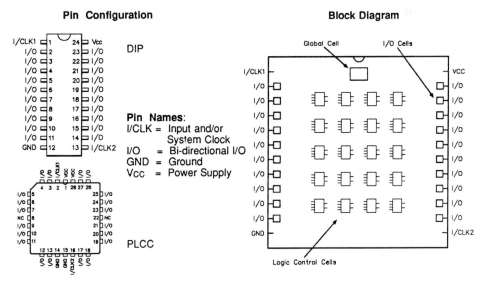

Figure 8.5 PEEL Array architecture.

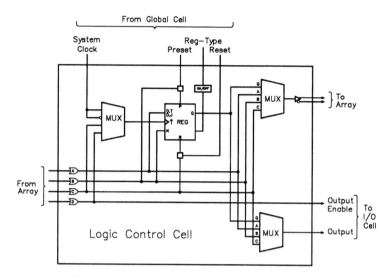

Figure 8.6   PEEL Array Logic Control Cell.

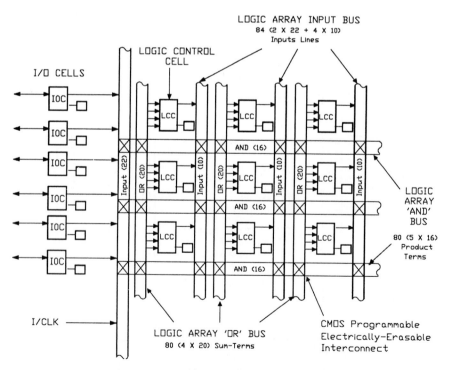

Figure 8.7   Distributed logic array matrix.

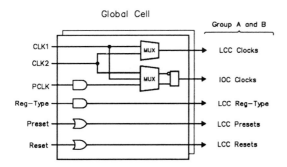

Figure 8.8   PEEL Array Global Cell.

8.2.1 PEEL Array Design Software

The PLACE Architectural Editor assists in designing with PEEL Array products. PLACE presents a graphic architectural image (Figure 8.5) on a PC screen. A standard mouse interface permits the designer to point at specific regions within the architecture, isolate LCC input points and write logic equations for the function at that point. The designer is literally manipulating the architecture of the final device in this type of design session. I/O pins are selected, names assigned and output signals formed with logic equations.

Functions are made by direct assignment to a specific LCC input point. Then, the LCC output is handled similarly. The internal LCC configuration is altered by screen images permitting cell configuration of flip flops as D, T, J-K, and so on. Once the design is done, the PLACE compiler creates a JEDEC compatible fusemap. The fusemap is downloaded to a third-party programmer that programs the device.

8.2.2 PEEL Array Performance

The PEEL Array family has two members at the time of this writing, the fastest parts are described here, with typical values. The input time delay is

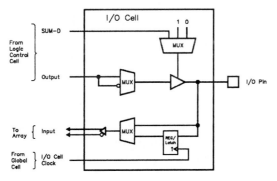

Figure 8.9   PEEL Array I/O Cell.

TABLE 8.2 PEEL Array Capacity Table

Function	Cells Used
4 input AND	1 gate
4 input NAND	1 gate
4 input NOR	1 gate
4 input OR	1 gate
4 to 1 Multiplexer	5 gates
4 bit Shifter	4 flip flops
4 bit Counter	4 flip flops and 4 gates

Note: This is a very rough table because extraneous gates to connect the flip flops are not included.

2 nanoseconds, output is 5 nanoseconds, and the internal gate delay is 13 nanoseconds. The flip flop setup time is 3 nanoseconds and the corresponding clock to Q is 11 nanoseconds. This gives a calculated toggle rate of 71.4 MHz. These delays include interconnection metal delays.

8.2.3 PEEL Array Summary

The PEEL Array family is an extension of the PLA (Programmable Logic Array) architecture, with buried flip flops and cascaded arrays. Again, the trend is toward faster, larger parts. Because this part is CMOS and may be scaled, it has the potential of being expanded in number and capacity.

Table 8.2 summarizes PEEL Array functional capacity. This table can be easily supplemented, building up larger blocks from these small pieces. As usual, capacity estimation occurs by tallying with the usual procedure.

8.3 ERA

Plessey Semiconductors has manufactured an FPGA product family incorporating static RAM-based interconnection with fine-grain functional cells based on a two input NAND gate. Named the Electrically Reconfigurable Array or ERA™, the architecture targets the fine grain functionality of a CMOS gate array.

Two ERA cells are shown in Figure 8.10. These cells reside in a large array of similar cells. Eight interconnect lines arrive at an eight-to-two MUX. The MUX is controlled by a ten bit SRAM, selecting among the cell inputs. The SRAM is the configurable part of the ERA. Also included in the cell is a single bit latch function that incorporates the two input NAND. Master-slave flip flops are made by cascading two ERA latch cells. In this

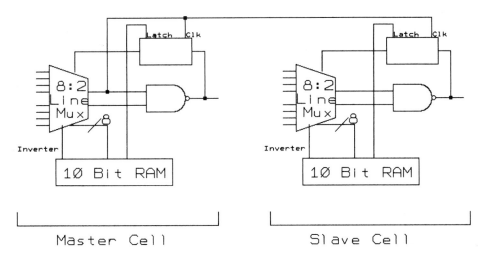

Figure 8.10 ERA cell schematics.

situation, one latch acts as the master latch and the other is the slave, as shown in Figure 8.10.

The interconnect scheme is hierarchical. Figure 8.11 shows how various outputs route through local interconnect (nearest neighbors), short range horizontal busses (across ten cell groups) and long range horizontal busses (spanning the die). Local interconnect best forms hard macros, while short range busses can interconnect physically adjacent macros. Higher level functions are built from lower level ones being connected with long range busses. The ERA 60100 has 2500 cells with 100 long range and 750 short range busses. There are 12,500 local interconnects on the ERA 60100.

Surrounding the ERA core of logic cells is a ten bit bidirectional peripheral bus. Information passes from the core to the bus and onto I/O pins, or vice versa. The peripheral bus is used to transmit global clock and reset signals for the chip. Access to the I/O pins is not restricted to the peripheral bus, but may occur within the core at key sites. The peripheral bus may also be used internally, without using I/O pins.

Figure 8.12 shows the basic ERA I/O cell. Output data heads toward the pin through a driver that has optional slew rate control. Input data arrives through a hysteresis receiver. Note the transmission gate access path to the internal ten bit peripheral bus. The transmission gate permits multiplexing of data directly onto the bus.

Following a signal through the ERA 60100, it arrives at an input (tpd = 2.5 nsec, typical) passes through any number of two input NANDS (tpd = 2.5 nsec/NAND, typical) and finally passes to the output. The speed of the output cell depends on whether or not it is slew rate controlled. The

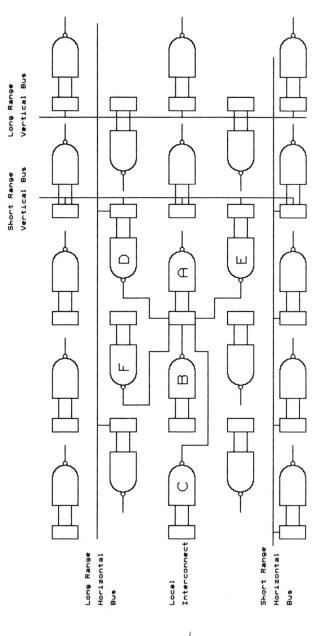

Figure 8.11 Simplified ERA internal interconnect.

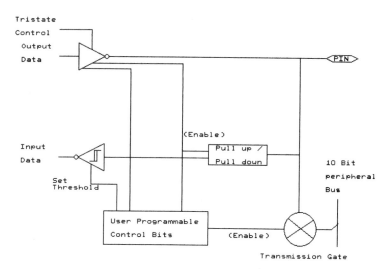

Figure 8.12   Simplified ERA I/O structure.

output speed is typically 5.0 nanoseconds uncontrolled and 7.0 nanoseconds for a slew rate controlled output.

Of course, the speed is also a function of capacitive loading. Manual timing estimates can be derived. The upper toggle limit on ERA flip flops nears 200 MHz. Remember, high toggle rates do not show performance, but rather the potential for performance.

8.3.1 ERA Design Software

The ERA design software strongly tracks a classic gate array flow. Cell and macro libraries are included for the capture, simulation, and layout sequence. Naturally, delays are extracted for back annotation. Once the optimized layout is complete, the generation of a binary configuration image occurs. The download file can be programmed into an EPROM that is available to configure the ERA.

The ERA downloading process is not unlike the LCA procedures described in Chapter 4. Using internal ERA counter resources, the ERA controls Erasable Programmable Read-Only Memory addressing to directly load itself. Saving ERA pins, the counter may be taken outside the part to control the EPROM. Alternately, a microprocessor can be used to sequence EPROM data loading into the ERA configuration memory. Four different downloading procedures are offered. The choice should be made depending on resources available to support the download.

A particularly intriguing capability is that the ERA may be partially reconfigured. Design sections can be updated, while other sections go untouched. Reconfigurable designs have not been too important in recent times, but the day may arrive when an FPGA is used to access and test other sections of a system, then be reconfigured to perform a different function altogether. This frontier is just opening.

8.3.2 ERA Performance

The ERA performance is the only performance in this chapter that doesn't include interconnect metal time delay. This is because the part has hierarchical interconnection, so time delays reflect the exact connections made. The input time delay is 2.5 nanoseconds, output delay is 5 nanoseconds and the internal cell delay is also 2.5 nanoseconds. The setup time is 0.2 nanoseconds and the clock to Q, as calculated from the toggle frequency, is quoted at 200 MHz. Taking the reciprocal of the sum of the setup plus clock to Q times and solving for the latter from the toggle frequency gives 4.8 nanoseconds for the Tckq.

8.3.3 ERA Summary

The ERA is an interesting family that Plessey has positioned to work in collaboration with their existing gate array products. The ERA architecture was originally developed by Pilkington Microelectronics Ltd. and the ERA is sometimes called the "Pilkington Architecture." Both Toshiba and Motorola have developed versions of this architecture. The claim is that automatic transition from the ERA netlist to a Plessey gate array is straightforward. Many designers are hoping for this approach, and this angle may be just right for quick access to the PLD designer market. Table 8.3 summarizes the cell usage in the ERA for capacity estimation. To expand the table, the designer must use two input NAND gates, or latches, because that is all ERA has.

8.4 FPGA-PLUS ARRAY

PLUS Logic has defined an EPROM based FPGA product family with the part prefix FPGA—the parts are also called "PLUS Array" parts. The first part, the FPGA 2020, includes eight Functional Blocks (FB) with a Universal Interconnect Matrix (UIM) and additional features in an 84 pin package. Figure 8.13 shows the FPGA architecture. Signals enter the chip through input or I/O pins. Signals then enter the Functional Blocks. Functional Block logic operates on signals, connecting between FBs through the UIM. Finally, the signals exit at the output pins.

TABLE 8.3   ERA Capacity Table

Function	Cells Used
4 input AND	6 NANDs
4 input NAND	5 NANDs
4 input NOR	10 NANDs
4 input OR	9 NANDs
4 to 1 Multiplexer	25 NANDs
4 bit Shifter	8 Latches
4 bit Counter	8 Latches and 40 NANDs

Note: Edge triggered D flip flops are made from the latch portion of the cell (Chapter 1), and the count cell method described in Chapter 4 is used to estimate the 4 bit Counter. The Exclusive-OR in the count cell takes 4 NANDs to make.

Figure 8.14 shows the internal structure of an FB. Signals from the UIM enter the FB and encounter an AND array. The AND array outputs then drive two OR arrays. One OR array is "shared" within the FB and one OR array is "privately" available to dedicated output cells. The private terms can be used to control an associated flip flop, perform logic, or both.

As the signal progresses through the programmable portion of the FB-heading to an output, it encounters a combinational cell called the Logic Expander (Figure 8.15). The Logic Expander can accept three inputs. One input comes from the shared OR term, one comes from the private OR term and one dedicated "carry-in" input comes from an adjacent cell. The Logic Expander generates one output that drives the flip flops D input, and a carry out to the next Expander's carry in input. Arithmetic functions (add or

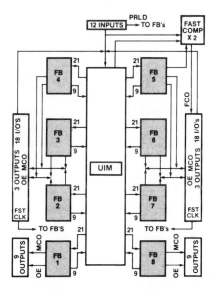

Figure 8.13   FPGA 2020 architecture.

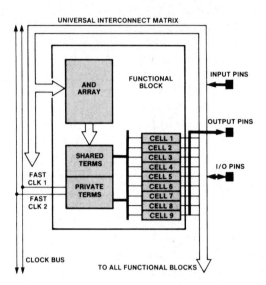

Figure 8.14   FPGA Functional Block.

subtract) fit well in this arrangement. This carry approach is similar to the LCA 4000 CLB approach.

The Logic Expander can make any logic function of two input variables, suggesting a RAM implementation. Details of making functions in a RAM are shown in Chapter 4. The Logic Expander adds in a third logic layer in the signal path, which is unique. The power of an additional flexible cell must be traded off against the liability of a third logic level, with the Expander.

From a global interconnect viewpoint, the UIM resembles the MAX PIA. The UIM also exhibits time invariant interconnection delay. The UIM

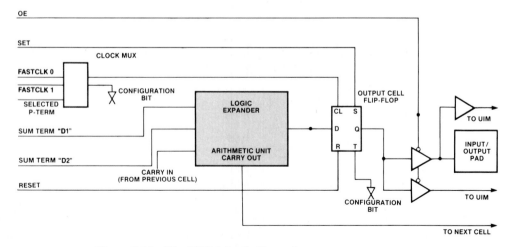

Figure 8.15   The FPGA Logic Expander.

operates as an internal bus and wire ANDs functions. Think of entry into an FB from the UIM as being from a 126 input AND gate.

Two sources of minimum skew fast clocks are available to each internal flip flop cell. Flip flop clocking rates are currently at 33 MHz and 40 MHz for the FPGA 2020. These rates include the transition logic in front of the flip flops, so toggle rates should be higher than these values.

Incorporated on the FPGA 2020 are also two FastCompare™ circuits targeted at high speed decode of up to twelve bit operands. The unlatched propagation delay for FastCompare on the FPGA 2020 is initially specified between 5 and 15 nanoseconds. These high speed comparators have similar application to the fast wide gates in PML and on the LCA 4000.

8.4.1 FPGA Design Software

The PLUSTRAN™ software follows the classic programmable gate array flow with simulation, optimization and download to an external EPROM programmer. Personal computer based, with higher workstation platforms planned, it supports a respectable library of TTL-like schematic cells and higher level macros. Several library cells allow direct mapping to the Fast-Compare logic cells. Several of PLUSTRAN's modules for technology mapping and netlist optimization have quaint names like the Muncher and the Integrater.

8.4.2 FPGA Performance

As a point of reference, consider the FPGA-30 specifications for comparison. The input time delay is 7 nanoseconds, output time delay is 10 nanoseconds and internal cell delay is 8 nanoseconds. The setup time is 25 nanoseconds and the clock to Q time delay is 5 nanoseconds. The toggle frequency is 33 MHz. These values include interconnection delay, and the high speed comparators have not been included in the comparison specifications.

8.4.3 FPGA Summary

The FPGA-PLUS Array products are, again, a family of parts. This suggests that a designer can learn to use one family member and find that skills carry over to the use of other parts. The approach also permits incremental design. Incremental design means two things. First, compile a piece of a design, get it working, add more and get that working, and so forth until the FPGA is expended. It also means that a design can be targeted to one device, and if it overflows, swiftly moved to another part in the same family—with no

TABLE 8.4 PLUS Array Capacity Table

Function	Size Factor
4 input AND	0
4 input NAND	0
4 input NOR	2
4 input OR	2
4 to 1 Multiplexer	3
4 bit Shifter	6
4 bit Counter	6

Rounding and taking liberties with the wire AND of busses may account for some of the 0 values shown. Values given are taken from the PLUS Logic Design Guide. Each PLUS Array part has a maximum size factor budget, and tallies are compared to it.

surprises. The PLUS family of FPGA parts continues to grow and the support for the parts continues to expand, as well.

Table 8.4 presents a summary of the PLUS Array capacity estimation table. In this case, the values given are not in actual cells, but in units that PLUS Logic calls "size factor." Size factor is calculated based on the usage of the Function Blocks. Each FB has twenty-one inputs and nine outputs. Fed back signals use up inputs to the FB. To calculate size factor, two numbers are first found. One number is the total number of component outputs used. The other is the number of component inputs—including signals fed back into the FB, multiplied by 9/21. The size factor is the greater of these two numbers.

As an example, an eight to one multiplexer similar to the 74151 has two outputs and twelve inputs. The inputs are the eight data lines into the cell, plus three inputs to select among the eight data lines, plus one enable input. The number of outputs is two. The number of inputs (12) times 9/21 is 5 and 1/7. The folks at PLUS Logic round this to a size factor of five.

During the writing of this text, Plus Logic was acquired by Xilinx. The stated rationale was that Xilinx had a gap in the lower density parts that would be nicely filled by a CPLD (foldback) architecture. It was also stated that having a common design tool would be beneficial. To date, Xilinx was the first to include both basic architectures.

While incorporating the PLUS logic products into the Xilinx product line, some changes were made. First, the FPGA parts were redesigned and renamed. The PLUS logic FPGA parts are currently called the XC7236, XC7272, XC7236A and the XC7272A. The A designations indicate faster parts, with the same functionality as the original parts. To complement the XC7200 parts, an additional family of parts has been derived from the basic XC7200 architecture, namely, the XC7300 family.

The XC7300 is a family of parts that incorporates a High Density Function Block similar to that of the XC7200 family, with the UIM and expanders, but also includes smaller Fast Function Blocks (FFBs) that operate considerably faster than the High Density Function Blocks. The new architecture, dubbed the Dual Block Architecture, is shown in Figure 8.16. Figure 8.17 expands the detail of the High Density Function Block, and Figure 8.18 shows the Fast Function Block. By eliminating the expander and permitting direct access to the Fast Function Block from external pins, some Tpd values are as fast as 7.5 nanoseconds.

The Fast Function Block is streamlined for speed and targeted for applications like high-speed address decode and very fast state machines. Naturally, there is a price for the speed, namely, density. The Fast Function Block has four product terms assigned to each macrocell flip flop D input, with a fifth available for either driving the asynchronous set input or driving

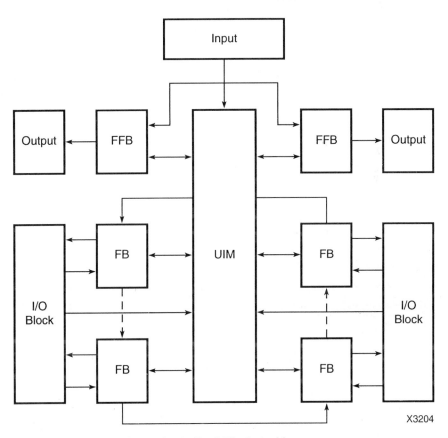

X3204

Figure 8.16 Dual Block Architecture.

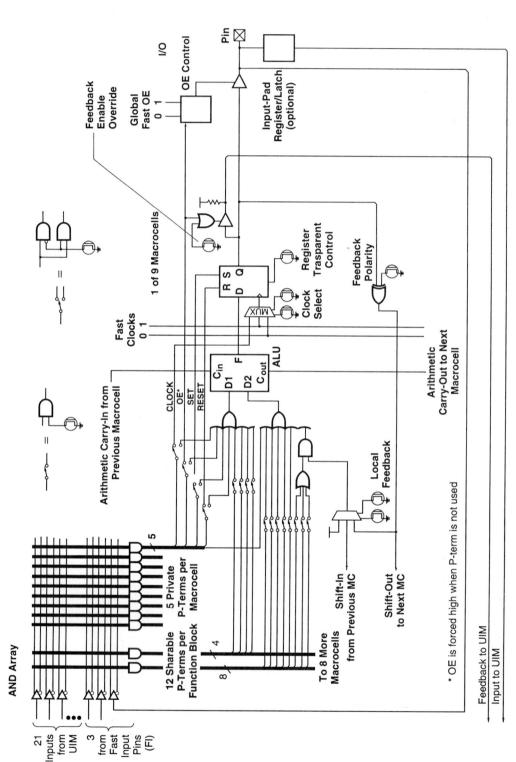

Figure 8.17 Dual Block Architecture High Density Function Block macrocell.

X1829

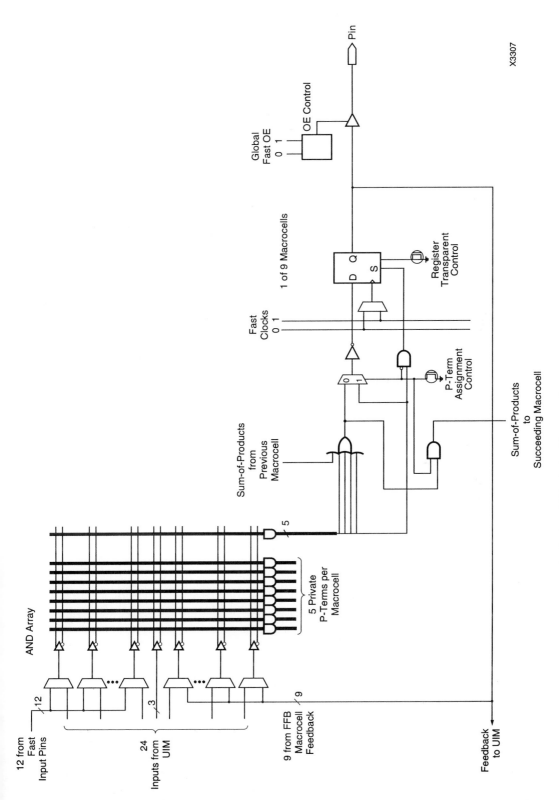

Figure 8.18 Dual Block Architecture Fast Function Block macrocell.

D when the other four product terms are directed to neighboring macrocells as shown in Figure 8.19. Within a nine macrocell Fast Function Block, it is possible to assign four product terms in a cascade fashion to a neighbor, with the cascade rippling through the whole function block. Each assignment of the four product terms incurs a 1 nanosecond time delay, but it is possible to accumulate up to 36 product terms at a macrocell with a net time penalty of 8 nanoseconds. When product terms are reassigned in this fashion, the fifth product term remains and can be used with product terms generated in the UIM to form logical sums of products at the macrocells.

The High Density Function Block has also been speed improved. Figure 8.20 shows the expander (or function generator) in more detail. Note that the carry in and carry out signals are clearly shown and that the sum of products signals enter pins D1 and D2 on the function generator. The function generator can be configured into any of sixteen distinct binary logic functions, but the most common is that of an adder. Across a function block, the total penalty for the carry signal is 6 nanoseconds. Compare this to FPGAs or CPLDs without special carry logic and datapaths to support them. It is possible to build accumulators that operate at 55 MHz and multiplier

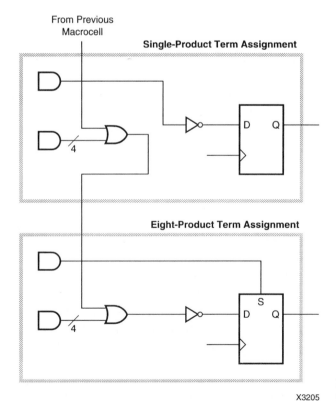

X3205

Figure 8.19   Fast Function Block product term sharing.

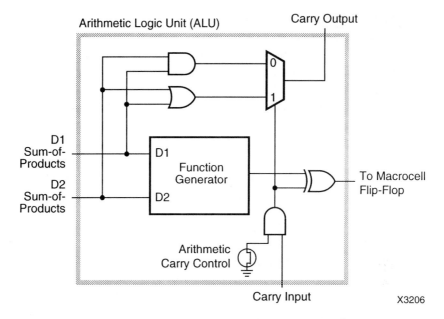

Figure 8.20   High Density Function Block Function Generator.

accumulators that operate above 30 MHz. This carves a nice niche for this family when applied to digital signal processing, data communications and graphics operations.

The Dual Block Architecture and the XC7200 family are supported with the standard Xilinx development flow, permitting common library development as well as a unified design environment. Both the LCA family and the XC7000 families have an identical user interface and address third-party support in similar fashions. This appears to be the way of the future.

8.5 SUMMARY

The products described in this chapter underline the accepted truth that there is much demand for more FPGA architectures in the market today. Most of the products are variations on CMOS technologies, many are foldback architectures, some have channels and foldback structures, and all have similarities. There are still more, yet to come (see Chapter 9).

The gate array flow is fairly standard among all of the products, and a family approach is the rule, not the exception. This chapter does not include the latest entries, but rather those that have gained some presence in the design world today. There will be others to enter this arena, and some of

TABLE 8.5   Comparative Performance Key Parameters

Parameter	PEEL	ERA	FPGA	ERASIC	XC7300
Tin	2 ns	2.5 ns	7 ns	3 ns	3 ns
Tout	5 ns	5 ns	10 ns	7 ns	4 ns
Tpd	13 ns	2.5 ns	8 ns	15 ns	2.5
Tsetup	3 ns	0.2 ns	25 ns	2 ns	2.5
Tckq	11 ns	4.8 ns	5 ns	13 ns	1.0
Ftoggle	71.4 MHz	200 MHz	33 MHz	66 MHz	125 MHz

these products may perish in today's competitive world. The common prevailing trend is that new parts must be larger and faster, with more pins.

Table 8.5 gives a quick summary of all products in this chapter, from a speed viewpoint. Remember that values given reflect recent technical information, which becomes dated. Three out of four of the products shown include interconnect metal. Some parameters were derived, for comparison. The output cell time delays may be taken with a grain of salt, because each manufacturer specifies the external drive circuitry and test conditions differently. The values shown are the key ones needed to assess any FPGA product.

Until this point, a discussion of gate count equivalents has been avoided. Tables 8.1 through 8.4 are function tables that describe how many cells are needed to make a particular function. The values do not translate well to gates, as Table 8.4 shows in particular. Because there are no standards for comparison among the products, one is motivated to find another basis of comparison. This comparison basis is addressed in the chapter on Benchmarks and Metrics.

PROBLEMS

1. Estimate the number of Dual Block macrocells needed to build the Chapter 7 logic analyzer.

2. Show how many ERA cells are needed to build an eight bit counter using the count cell method of Chapter 4.

3. The ERASIC uses NOR gates to form functions. Show a two bit adder configured from ERASIC NOR gates.

4. Estimate the speed of a four bit comparator built using the ERASIC, ERA, PEEL Array and the Xilinx XC7300 parts.

9

Newcomers

9.0 PREVIEW

Recently, the FPGA market began to change dramatically. Some have proclaimed that the FPGA architecture wars are over. Several older vendors shifted their approach and newer FPGA products emerged from startups. These new products were targeted toward specific markets. For instance, QuickLogic arrived with what may be the "speed king" FPGA, but Crosspoint Solutions focused on ASIC migration as its main thrust.

This chapter explores those two, as well as the capabilities of Concurrent Logic's products and the Intel FLEXlogic™ family. Concurrent Logic's CLi 6000 is an updated version of cellular logic, and FLEXlogic is an intriguing CPLD combining EPROM and SRAM on a chip with microprocessor oriented features. As in Chapter 8, this chapter highlights only key features needed to assess these newcomers.

9.1 pASIC

QuickLogic's FPGA product is called the pASIC, and it combines a functionally complete logic cell with routing channels using an antifuse called the ViaLink. According to QuickLogic, the dielectric-based antifuse (as with PLICE of Chapter 6) suffers from two weaknesses. First, because the dielectric is very thin, the capacitance of each connection site is high. Second, the resistance of the breakdown region is greater than 100 ohms. The combination of these factors slows signals down appreciably, especially if a signal passes through several fused sites. Because of this, QuickLogic developed an antifuse that exhibits lower impedance, slowing the signal much less. According to QuickLogic, the ViaLink creates a column of tungsten, titanium and silicon alloy with a typical resistance of only 50 ohms.

Figure 9.1 shows the pASIC logic cell, which multiplexes a mixture of wide and narrow input gates into or around a D flip flop. Note that the cell has five outputs, of which four are combinational. Figure 9.1 has two six input AND gates, four two input AND gates, a D flip flop and three two-to-one multiplexers. The asynchronous inputs to the flip flop go outside the cell, where they get connected to other signal inputs in the routing channels. The clock can be handled similarly.

Figure 9.2 shows how several such cells connect in the routing region. Note that the outputs wrap directly back into the channel along with the inputs, so that feedback for a cell occurs in the routing channel.

As seen with other dense architectures, additional test circuitry is helpful. The pASIC is the second entry in the FPGA world to recognize and implement scan design, which configures internal cells into a giant shift register chain. When in test mode, the shift register allows designers to observe or drive internal nodes.

9.1.1 pASIC Design Software

The pASIC Toolkit is a framework of design tools including both vendor-provided compile tools and the ability to interface to third-party capture and simulation tools. Initially offered on personal computers running in a Micro-

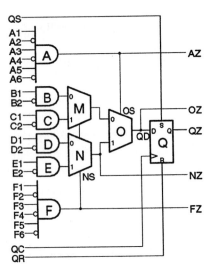

Figure 9.1 pASIC macrocell.

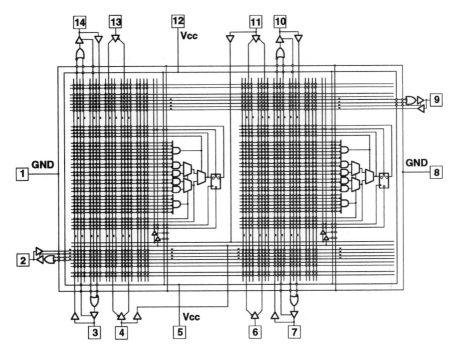

Figure 9.2 pASIC architecture.

soft Windows environment, the pASIC Toolkit provides a complete gate array flow. The pASIC Toolkit also includes Automatic Test Vector Generation (ATVG) to work with the pASIC scan design circuitry.

QuickLogic provides the Seamless pASIC Design Environment (SpDE) that includes the A.P. & R. (Automatic Placement and Routing) software, the modeler, verifier, timing analyzer, and programmer interface. Figure 9.3 shows the software flow, with the SpDE embedded into the pASIC Toolkit. The technology mapping (or fitting) is called the "packer" in Figure 9.3, and there is a hierarchical router. The router is actually three separate pieces, with a global router, a detail router, and a clock router, to optimize clock nets for minimum delay and skew.

Because the pASIC cell has multiple outputs, it is possible to have several small functions assigned independently to each cell. For instance, there are two distinct six input AND gate functions, that have logic outputs that also control the multiplexer for the flip flop. The packer can break functions up and target them to land in a single logic cell.

9.1.2 pASIC Performance

The pASIC is currently built with a one micron CMOS process, and makes logic functions having a delay of about 5 nanoseconds. Counter rates are

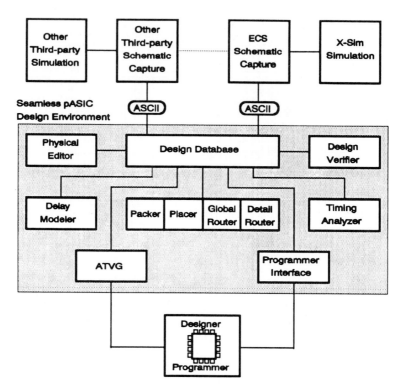

Figure 9.3   Seamless pASIC design environment.

quoted in excess of 100 MHz. Table 9.1 summarizes the individual cell delays for the fastest pASIC family members. The pASIC FPGAs are offered in slower speeds, as well.

9.1.3 pASIC Summary

The tradition for FPGAs is to cast entire families of FPGAs, at the first announcement, and pASIC is no different. The current goal is to make a series of parts in packages from 40 to 160 pins, having 48 to 384 cells, with arrangements shown in Figure 9.4. Table 9.2 shows the device numbers, with the corresponding number of logic and I/O cells, input pins and available package pins. Table 9.3 shows the cell usage for the standard table of SSI/MSI functions used throughout the text. This is the initial pASIC 1 family.

In theory, the ViaLink is scalable along with the rest of the pASIC cell structure. There is nothing conceptually to keep successive generations of the pASIC structure from growing and increasing steadily in performance.

TABLE 9.1 Basic pASIC Timing

Parameter	Minimum	Typical	Maximum
Tpd clk buff	4.0 ns		5.5 ns
Tinput pad	1.5 ns		1.9 ns
Tpd output (fast)			3.3 ns
Tpd output (slow)			3.5 ns
Tpd	3.6 ns		8.3 ns
Tsetup	3.9 ns		3.9 ns
Tckq	1.8 ns		6.4 ns

Note: Min/max values are for fanouts of 1 and 8, respectively.

9.2 CLi

Back to the RAM structure for function interconnection. Based on the architectural work of Fred Furtek's Labyrinth design, the CLi6000 has evolved into an intriguing first member of another family of FPGAs. A striking difference here is that the interconnect structure is regular and cells are primarily connected by adjacent placement to nearest neighbors.

Figure 9.5 shows the CLi cell architecture, with Figure 9.6 showing the bus interconnection architecture. The CLi logic cell is shown in Figure 9.7. Note that Figure 9.7 refers to AN, AE, AS, AW, as input points. These are the north, east, south and west neighbor cell output points. There are other operands available from adjacent cell B outputs.

Each cell accepts one of four neighboring cell A outputs, and one of four neighboring cell B outputs. In turn, each cell generates four copies of each A output and each B output to neighboring cells. Once the operands arrive in the cell, they can be combined through the internal gating to form a logic function of two input variables. The A outputs are driven from a four to one multiplexer that gets inputs from the gates (or flip flop) above them. Likewise, the B outputs are driven from the four to one multiplexer and gates above them.

The A function can be the logical AND of an A input (or "1"), with an input brought into the cell from the right side labeled NS1, NS2, EW1 or EW2. These four inputs (NS1, NS2, EW1, EW2) arrive by local buses that permit cells to skip over each other. The A output can also be generated by ANDing a B input with the NS1, NS2, EW1 or EW2 signals. There is a possible path permitting A, B, NS, EW signals to be Exclusive-Ored or to be loaded into a D flip flop.

The B signals encounter a different set of Boolean operations, but a NAND path going into the B multiplexer, ensures that the cell is functionally

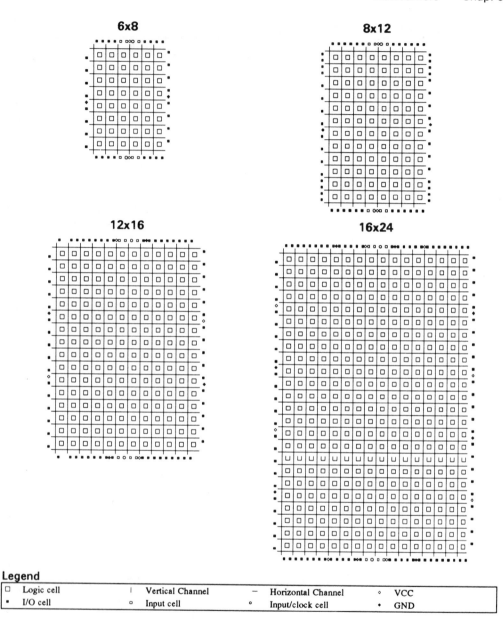

Figure 9.4 pASIC 1 chip arrangements.

complete. Each logic cell multiplexer is controlled by a static RAM cell, not shown.

As suggested above, entry to the cell can be from adjacent neighbor A and B outputs, or a system of local buses. Exit from the cell may also be to the local buses from the A output, assuming no contention. The local buses are arranged between rows and columns of the cells. The vertical buses NS1

TABLE 9.2 pASIC 1 Family Members

Device	# Logic Cells	# I/O Cells	Dedicated Inputs	Pins
QL6X8	48	32	8	44
QL8X12	96	56	8	68
QL12X16	192	68	8	84
QL16X24	384	104	8	160

and NS2 are available to each column of cells. The horizontal buses EW1 and EW2 are available to each row of cells. An additional bus line is parallel to each local bus, and is called an Express bus. The Express bus is not connected directly to the cells like the local buses. Express buses are accessed by the local buses, but not the cells.

Signal routing through the CLi cells is possible and interesting. It is possible to enter on A inputs, exit on A outputs; enter on B inputs, exit on B outputs; enter on A inputs, exit on B outputs; enter on B inputs, exit on A outputs; or several combinations of entry and exit from A, B and the local buses.

TABLE 9.3 pASIC Functional Equivalents

Function Description	pASIC Resources
1. Basic Logic Gates	1/4 to 1/2 cell
2. D flip flop (edge triggered)	1 cell (logic remains)
3. D latch (transparent)	1/2 cell
4. J-K flip flop (edge triggered)	1 cell
5. Decoders	
a. 2 to 4	2 cells
b. 3 to 8	4 cells
c. 4 to 16	8 cells
6. Multiplexers	
a. 2 to 1	1 cell
b. 4 to 1	1 cell
c. 8 to 1	2 cells
d. 16 to 1	3 cells
7. Comparators (equality only)	
a. 2 bit	1 cell
b. 4 bit	2 cells
8. Registers (serial load)	
a. 4 bit	4 cells
b. 8 bit	8 cells
9. Counters	
a. 2 bit	2 cells
b. 4 bit	4 cells

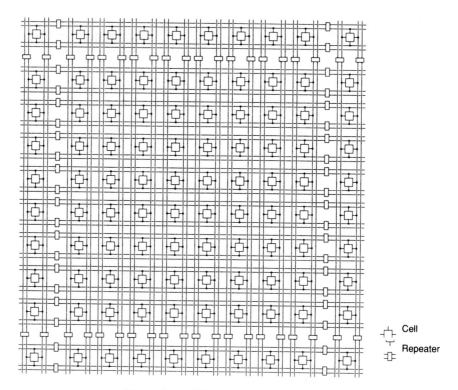

Figure 9.5 CLi connection architecture.

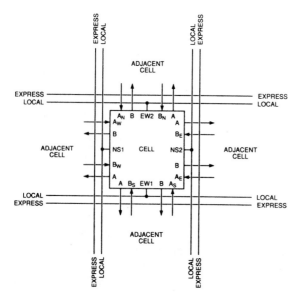

Figure 9.6 CLi cell-to-cell and cell-to-bus connections.

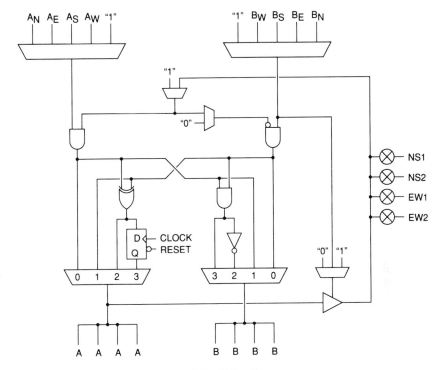

Figure 9.7   CLi cell structure.

Additional on-chip resources include global clock distribution and global flip flop asynchronous resetting. The I/O cells can be configured to mimic Open Collector outputs, have three-state control and either slow or fast slew rate. Three-state control is a logic variable tied to vertical or horizontal buses. Slew rate control is a simple bit associated with each output pin.

The CLi can be configured by an external EPROM, a microprocessor or another source. Internal CLi circuitry handles the configuration automatically.

9.2.1 CLi Design Software

CLi design software (Figure 9.8) is called the Integrated Development System (IDS). As expected, it combines industry standard design capture and simulation packages (currently ViewLogic) with vendor generated A.P. & R. software and netlist handling utilities. The IDS includes all necessary design rule checkers, back annotation and timing estimators as well as timing analyzers. The usual logic optimization and technology mappers are included, as well as layout floorplan editors, so you can influence the exact

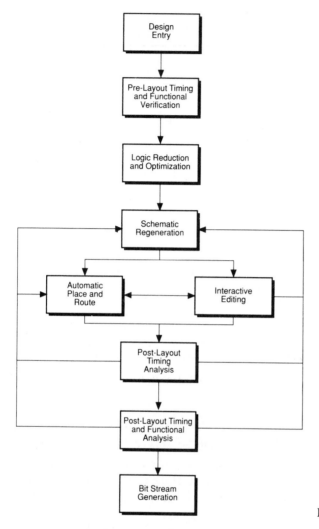

Figure 9.8 IDS flow chart.

arrangement of the final design. The result of all of this is a bit configuration file that is downloaded into the CLi.

9.2.2 CLi Performance

Currently built on a one micron CMOS process, the performance is strongly a function of the final design arrangement. Very regular logic functions achieve highest performance, by minimizing routing metal. Cell propagation delays are between 2 and 3.5 nanoseconds, input delays between 1.5 and 2.5 nanoseconds and outputs between 5 (fast) and 8.4 (slow) nanoseconds. Table 9.4 summarizes the CLi 6000 speed.

TABLE 9.4   Basic CLi Timing

Parameter	Minimum	Typical	Maximum
Tpd clk buff	1.5 ns		2.5 ns
Tinput pad	1.5 ns		2.5 ns
Tpd output (fast)			5.0 ns
Tpd output (slow)			8.4 ns
Tcell	2.0 ns		3.5 ns
Tsetup	2.1 ns		3.5 ns
Tckq	1.6 ns		2.7 ns

Note: Interconnection delays are not included; maximum values are given. Values shown are in nanoseconds.

9.2.3 CLi Summary

Again, a family of parts is in development. Table 9.5 shows the CLi family and Table 9.6 summarizes the CLi 6000 cell capacities for the standard functions.

A couple of additional points are particularly worth mentioning, however. The CLi architecture is so regular that designs could be done with little regard to where they land. It is possible to put the same design into several small chips, or cascade big and small CLi parts. This is because the chip exit points look like the next chip entrance points. The cells are all identical, so designs could be done from one chip to the next, crossing chip boundaries.

Another point with regard to the regularity of function and connection is the handling of highly regular applications. The CLi is particularly suited for video, graphics, animation, or parallel processing (systolic and wavefront) applications. In each of these applications, computations occur frequently with data residing in adjacent neighbor cells. The CLi fits this computation model very well.

Concurrent Logic was recently purchased by Atmel Corporation, a manufacturer of CPLDs and ASICs. The CLi architecture complements the Atmel CPLD family by adding a dense, flip flop rich, highly regular FPGA to their current product line.

TABLE 9.5   Partial CLi Family Configurations

Device	CLi6001	Cli6002	CLi6003	Cli6004	CLi6005	CLi6006
Logic Cells	576	1024	1600	2304	3136	4096
Registers	576	1024	1600	2304	3136	4096
I/O	64	96	108	108	108	128
Row X Columns	24X24	32X32	40X40	48X48	56X56	64X64

TABLE 9.6 CLi Functional Equivalents

Function Description	CLi Resources
1. Basic Logic Gates	1 cell for 2 inputs
2. D flip flop (edge triggered)	1 cell
3. D latch (transparent)	6 cells
4. J–K flip flop (edge triggered)	8 cells
5. Decoders	
a. 2 to 4	10 cells
b. 3 to 8	24 cells
c. 4 to 16	48 cells
6. Multiplexers	
a. 2 to 1	1 cell
b. 4 to 1	20 cells
c. 8 to 1	63 cells
7. Comparators (equality only)	
a. 2 bit	6 cells
b. 4 bit	9 cells
8. Registers (serial load)	
a. 4 bit	4 cells
b. 8 bit	8 cells
9. Counters	
a. 2 bit	4 cells
b. 4 bit	8 cells

Note: Some functions can be improved using the bus structures.

9.3 FLEXlogic

Intel Corporation is best known for its dominance of the microprocessor world. In support of that position, much of the Intel PLD effort is directed toward supporting that microprocessor market. With this success in hand, Intel chose to attack the FPGA market with a dense architecture that was instantly recognizable for microprocessor designers, and offers a distinguishing set of features.

Figure 9.9 shows the architecture of the iFX780. It contains eighty macrocells arranged peripherally around a global interconnect region. The eighty macrocells are clustered in groups of ten macrocells in eight groups called Configurable Function Blocks (CFBs). Each CFB constitutes a 24V10 type architecture, similar to the industry standard PAL22V10. For the uninitiated, the nomenclature means that the block has twenty-four possible inputs, ten outputs (actually bidirectionals) and arranges its product terms in variable patterns.

Figure 9.10 shows the interior of a CFB, with the distribution of product terms among the macrocells. In particular, note that the macrocells on each

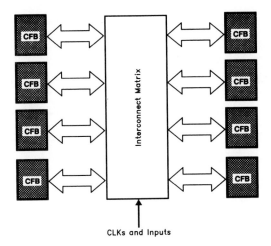

CLKs and Inputs

Figure 9.9 iFX780 architecture.

end of the CFB have twelve dedicated product terms, ORed with two dedicated product terms and finally selectively ORed with two product terms from an adjacent macrocell. This takes the total available product terms to sixteen for each end macrocell within the CFB. Macrocells on the interior have two groups of two product terms dedicatable, and may share additional pairs from adjacent macrocells. With this patented arrangement, any interior macrocell may be configured to have two, four, six or eight macrocells. Each macrocell D flip flop may be configured as a T or J-K flip flop, as needed.

Within a CFB, there is also a special arrangement of Exclusive-NOR gates tied to the CFB inputs (Figure 9.11). Each CFB input also feeds one EX-NOR leg, so that fast twelve bit comparators can be built. Because there are only twenty-four total inputs, this limits the bit compares, but for today's microprocessors, twelve bit compares make sense for high order address lines. The results of the EX-NOR compares are tied into a large twelve input AND gate within the CFB, completing the compare operation for external use as a memory select signal. Using inputs for comparison limits their availability for application to macrocells.

At this point, it has been shown that the CFB may be used as a 24V10 or a fast twelve bit comparator. There is one more important use for the CFBs—embedded static RAM. Each CFB can be configured to form a 128×10 bit RAM. The RAM blocks preclude CFB usage as a classic logic function, but recalling Chapter 1, the RAM can form any ten combinational functions of seven inputs, if need be. As expected, the RAM configuration makes use of the CFB inputs to pass the address, data and RAM control signals to the CFB. RAM control signals include the familiar /OE, /WE and /BE signals. Using the Output Enable (OE) and Block Enable (BE) inputs, it is possible to stack the CFB RAMS into deeper or wider structures and connect to other CFBs forming stacks and queues.

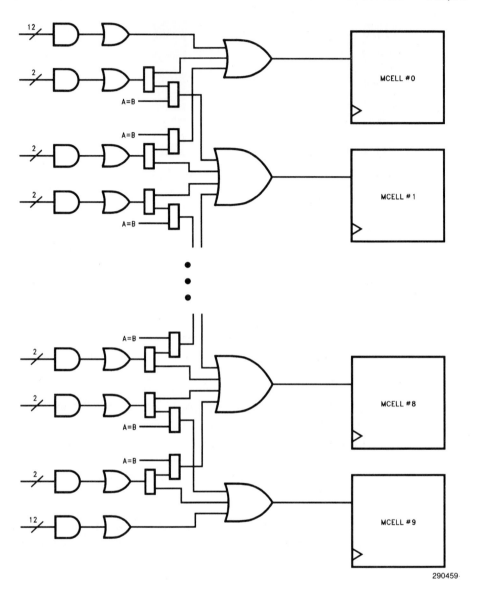

290459

Figure 9.10   FLEXlogic CFB.

Additional FLEXlogic features include operation of each CFB selectively at 3.3 volts or 5 volts, special clock skew options and JTAG boundary scan. An interesting capability that FLEXlogic provides is the ability to develop a design, download it into the part where the design is formed in RAM, perform in circuit debug and not program the EPROM cells until the design is debugged. Similarly, a design can be overlayed—in circuit—on top

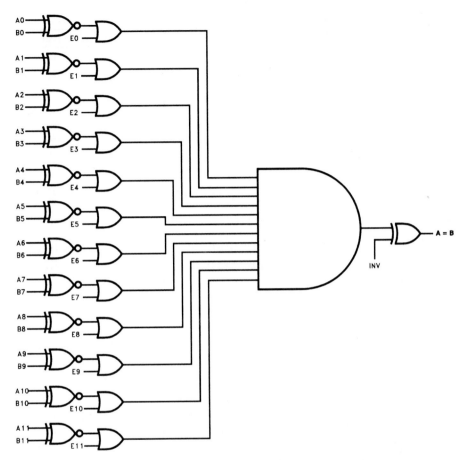

Figure 9.11   FLEXlogic CFB comparator structure.

of a design that was originally in the EPROM cells. Currently, the FLEXlogic parts are not EPROM reprogrammable, but the overlay capability may make this less necessary.

9.3.1 FLEXlogic Design Software

PLDshell Plus is Intel's design software package. It includes design capture for the entire Intel PLD product line using a superset of the familiar PALASM syntax. PLDshell Plus estimates, optimizes, and compiles designs into any of the FLEXlogic parts, and provides a graphic display, functional simulation. Unlike the other entries in this book, PLDshell currently does not include a detailed timing simulator with back annotation. Part of the rationale here is that the current architectures have deterministic timing, so the relative simulation is adequate. This remains to be demonstrated in the

TABLE 9.7   Basic FLEXlogic Timing

Parameter	Minimum	Maximum
Tpd input to output		10 ns
Tpd compare		10 ns
Tsetup synchronous	6.5 ns	
Tsetup asynchronous	2.0 ns	
Tckq synchronous		6 ns
Tckq asynchronous		12 ns
Thold synchronous	0 ns	
Thold asynchronous	5 ns	
Taa (RAM access)		15 ns

long run, but a very critical feature of PLDshell Plus is simply that, unlike the rest of the software in this text, it is currently offered free of charge.

9.3.2 FLEXlogic Performance

The introduction to this chapter suggested that QuickLogic was positioned as the "speed king" of FPGAs. This position is strongly challenged by FLEXlogic, which achieves a pin to pin speed of 10 nanoseconds. The interesting attribute of FLEXlogic is that the 10 nanosecond number is from any input pin to any output pin, regardless of where the pins are on the chip. That is, the pins may be within the same CFB or tied to different CFBs. The access time of the SRAM is somewhat slower, with that value being 15 nanoseconds. Flip flops are quoted to operate with up to 80 MHz clocks. Table 9.7 summarizes the FLEXlogic performance, and Table 9.8 summarizes the rate at which logic functions are used in the iFX780.

Note that the flip flop specifications of Table 9.7 indicate both synchronous and asynchronous clocks. Synchronous clocks are driven from a clock pin, while asynchronous clocks arrive from the programming array. There is a third method, not shown, that is a delayed clock. The delayed clock is appropriate for situations that occur most frequently with interfacing an address or data bus to a microprocessor.

9.3.3 FLEXlogic Summary

AMD's MACH family and ATMEL's ATV family are two other architectures with similar architectures to the FLEXlogic family. All would be considered CPLDs by this book's definition, and all capitalize on the instant recognizability of a clustered 22V10 type architecture. Intel has distinguished itself in providing a high speed, dense architecture that is both EPLD and

TABLE 9.8 FLEXlogic Functional Equivalents

Function Description	FLEXlogic Resources
1. Basic Logic Gates	1 cell
2. D flip flop (edge triggered)	1 cell
3. D latch (transparent)	1 cell
4. J-K flip flop (edge triggered)	1 cell
5. Decoders	
a. 2 to 4	4 cells
b. 3 to 8	8 cells
c. 4 to 16	16 cells
6. Multiplexers	
a. 2 to 1	1 cell
b. 4 to 1	1 cell
c. 8 to 1	1 cell
7. Comparators (equality only)	
a. 2 bit	1 cell
b. 4 bit	4 cells
8. Registers (serial load)	
a. 4 bit	4 cells
b. 8 bit	8 cells
9. Counters	
a. 2 bit	2 cells
b. 4 bit	4 cells

SRAM based. The FLEXlogic family is slated to continue growth, with additional parts having more logic and pins, as well as less logic and pins than the current parts.

9.4 CP20K

When the term Programmable Gate Array was coined, it was done so to make the LCA more tangible to the average logic designer. What has happened since then is remarkable from a diverse architectural viewpoint. However, one company—Crosspoint Solutions—has taken the term Field Programmable Gate Array and built an architecture as close to a CMOS gate array as is possible. Literally building the gates from transistors and anti-fuses, the CP20K directly tracks real gate arrays. Crosspoint Solutions' target market is the one expecting design migration, to a real gate array.

Again, this is a family of parts, but the structure of each is similar. Contained in the CP20K family are a series of transistor building blocks called Transistor-Pair Tiles (TPT), and RAM-Logic Tiles (RLT).

The TPT (Figure 9.12) is the building block most closely resembling a CMOS gate array cell. TPTs permit signal entry from a routing channel to the transistor columns, where logic functions form and exit back to the routing channel.

RLTs (Figure 9.13) are coarser grain structures included to efficiently make RAM blocks, multiplexers, and Exclusive-ORs/NORs. The design software decides whether to build a function from the TPT or RLT pieces, depending on efficiency and expediency. Because the cells are fine grain, logic functions are "built up" rather than "stripped down."

Connections are made primarily within the routing channels of the FPGA (Figure 9.14), using antifuses similar to the Vialink. Performance is

Transistor-Pair Tile (TPT)

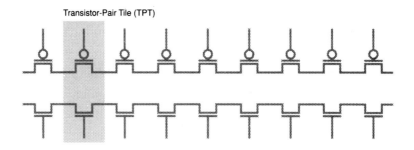

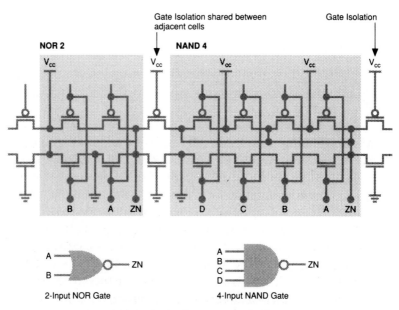

Figure 9.12 Transistor-pair tiles.

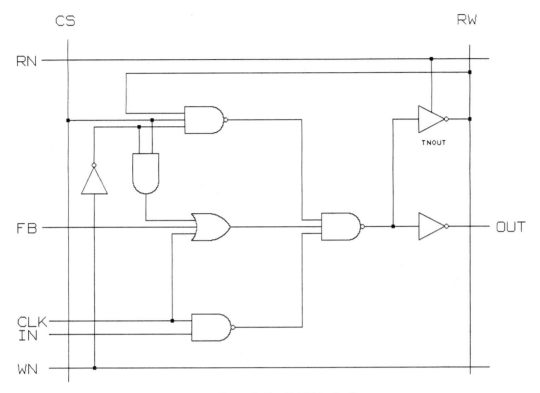

Figure 9.13   RAM-logic tile.

dictated by antifuse impedance, so an unprogrammed antifuse has low capacitance and high resistance; a programmed one has low capacitance and low resistance.

Cells also may be connected by abutment, using V-shaped lines called chevrons. The chevrons permit direct connection within the TPT and RLT logic rows. Chevron interconnection uses shorter metal runs, so less speed degradation occurs with their use.

RLTs are aligned within their rows permitting efficient connection as user configurable RAM chunks. Common column select lines, read/write data lines, read select, and write select signals are regularly spaced nearby permitting tight RAM connection. The RLT has eight ports: six are inputs, one is an output and one is bidirectional.

The CP20K I/O cell (Figure 9.15) is possibly the most elaborate one to date. The I/O cell can be used for input, output or bidirectional transfer, and includes slew rate control. On top of that, the output can be programmed to sink or source 4,8 or 12 mA and can select between CMOS or TTL input signals. There is also an output latch available at each pin site.

System clocks are very flexible on the CP20K, with four configuration options. Figure 9.16 shows the elaborate substructure of the clock system

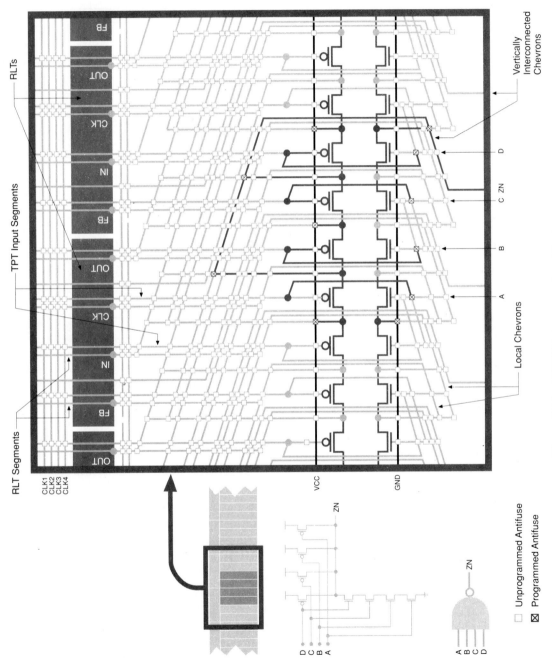

Figure 9.14 CP20K interconnect architecture.

206

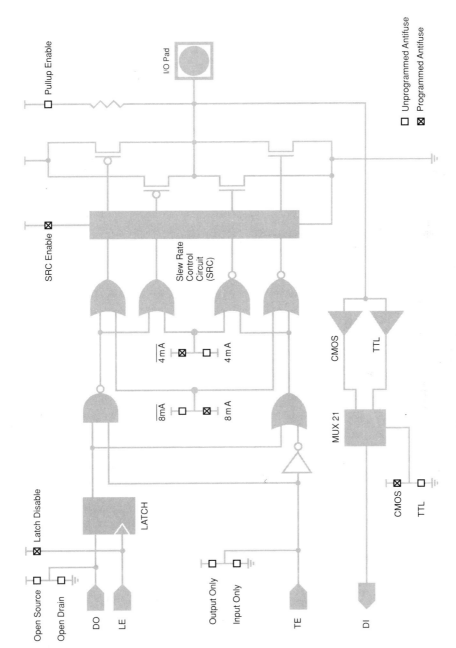

Figure 9.15 CP20K I/O cell structure.

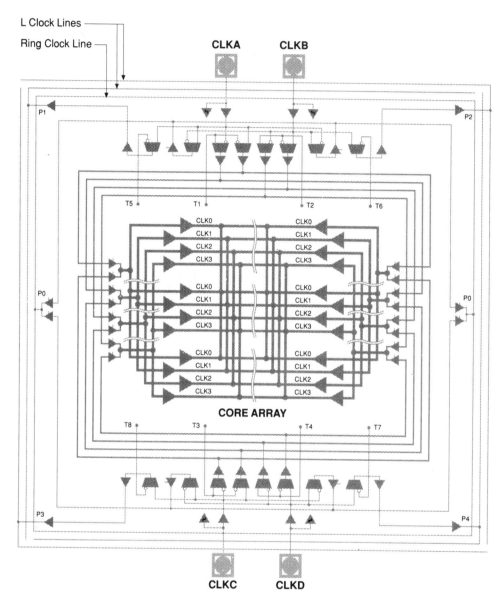

Figure 9.16 CP20K clock structure.

within the CP20K. There is a ring surrounding the entire die, which may be accessed by each I/O latch. There are four clock input pins (CLKA, CLKB, CLKC, CLKD) that enter the chip and access the internal clock driver circuitry. Eight internal clock points can also access the clock drivers.

The clock drivers increase the strength of a clock signal. The driver then passes the signal to the surrounding ring or one of two L shaped bands passing

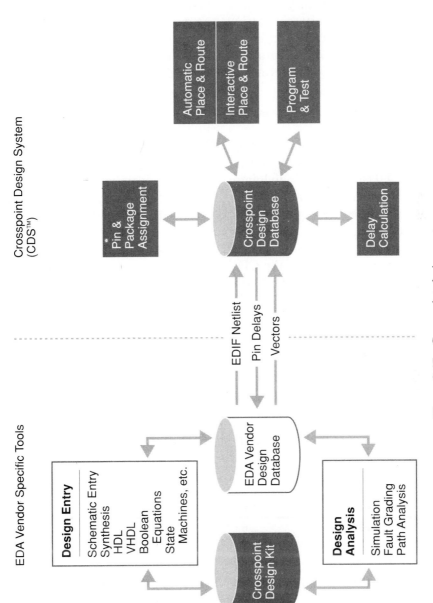

Figure 9.17 Crosspoint design system.

around half the chip. Clock input pins can be used for ordinary signals, and the internal clock points can pass global resets around the chip, instead.

Testability with the CP20K is addressed by implementing the I.E.E.E. 1149.1 JTAG Boundary Scan Architecture Standard. As mentioned for the LCA 4000, boundary scan permits the pins of a device to be configured as a large shift register, controlling, and monitoring the chip. Crosspoint Solutions has added some features in addition to the basic standard, with a thirty-two bit user configurable register and a device identification register.

9.4.1 CP20K Design Software

Crosspoint Design Environment (CDE™) adds the usual gate array imperative tools to industry standard design capture and simulation tools. The basic CDE flow is shown in Figure 9.17, which oversimplifies the actual flow. Naturally, CDE includes both automatic and interactive place and route software, along with pin and package assignment, delay extraction/calculation and program/test software. Communication occurs between CDE and the capture/simulate/synthesis tools by way of EDIF netlists, pin delays and test vectors. The goal of the CDE package is to make an antifuse table that is then downloaded to the Crosspoint FPGA Programmer/Tester. CDE is written in C++ and designed to be transportable to multiple workstation environments.

9.4.2 CP20K Performance

The CP20K has an interesting angle on performance (Table 9.9). It was implemented in a 0.8 micron CMOS technology using antifuse programming. Because the antifuse impedance exceeds that of metal connections, the CP20K is slower than a comparable CMOS gate array of the same feature

TABLE 9.9 Basic CP20K Timing

Parameter	Intrinsic	4 Loads	8 Loads
Tpd clk buffer	6.69	(derates with load capacitance)	
Tinput buffer	1.65	2.0	2.4
Tpd output (fast)	3.7	(derates with load capacitance)	
Tpd output (slow)	4.23	(derates with load capacitance)	
Tpd 4 in NAND	1.46	2.2	2.9
Tsetup	3.15	3.15	3.15
Tckq	2.84	3.3	3.7

Note: These values are typical, with load and corresponding interconnect capacitance as shown. Output and clock buffers must be rated for capacitance instead of internal cell loads. All values are in nanoseconds.

TABLE 9.10 CP20K Cell Capacities

Part #	TPT Count	RLT Count	I/O Pads
CP20220	1760	440	91
CP20420	3584	896	130
CP20840	6696	1674	180
CP21200	9504	2376	219
CP21600	12672	3168	250
CP22000	15876	3969	270

size. With this in mind, Crosspoint has positioned the CP20K to be performance comparable to a 1.2 or 1.5 micron CMOS process—larger featured, therefore slower. Care has been taken to assure the availability of commercial gate arrays capable of handling Crosspoint FPGA designs. These gate arrays map closely to the Crosspoint architecture.

9.4.3 CP20K Summary

The CP20K family is summarized in Table 9.10, where some members are being delivered. Table 9.11 shows the number of cells needed to form the

TABLE 9.11 CP20K Functional Equivalents

Function Description	CP20K Resources
1. Basic Logic Gates 2 to 6 input NAND	3–11 TPTs
2. D flip flop (edge triggered)	3 TPTs and 2 RLTs
3. D latch (transparent)	7 TPTs or 1 RLT
4. J–K flip flop (edge triggered)	17 TPTs or 3 RLTs
5. Decoders	
a. 2 to 4	14 TPTs
b. 3 to 8	38 TPTs
c. 4 to 16	88 TPTs
6. Multiplexers	
a. 2 to 1	6 TPTs or 1 RLT
b. 4 to 1	16 TPTs
c. 8 to 1	8 TPTs and 7 RLTs
7. Comparators (equality only)	
a. 2 bit	6 TPTs
b. 4 bit	17 TPTs
8. Registers (serial load)	
a. 4 bit	12 TPTs or 8 RLTs
b. 8 bit	24 TPTs or 16 RLTs
9. Counters	
a. 2 bit	11 TPTs and 4 RLTs
b. 4 bit	30 TPTs and 8 RLTs

small design suite that have been used for comparison. As usual, the family is scalable, so future additions with smaller features are to be expected. RAM configurations are available as hard macro cells, built up from the RLTs.

The success of migrating designs to CMOS gate arrays from Crosspoint FPGA solutions remains to be demonstrated, but the architectural approach is promising. It is fitting that this discussion end with a product that so strongly resembles a real gate array.

PROBLEMS

1. Johnson counters (aka "Moebius" counters) have an interesting property. They are formed as a shift register where each flip flop Q output feeds the next flip flop D input, except the last member of the chain returns its /Q output to the first member's D input. As clocks occur, the shifter changes states, and there is a finite number of states in the counter. Why might Johnson counters be particularly important to an architecture like CLi? Why would they also be of use with other FPGAs?

2. Crosspoint Solutions' CP20K and the Plessey ERA are both supposed to ease the migration of designs from FPGA versions to gate array versions. Compare and contrast the two approaches.

3. Returning to the Johnson counters of problem 1, compare a three bit counter using standard methods with a similar counter built from a Johnson counter. To make the comparison fair, the outside world should see the same binary variables, so some encoding may be needed. Which counter operates faster (clocking rate)? The count sequence should be 000, 001, 010, 011, 100, 101, 110, 111, 000.

4. Derive a one bit count cell appropriate for use with CLi.

5. Justify the cell counts for Table 9.3, for the pASIC.

10

Benchmarks and Metrics

10.0 INTRODUCTION

Benchmarks are a relatively easy means of making decisions when criteria are complex. Benchmarking FPGAs involves using a relevant set of test designs. The test designs, or benchmarks, model real designs for the sake of making a decision.

In the past, computer systems' benchmarks were programs with key properties like intense floating point calculations or binary vector manipulation. A computer analyst used the benchmark program's performance to make buying decisions.

The benchmark procedure was often adequate—assuming the benchmarks reflected what the computer system would be doing. Many times, the benchmarks did not reflect realistic system behavior, and they were misused. FPGA benchmarks are treated similarly.

Design benchmarks can be used and misused like computer program benchmarks. The difficulty of assessing speed and capacity for an FPGA increases because manufacturers don't specify gate counts and propagation delay consistently. Rather than homogenize FPGA specifications, some try to solve the problem with benchmark designs. Many designers prefer suites of benchmarks.

An alternate approach to benchmarking is using metrics. Metrics present an analytic framework to evaluate designs. Both methods have their merits and weaknesses. This chapter proposes a small set of benchmarks and metrics and shows their use.

10.1 BENCHMARKS

Picking an appropriate set of benchmarks that permits comparison among FPGAs is critical for selecting a candidate. Gate array manufacturers barely have such a benchmark system. The JEDEC JC-44 committee proposed a set of test designs (essentially hard macros)—but these are not complete designs, as a good benchmark should be. Instead, the JC-44 benchmarks are items like RAM patches, shift registers, arithmetic units and binary rotators. The JC-44 benchmark goals were spelled out clearly, but many were directed at assessing the design software rather than the gate array's speed or capacity. Recognition of the software role is important, but another issue.

For most readers of this book, what is needed is a set of benchmarks that target FPGA design comparison. Some appropriately relevant designs to address that task are needed. Many digital designers are concerned with systems resembling Figure 10.1. This microprocessor system could be a small industrial control station, a minicomputer or an engineering workstation, depending on the specific processor and peripheral configurations. It should be noted that the CPU interfaces to a Local Area Network (LAN), a disk, a graphics display, dynamic RAM (DRAM), EPROM/Static RAM and an I/O bus.

These interfaces are common in modern systems. Many of them are specified to current industry standards. In particular, those that are not are strong candidates for FPGA devices.

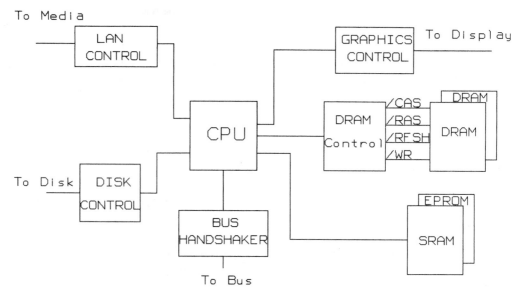

Figure 10.1 Typical microprocessor system.

The core function of each interface given is an appropriate benchmark because it embodies the essence of that interface. The benchmarks omit particular features that distinguish them among specific interfaces. For instance, the DRAM controller should be altered to interface to the most common high performance DRAM products available. Whether the DRAM benchmark supports static ROW/Column, nibble mode or other features is not important for selection as a benchmark.

The proposed benchmark functions are shown in Figures 10.2 through 10.4. They are only core functions. In particular, note that the bus handshaker is the simplest and the Universal Asynchronous Receiver/Transmitter (UAR/T) is the most complex.

The UAR/T is not mentioned specifically in Figure 10.1. The UAR/T is a key building block of the LAN controller and the Disk controller. How the UAR/T does a specific encoder/decoder operation is the main distinction between a LAN and Disk controller. When you build the final design, it is the designer's option to designate the details that fit specific needs.

10.2 THE DRAM CONTROLLER BENCHMARK

The DRAM controller benchmark is probably the most common design implemented in the gate array world of the past. It became a common gate array design because DRAM manufacturers were slow to market supporting controllers for their DRAM products. Designers resorted to using lots of discrete logic to tailor solutions for specific DRAM configurations.

Some designers included fancy memory management options while others kept their DRAM controllers simple. When standard products became available, many designers had already made gate array solutions based on discrete logic solutions. These designs had features that the DRAM controller vendors had not anticipated. With the coming of new DRAM and VRAM (video RAM) devices, having even newer features, the cycle repeats. This time the DRAM controller is in the realm of the FPGA.

Figure 10.2 shows a simple DRAM controller. It includes an eighteen bit transparent latch, for holding microprocessor addresses. CPU signals attach to the controller State Machine which latches addresses at the appropriate time. The addresses pass to a multiplexer where nine bits are selected—again, controlled by the State Machine. The ability of the FPGA to handle the address path shows it supports internal data manipulation. Data manipulation is important in modern logic design.

To handle DRAM refresh, there is an eighteen bit counter cycling through row and column addresses, periodically strobed by the State Machine. The State Machine can be interrupted from its ordinary operations

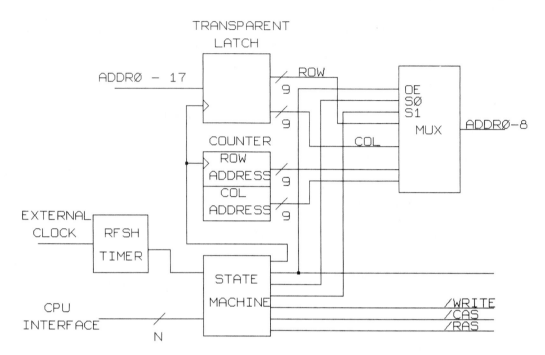

Figure 10.2   DRAM controller benchmark.

by the internal Refresh (RFSH) Timer. The State Machine is a collection of gates and flip flops interfacing the microprocessor signals with the DRAM modules. The State Machine also makes the row and column address strobes (/RAS and /CAS) as well as the write strobe that loads data into the DRAMs. The State Machine output enable signal asserts the chip enable inputs on each DRAM. An external clock sets the refresh interval. Design requirements for a specific system are left to the designer.

    Why is this a good benchmark? It is a typical FPGA application found in many systems. The DRAM controller includes several blocks that are good speed and function capacity indicators. First, critical path assessment can be done by finding the time delay from address inputs (through the latches) to address outputs (through the multiplexer). Second, an eighteen bit (or possibly two nine bit) counters demonstrate the ability to build deep, synchronous counters. The counter feature is appropriate for other applications, as well. Third, the refresh timer may be efficiently made with a ripple counter, or a synchronous counter. A ripple counter uses only flip flops with independent clock inputs (no extra gates). Alternately, the refresh timer can be a synchronous counter like the row/column address counter.

    The State Machine is usually synchronous with a half-dozen flip flops and transition logic gates. The State Machine may require all flip flops to be clocked in strict or skewed phases. The ability of the FPGA to support these kinds of design techniques may be critical, and are typical of a large class of designs.

Based on the arguments presented above, the DRAM benchmarks require about fifty flip flops and/or latches and about 150 gates. The package requirement exceeds thirty-five pins, so the package must be at least a forty pin package. Most of the higher end products discussed so far could make this benchmark.

10.3 THE UAR/T BENCHMARK

The UAR/T benchmark (Figure 10.3) meets criteria similar to the DRAM controller. UAR/Ts are found in both disk and LAN controllers and were made by gate arrays in the past. The UAR/T has two independent machines, where one is the Transmitter and the other the Receiver.

Transmitter operation is simple. Byte data arrives in parallel at the XMIT Data Register, is passed to a shifter and serialized. The serial bit-stream is then encrypted, depending on the needs of the application. The

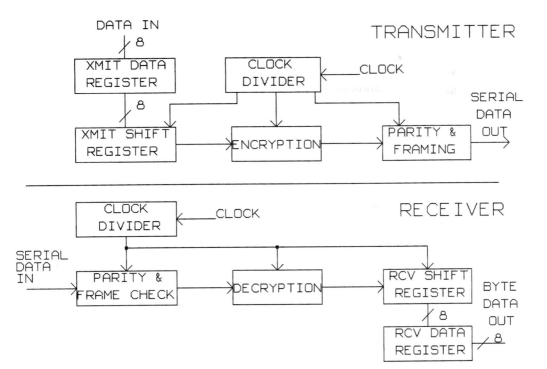

Figure 10.3   UAR/T benchmark.

encrypted bitstream may or may not have parity added into the information, but the data is then framed with special bits that signal the beginning and end of an information item before it is transferred onto the data line.

The Receiver reverses the process. Serial data arrives at the receiver where framing information is stripped, and the data's parity is checked. The stripped bitstream passes to a decryption unit and on to an RCV shift register. The shift register passes parallel bytes to the RCV data register and the outside world.

The requirements for the UAR/T include setting up a datapath (through the parallel and serial registers), implementing special state machines (that is, the circuitry for encryption/decryption, parity and framing) and supporting clock division. Some UAR/Ts may incorporate the familiar sixteen X sampling rate (of the serial data stream) that can make the clock divider more interesting.

The UAR/T incorporates multiple state machines that may all be synchronized to independent clock sources. Clock independence shows flexibility in the FPGA clocking circuitry for handling multiple internal state machines. Pinning requirements are typically less than those of the DRAM controller, but at least forty pins allow additional features to be included. Some features could indicate whether data is available, or parity and framing errors have occurred on either the Transmitter or the Receiver. The UAR/T structure is found in disk controllers, LAN controllers, modems and terminal communications equipment, to mention a few applications.

10.4 THE BUS HANDSHAKER BENCHMARK

The bus handshaker is the loosest of the chosen benchmarks. It is also the smallest and may be the easiest to expand in many different directions. The diagram in Figure 10.4 includes the familiar bus request, Read, Write, Address and Data Enable flip flops. More signals could be added, to distinguish Memory from I/O cycles, multiple word transfers, etc. This sort of benchmark focuses on the ability of the FPGA to deal with independent flip flops. Are there clocking options that permit quick bus access by asserting the Bus Request signal on the rising clock edge? Can the Read or Write flip flop release on the falling edge of the same clock? Can flip flops be reset independently with an asynchronous input or must they be reset by the next clock? These specific questions may be critical to a given design. More interesting things could be added to this design, such as DMA control or Interrupt control and vector encoding, but those embellishments are left to the designer.

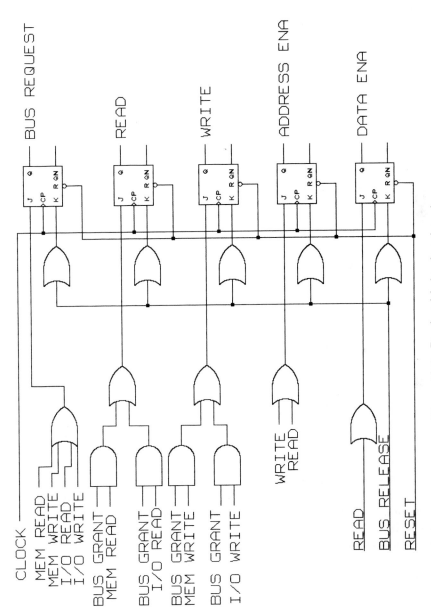

Figure 10.4 Bus handshaker benchmark.

10.5 A PRACTICAL METHODOLOGY

The proposed benchmarks are in reality only templates for benchmarks. If these benchmarks make sense, the FPGA designer should recast them to meet specific needs. For instance, the DRAM controller could be the company standard VRAM interface design—many companies have such standards. The bus handshaker could be the company standard bus, not an industry standard one.

Conversely, the bus handshaker could be almost any appropriate industry standard, as long as it is appropriate for the designer's needs. The UAR/T could be modified, as well. For the sake of discussion, assume that the customized benchmarks can be easily defined. The next step is to use them to help in the selection of an FPGA.

Recognizing that many FPGA designers use inexpensive schematic capture software, many of the FPGA manufacturers have made cell library conversion software for them. By judiciously capturing the benchmarks with one of these tools, there is a strong possibility the vendor FPGA software can directly translate the schematic. The design can then compile onto the chosen FPGA. This creates a transportable design benchmark that can be moved from one design environment to another. At some point in the future, such benchmarks may be written in VHDL and be even more transportable than schematics.

Many designers have had very good first-time success by using low-level logic cells, made from just a few specific FPGA cells. Those cells, described in the function capacity tables in Chapters 3 through 6, are an appropriate level. Building the benchmarks up from low level cells is also straightforward. The next step is to get the benchmarks compiled on several FPGAs, for comparison.

A particularly intriguing idea is that many vendors will accept a design and compile it free of charge. Designers are more likely to purchase an FPGA software package knowing their design compiles. If time and manpower do not permit this approach, some vendors offer the free use of their software for evaluation purposes. Either way, designers must generate the benchmarks and simulations, for their personalized benchmarks.

After the benchmarks are compiled, it is also necessary to determine that the FPGAs work. Careful attention to test vectors and general testability must be given. Clearly, the benchmark performance is critical in the decision process, but other factors enter into the decision.

10.6 ADDITIONAL BENCHMARK APPROACHES

The benchmarks given may not be appropriate for all situations. They may be taken as guidelines or simply templates for other benchmarks. The designer also may wish to implement more register or gate intensive bench-marks.

To minimize the number of separate designs that must be tested on each candidate FPGA, it is better to be specific than prolific. A few good bench-marks representing the required design style give more insight than a large number of poorly chosen designs.

Recently, some organized benchmarking efforts have surfaced. MCNC (Microelectronic Center of North Carolina) and PREP (Programmable Electronics Performance) have proposed benchmark suites with strong cooperation from several FPGA manufacturers. In particular, PREP Corporation has proposed a suite of benchmarks targeted at assessing capacity and speed.

The PREP ground rules are well defined. Gates are defined based on a two input NAND gate (ala gate arrays), and impartiality is a target. The PREP benchmark suite includes:

a. A data path with eight 4:1 muxes, an octal register and an eight bit shifter.

b. A timer/counter built from a 2:1 mux, two eight bit registers, an eight bit loadable counter and an eight bit comparator.

c. A small state machine (Mealy type with eight states, eight inputs and eight outputs).

d. A large state machine (Moore type with sixteen states, eight inputs and eight outputs).

e. A four-by-four bit multiplier and eight bit accumulator.

f. Sixteen bit accumulator.

g. Sixteen bit synchronous counter (like 741s163s).

h. Memory address decoder with sixteen inputs and eight select outputs.

Capacity is measured by the number of copies of each benchmark that can be dropped into a given FPGA. Equivalent gate counts are given for the benchmark. The designer's job is to assess whether the FPGA has enough gates to meet specific needs.

This author believes that more meaningful benchmark patterns would be combinations of the benchmarks forming whole subsystems. For instance, a benchmark including an accumulator, a datapath, and an address decoder might actually occur in a design. This would be more realistic than having six accumulators poured into a single FPGA, which is unlikely to ever occur.

It may be noted that the benchmarks should not be restricted to single chip solutions. Sometimes, no single FPGA product has precisely the re-quired speed and capacity for an efficient solution meeting all criteria.

As sophisticated as the design tools are today, it is to be expected that FPGA users will have to make tradeoff decisions even when using transportable benchmarks. The design process is not yet "push button."

In earlier chapters, it was shown that designs could be analyzed in terms of their relative gate or cell counts using tally methods. The approach involves breaking the design into small pieces that were tabulated, and added up to get a total. With this in mind, it makes some sense to cast a table showing gate capacities of FPGAs.

Dennis McCarty, at ACTEL, published a chart with his tally of the gate equivalent capacity of several popular FPGA parts. Table 10.1 is a subset of McCarty's chart, including only parts that have been discussed in this text. McCarty's approach is reasonable, in that he uses equivalent two input NAND gates as his building blocks, and proceeds from there. Naturally, his tallies differ somewhat from other published marketing reports by the FPGA manufacturers themselves, so they could be considered to be controversial.

Now this is a chart of capacities and a method to determine the design's requirement. This should be enough to determine whether a design will fit a particular FPGA. Unfortunately, the abilities of the technology mapper (Chapter 2) and the design optimizer (fitter, also Chapter 2) come into play. It would be nice if there was a way to correlate a specific FPGA architecture to our design, and determine whether it will fit or not. That is the goal of design metrics.

10.7 DESIGN METRICS

Recent work in evaluating FPGA architectures has evolved a small set of metrics which may prove to be useful in estimating whether a specific design will fit a particular FPGA. Based on the work of Jonathan Rose and Steven Brown, Jay Sturges at Intel has proposed a direct and simple approach.

Sturges' metrics are admittedly still under development, but are easy to understand and apply. The idea is that any FPGA architecture can be described by a set of metrics which correlate with the ability to map a design onto the architecture. The current choice of metrics includes a "connectability" metric (Ic), a "routability" metric (Rc) and a usability metric, U.

Sturges has chosen the same basic partitioning of the FPGA world as that taken in Chapter 1 of this text, namely, channeled (FPGA) and foldback (CPLD) architectures. Because of this partitioning, there are two versions of the three metrics, depending upon the basic structure of the architecture. It remains to be seen what will happen with hybrid versions of the architectures. Examine the basic ideas of the three metrics for the two architectural groups.

TABLE 10.1   FPGA Capacity Table

Vendor	Device	Dedicated FF	% Used	# Gates	# I/O
Actel	1010	0	.90	916	57
	1020	0	.90	1697	69
Altera	5064	64	.90	770	36
	5128	128	.90	1530	60
ICT	7024	40	1.00	530	22
	7040	48	1.00	640	30
PlusLogic	2020	144	.90	1255	72
Signetics	2552	52	1.00	575	53
Xilinx	3020	128	.90	630	64
	3030	200	.85	930	80
	3042	288	.80	1180	96
	3064	448	.70	1860	120
	3090	640	.65	2270	144

Source: Dennis McCarty, *Actel Databook*, 1992.

10.8 CPLD ARCHITECTURE METRICS

The first metric is the "interconnectability" metric, Ic, given in Equation 10.1. Ic is composed of three other parameters: S, B and F. S is the total number of routable and usable resources in the architecture, B is the number of blocks (or segments) in the architecture and F is the channel width feeding each block.

$$Ic = S/(B*F) \qquad \text{(Eq. 10.1)}$$

Taken grossly, S is the number of signal sources—inputs, outputs and bidirectional signal lines that span the FPGA. S also includes the outputs of any macrocells that feedback to the internal connection region of the part. Think of S as the maximum number of signals entering the connection region. Assuming the FPGA has clusters of function blocks, B is the number of such blocks. Finally, F is the potential number of inputs that may feed each block—the fanin.

As an example, the MAX EPM5064 (Chapter 5) has 72 signal pins ($S = 72$) and four LABs (hence, $B = 4$), and each LAB has 24 input entry points ($F = 24$). This permits a calculation of $Ic = 72/(4*24) = 0.75$.

The second metric is the routability metric. This metric has a simple expression:

$$Rc = Ic/P \qquad \text{(Eq. 10.2)}$$

As before, Ic is calculated using Eq. 10.1 and P is the probability of obtaining a given connection. As might be expected, the probability of obtaining a given connection is derived from the total number of possible connections that can be made. The probability P of obtaining a given connection is the weakest aspect of metrics. P is a strong function of the ability of design software to take advantage of the architecture. For foldback architectures, usually assume that P is one, and less for channelled ones.

The third metric is the usability metric, U, which suggests the probability of being able to route a particular resource. Equation 10.3 gives an expression for U. The parameter D is the

$$U = 1 - [(1/Rc) + (D/S)] \qquad \text{(Eq. 10.3)}$$

number of dedicated routing channels for a given set of resources. In this case, D is the local feedback paths within an LAB on a MAX architecture. Sturges has suggested that a value of zero is ideal for the U metric, with values greater than zero corresponding to the probability of failing, and negative values indicating architecture overkill.

To complete the example metrics for the MAX EPM5064, the results are summarized as follow:

$$S = [9 + (16*4) + (7*4) + (32*4)] = 229$$

$$B = 4$$

$$F = 24$$

$$D = [(32*4) + (16*4) + 9] = 201$$

$$Ic = 229/(4*24) = 2.38$$

$$Ec = 1/2.38 = .42$$

$$Rc = 2.38/1 = 2.38$$

$$U = 1 - [(1/2.38) + (201/229)] = -0.29$$

10.9 FPGA ARCHITECTURE METRICS

Going back to the work of Rose and Brown, Jay Sturges cast a slightly different version of the metrics for channeled architectures. In particular, the parameter B is replaced by Bf, where its expression is given as follows:

$$Bf = [(Fs*n)*(Fc*m)]/W*(v*h) \qquad \text{(Eq. 10.4)}$$

where

$n =$ the number of switch boxes

$W =$ the average number of tracks per channel

$v =$ the number of vertical channels

$h =$ the number of horizontal channels

$m =$ the number of connection boxes

$Fc =$ the number of fanout channels

$Fs =$ the number of connections available to each incoming resource

With this definition, the channeled version of the interconnectability metric, Ic is given with Equation 10.5:

$$Ic = S/Bf \qquad \text{(Eq. 10.5)}$$

The routability metric Rc is identical to Equation 10.2, but the probability of obtaining a connection is even harder for channeled architectures. Sturges suggests taking the probability as an average of Fs and Fc, but a more realistic value is likely to be more complex. The usability metric is identical to Equation 10.3.

At this point, a number of questions should have arisen. For instance, where do v and h come from? How does the designer know what value W will be? It appears that many of these parameters have been held back by manufacturers.

Calculate the metrics for the ACTEL 1010. Initially,

$$n = 5$$

$$m = 59$$

$$v = 59$$

$$h = 5$$

From these, calculate:

$$S = (n*m) = (5*59) = 295$$

$$Fs = (13*59) = 767$$

$$Fc = (5*7) = 35$$

$$W = [(22 + 13)/2] = 17.5$$

$$D = 0$$

$$Bf = [(767*5)*(35*59)]/(17.5*59*5) = 1534$$

$$Ic = 295/(1534) = 0.19$$

$$Ec = 1/(0.19) = 5.26$$

$$Rc = 0.19/0.70 = 0.27$$

$$U = 1 - [(1/0.27) + (0/295)] = -2.7$$

The values for v and h were derived from technical conference papers rather than from the ACT 1010 data sheet. Table 10.2 summarizes the metrics for several commercially available parts, with values derived from sources other than the data sheets. As FPGA suppliers become more involved with design metrics, they will probably supply at least the complete metric values at some point in the future.

A very important step remains to be done with metrics, and that is correlating them to specific designs. Work is being done here, with the goal of examining a design netlist and arriving at a probability of whether it will

TABLE 10.2a Some CPLD Metrics

Device	Pins	S	B	F	D	Ic	Ef	P	Rc	U
MAX5064	44	72	4	24	64	0.75	1.33	1	0.75	-1.22
MAX5128	68	136	8	24	128	0.70	1.42	1	0.70	-1.36

TABLE 10.2b Some FPGA Metrics

Device	Pins	S	Fs	Fc	n, m	W	v, h	Bf	Ic	P	Rc	U
3020	44	128	5.4	2.5	77, 64	5	9, 9	164	0.77	0.70	1.1	0.10
1010	44	442	767	35	5, 59	17.5	59, 5	1534	0.28	0.70	0.41	-1.4

Note: 3020 is the LCA 3020 and 1010 is the ACT 1010.

fit into a specific FPGA. Much of this type of work has been done over the last twenty-five years in the semicustom world for gate arrays and standard cells. It is interesting to note that empirical work done at I.B.M. in the 1960s by E. F. Rent still has application in this area, and it may form the basis of FPGA metrics.

10.10 CONCLUSIONS

Ideally, designers should be able to drop netlists for their designs into a mysterious software package and have the program pop out the best available FPGA selection for their design. Unfortunately, that day is still not here. However, several vendors are working hard to make that scenario happen. Until that time, using an appropriate set of benchmarks and metrics is the most logical starting point for making an FPGA selection.

PROBLEMS

1. Propose an appropriate set of benchmarks for making DSP designs with FPGAs. Three or four blocks will probably be fine, and the block diagram level will be appropriate. Hint: Look at basic Finite Impulse Response and Infinite Impulse Response Circuits.

2. Digital Communications and Local Area Network systems have their own specific basic building blocks. Propose a set of reasonable benchmarks (again, three or four blocks) that could be used to evaluate the viability of FPGAs in these systems.

3. Graphic and video data compression systems often use digital systems that compress by eliminating repeated data patterns. Take a look at this problem, and some commercially available chips that solve it, and propose a couple of FPGA benchmarks that make sense for compression.

4. Discuss why the commercially selected benchmarks in problems 1, 2 and 3 may be less than useful in very specific application areas. For instance, why might the PREP benchmarks not be useful for evaluating a design for an encryption engine? If an encryption engine is too obscure, pick a data communication interface.

11

Decisions

11.0 INTRODUCTION

The goal of this chapter is to present a simple approach for deciding which FPGA to buy. It is assumed the designer wishes to use an FPGA and support software, and has developed a benchmark set as described in Chapter 10. One should not rely on a "dry lab" estimate alone. Simplistic estimation will not guarantee the design fits the FPGA or meets the speed needs. If an estimate of speed and capacity is so obvious, then almost any of the choices will probably work. Then, the decision can be based on cost and delivery alone. If that is not the situation, other criteria come into play.

11.1 DECISIONS

Decisions are not always made for the best reasons when selecting an integrated circuit. The choice may depend on architecture, technology or understanding. The choice may also be emotional or rely on the appeal of the available development tools. The emotional aspect can be minimized by recognizing the importance of simply selecting the correct tool. No single FPGA fits all needs. If that were so, there would be only one product available. As it is, each manufacturer offers a selection of parts in different speeds, capacities and architectures. The appropriate criteria can become known so the correct contenders receive careful consideration. Consider the following standard selection criteria.

11.2 CRITERIA

This list includes criteria that users of semicustom and programmable devices have considered in the past. It is not complete and is in no particular order of importance. The criteria are simply ones that are common and useful for a wide class of designers.

1. Speed
2. I/O partitioning
3. Cost
4. Availability
5. Development tools
6. Power consumption
7. Testability
8. Board area
9. Second sourcing
10. Packaging
11. Technology
12. Architecture
13. Vendor
14. Understanding the architecture
15. Documentation
16. Reliability
17. Quality
18. Development time

The distinction regarding which criteria are intellectual versus emotional may be arbitrary. For some designers, speed is essential even in a slow application. Other designers get excited about untestable designs, so testability is key. Each criterion should be categorized regarding your specific needs. A simple decision matrix can be cast with assigned weights to each criterion. A simple score can be assigned to each solution. A final decision occurs by numeric scoring. Before casting the format, each criterion shall be clearly explained.

11.2.1 Speed

Speed is the propagation delay of internal cells within the FPGA. For simple functions this is obvious. Flip flop specifications include their toggle rate, but this must be derated for internal capacitive loading. Time delay for internal transition logic controlling state changes must also be included. As noted for the speed tables in Chapters 3 through 6, speed may be difficult to isolate because vendors specify their parts differently. Take care when comparing FPGAs with included routing delays to those that have these delays stripped out. This is why compiling the benchmarks and simulating them is so critical for speed assessment. Doing a paper study for speed assessment may easily prove to be wrong.

11.2.2 I/O Partitioning

I/O partitioning is defining the number and arrangement of input and output pins. Consideration must be given to the current drive of the output pins and input pin capacitance. These parameters affect performance.

11.2.3 Cost

Cost is a subtlety and comprised of many pieces. For instance, there is the cost of the integrated circuit, and support electronics for the circuit (capacitors, EPROMS, termination resistances). This must be included with the cost of programming hardware, development software, and learning time (at the designer's salary rate, with benefits and overhead). Included also should be failure rate analysis and the expense of field service and maintenance.

11.2.4 Availability

Availability is simply the ability to get the needed device. Circumstances such as whether it is available only through the manufacturer, through manufacturing representatives, distributors or parts brokers may be important.

11.2.5 Development Tools

Development tools include the software for capture, simulation and verification, as well as possible emulation. Programming equipment is included here. It may be possible to rent or borrow development tools rather than buy them. Typically, development tools are expensive enough to be a budgeted capital item. Development tools warrant management level understanding of their benefits and capabilities.

11.2.6 Power Consumption

Power consumption is important because FPGAs are larger chips in a digital system and can use a significant portion of the available power budget. Should the power budget be tight, the FPGA choice might dictate the system power supply. This can appreciably affect the total system cost. Naturally, the cooling system is linked to the power dissipation. Fans and system ventilation restrictions also are tied to this parameter.

11.2.7 Testability

The importance of testable FPGA designs depends on the manufacturing environment. If the FPGA is simply a prototype design for something that will be converted to a gate array, testability is less important at that time. However, if the FPGA design is targeted for high volume production, then the design should be as testable as possible. Having a high degree of observability and controllability (see Appendix) gives a highly testable design. The value of this will be seen when the design achieves production and field failure is minimal. Much money will be saved if the design is thoroughly tested.

11.2.8 Board Area

Should board area be tight, package choice and socket needs may be critical. Larger packages may require expensive sockets and occupy more board area than smaller packages. The designer will find that fewer vendors exist that can supply these larger sockets. There may be undesirable side effects, such as being forced to use a sole source socket vendor. The assessment of the value of board area is sometimes overdone. Remember that the "last square inches" of board area seem more expensive than the first ones do.

11.2.9 Second Sourcing

Second sourcing is an unusual idea. Second sourcing suggests that identical integrated circuits exist from different manufacturers. This is only possible if the degree of similarity is loose. Few of the FPGA products are really second sourced in the sense that the same silicon product is manufactured at different production sites. What most offer is a perceived second source. With a perceived second source, one producer offers silicon products that are sold to a second producer. The second manufacturer in turn resells the chips to the end customer, but is perceived as having produced the part. Today, several FPGA suppliers do not even possess silicon manufacturing capability. Incidentally, most gate array products do not have true second sources.

11.2.10 Packaging

The packaging issue is simply whether the silicon product exists in the desired package. Pin grid arrays, surface mount small outline, Plastic Leaded Chip Carrier (PLCC) and DIP are among the many choices. Not all FPGAs are available in all of them. Depending on the rest of the board components, FPGA choices in packaging may be restrictive. For instance, if an entire system is built using surface mounted packages in a robotic production line, the FPGA that is available only in a DIP may not be viable. Alternately, if the rest of a board uses DIP but the FPGA is offered in PLCC only, this may not be viable.

11.2.11 Technology

Technology is CMOS, Bipolar or BiCMOS today. There are currently no ECL based FPGAs and ECL is clearly a Bipolar technology. Technology choice is usually based on compatibility for interfacing the FPGA to the rest of the system. Technology choice is debatable because most of today's Bipolar and CMOS products are voltage-wise indistinct. Intermixing technologies is done successfully without regard for the older precautions. However, capacitance independent speed is more attainable from Bipolar products. Dense flip flop devices are usually made with CMOS products. Emerging BiCMOS products promise to bring the benefits of both technologies in the future, but many believe that CMOS is all that is needed.

11.2.12 Architecture

Architecture can be an important issue if the target problem is mismatched to the FPGA architecture. For instance, some architectures are better suited for random logic replacement, where others are suited for dense, structured-state machine design. Both architectures can perform the other's task, but with less than optimal results. Correctly assigning an architecture to a given problem can result in a tightly coupled, near optimal solution. Failing to match the architecture can result in a never-ending place and route nightmare.

11.2.13 Vendor

Vendor selection is emotional. Selecting a brand new high technology company's product includes the fears that it will not be around to support the design in the future. If the small company fails or is bought out by a bigger company, problems can occur. Choice of an older company may be comfortable, but it may include the older technologies on which the company is seeking to maximize profits. There is no certainty that an older company will not reorganize its FPGA product line out of existence. This has already happened at least once. There is no certainty that the smaller company will persist in the marketplace. Because the FPGA market is finite, some of the smaller companies will perish.

11.2.14 Understanding the Architecture

Understanding the architecture is necessary. Without understanding how the FPGA works, it is not possible to adequately assess its benefits and limitations. Most designers like the simpler architectures because they will one day have to debug the design. A clear understanding of the architecture suggests that the design can be completed and debugged on schedule. In turn, products can reach the marketplace within their target deadlines. At some point in the future, design software may be good enough to make architecture understanding less of an issue.

11.2.15 Documentation

FPGA documentation is of a fairly high quality from most vendors. Desktop publishing has improved the quality and technical contents of all silicon and software documentation. This permits inexpensive media that track the rapidly changing needs of modern designers. In general, documentation is not a major consideration. All manufacturers have recognized the high level needed and have spent the money to supply it. For responsive support, many manufacturers also support an online computer bulletin board service (BBS). The BBS permits designers access by telephone to factory support personnel and the latest online documents to update changes in existing documents and software.

11.2.16 Reliability

Reliability is generally very high. Not all vendors supply military quality products, requiring more stringent manufacturing and testing than ordinary commercial products. Military products command a premium price, but for situations requiring enhanced reliability, they are a must. Ordinary commercial and industrial quality products are generally acceptable for the EDP and instrumentation marketplaces in which current FPGA products tend to be designed.

11.2.17 Quality

Quality in the integrated circuit area is largely determined by the product compliance with published specifications. Manufacturing has advanced considerably as processes have become tightly controlled. Process parameters are also tightly tested. Most FPGAs are manufactured with advanced technologies using very precise equipment for their manufacture. Unless process shifts occur, the quality remains high. Perceived quality may be somewhat less than expected because many FPGA manufacturers do not specify their parts in a clear manner. That, however, is a marketing choice.

11.2.18 Development Time

Development time is proportional to the designer's understanding of the FPGA architecture and development software. This is a direct function of designer experience, development software maturity, and the difficulty of the problem. Designers who develop their expertise on small problems usually have fast development times. Approaching a first design with a cautious, systematic approach helps guarantee a reasonable development time.

11.3 SELECTION

Again, assuming the appropriate benchmarks have been compiled and simulated, there should be fewer FPGAs to consider. Knowing that all remaining contenders will work, the selection is simply scoring them and tallying. One might limit the criteria to the top five or ten discussed and weight ten points to the first five criteria and five points to the second five. This should give a reasonable spread. This weight assignment is the reader's choice. There may be other parties involved in the decision (such as purchasing personnel and test engineers that must deal with the choice). A chart as simple as the one below may suffice, with only three contenders and four criteria:

Contender #	Criteria 1	Criteria 2	Criteria 3	Criteria 4
1	score =	score =	score =	score =
2	score =	score =	score =	score =
3	score =	score =	score =	score =

Simply summing across the rows gives the winner. If a tie results, add more criteria until it is broken. A couple of things to remember:

1. Use pertinent criteria because this approach is simplistic.

2. Make certain that all contenders do meet the benchmark pretest. Whatever FPGA chosen will at least work. Naturally, this is an expensive and time consuming proposition.

3. Save the scoring criteria and results for comparison in future efforts.

4. Do not be surprised if the best solution requires more than one part or a mix of FPGA and PLD products. If extreme speed is needed, a PLD may be required.

5. Do not be surprised if you consistently pick your favorite device, on your favorite workstation, from your favorite vendor—we're all human!

11.4 CLOSING COMMENTS

There are no simple answers. In all likelihood, the FPGA decision will be made at the assessment of the benchmark set. With this chapter's approach, the reader now has a viable approach to select an FPGA. This method may be subjective and simplistic, but it is systematic and gives reasonable results.

PROBLEMS

1. Select five criteria and score four of the architectures covered in this text for building Figure 2.1.

2. Assuming minimum time to compare is the most important parameter for the logic analyzer, select among the MAX 7K, QuickLogic, LCA 4000 and Dual Block XC7300 families.

3. Propose a different selection strategy to that provided in this chapter.

12

Retargetting

12.0 OVERVIEW

Chapter 1 described a scene where a design was profitably moved from an FPGA to a CMOS gate array, for high volume production. Similar tales occur often, but the difficulty of translating to the gate array is often ignored. Details for design migration are usually oversimplified. Although there are many details to consider, the difficulty is decreasing as improved design tools become available. This final chapter clarifies design problems to be surmounted for successful design migration, which is also known as retargetting.

12.1 RETARGETTING

An underlying theme of this book is that digital designs can be made in a lot of ways. In a sense, an FPGA is treated like a blank canvas where the design is "painted" according to the constraints of the designer's needs and the FPGA's capabilities. Often, there is less concern with the FPGA's internal structure, and more with its speed and capacity.

Design flexibility was shown in Chapters 3 through 6, where a small design was implemented on each of four distinct FPGA/CPLDs—in different ways. Chapter 7 gave results for a larger design built on the different architectures, and the design comfortably fit any of the FPGAs used. In a way, this process was manual retargetting: the design was manually translated for each FPGA. Being able to reconstruct a design from one FPGA onto another is at the heart of retargetting, but the goal is to have an automatic procedure for retargetting.

Retargetting is also more general than migrating FPGA designs to gate arrays. Retargetting can be from multiple PLD designs into FPGAs, from one FPGA to another, among ASICs or as mentioned from FPGAs to

ASICs. In a sense, retargetting is making a compatible second sourced part, which is similar to having one design emulate another. This raises a question: How similar must the two versions be? The answer is similar enough that both versions work in the end system.

Designers have dealt with second sourced parts for years, but it should be remembered that part differences exist. For instance, when the digital world transitioned from 7400 series TTL in the early 1970s, the new Schottky and low power Schottky replacements were faster and had different power consumption characteristics. Their output switching characteristics also differed. Later that same decade, designers moved low power Schottky designs to CMOS, seeing different operating characteristics, again.

IC electrical behavior also differed among the various "compatible" manufacturers, raising designer awareness about subtle processing differences. With this in mind, from an electrical viewpoint, we should not expect a smooth road when moving designs from an FPGA to a gate array.

Fortunately, gate array style design tools are a common element between FPGAs and gate arrays. Tools are the critical element in the retargetting path. Designers are familiar with the design flow needed for FPGAs, and it strongly resembles that of gate arrays. Both flows describe designs with netlists. Both flows use back annotated simulation to determine design correctness. Both flows operate from personal computers or workstations. The following illustrates the overall retargetting process by examining a small example.

12.2 RETARGETTING EXAMPLE

This example was completed in great detail by Peter Meiser of the Philips Corporation in Germany. The design (Figure 12.1) was originally captured with Philips' SNAP (Chapter 3). Recall that SNAP uses an internal netlist. The design easily compiled into a PML part. The netlist was simulated and proven to work.

Next, the netlist was passed through a netlist conversion routine called PERC, which substituted one micron standard cells for PML cells. PERC simply uses a cell substitution table and replaces each PML cell with a corresponding standard cell.

Then, the design was converted to an EDIF 2.0 netlist format, where it could be understood by Compass (v8) design software from VLSI Technology, Inc. The Compass software can also reverse the EDIF netlist to a schematic, if needed.

Finally, the design was automatically placed and routed using the Com-

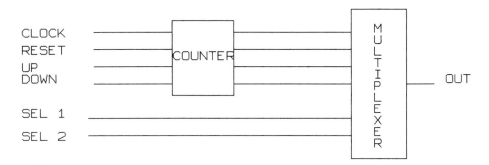

Figure 12.1 Small PML example.

pass software resulting in a layout as shown in Figure 12.2. From here, the interconnection delays were extracted and the netlist was simulated to determine whether or not it worked. Being small, it worked. If difficulty occurred, the layout and interconnections would have been changed and design iterations would continue until the design worked.

This approach used the EDIF 2.0 netlist as the common point between the FPGA and ASIC design flows. Other intersections are possible and desirable. For instance, if the design were initially made starting from VHDL, it could be compiled into either flow from the top. If the design had been captured using a standard TTL library, either flow could operate from there substituting appropriate cells as needed.

Where could the retargetting go wrong? Many places, but in particular, right at the cell substitution point. What would happen if there were no corresponding standard cell for a PML cell? This is likely because PML supports up to 256 input NAND gates and SNAP is written to flatten designs into two logic levels exploiting these gates. The solution to this problem is to make wide gates (manually or by synthesis) from smaller gates in the VTI library. This presents a new problem, namely, time delay incurred by stacking several small gates.

The new problem is often surmountable, but what happens if one encounters a cell for which there is no substitution? For instance, suppose a Xilinx LCA was the starting point, and it used long line drivers as busses. Many gate array manufacturers do not support three-state internal bussing because of testing difficulties. The most likely solution is substituting multiplexers for the busses. Multiplexers behave similar to busses, but not identically. As long as the retargetted design can adapt to the little discrepancies, the design can proceed. If not, retargetting will be difficult or maybe impossible.

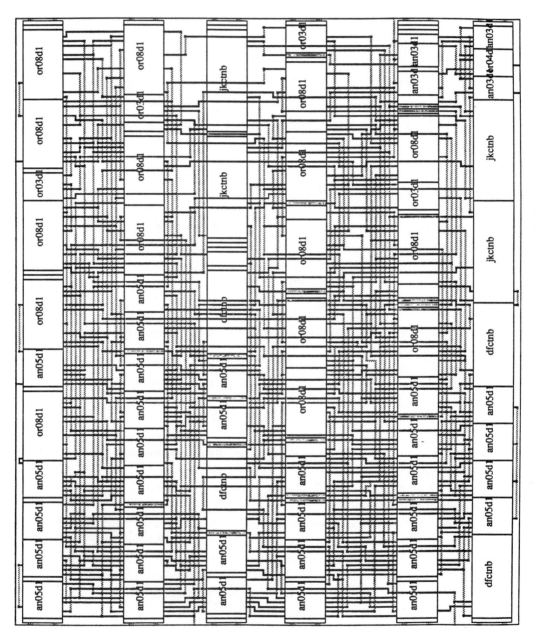

Figure 12.2 Retargetted standard cell design.

240

12.3 MORE GENERAL ISSUES

Cell substitutions are one problem and timing is another. FPGAs are slower than gate arrays of the same technology. There may be exceptions to this, but they are few. In general, the speed difference is probably good because the gate array needs all of the timing slack it can have in order to account for routing differences.

Real problems come with high speed. It has been said that below 30 MHz retargetting is simple. That may be an arbitrary speed limit, but there is some truth to it. As clock speeds climb, the setup time available for flip flops drops, but the need remains.

There is no way for a conventional gate array (except possibly Crosspoint Solutions) to take significant advantage of an existing FPGA layout. The gate array layout must start from scratch, because the connection restrictions and cell mappings are different from those of the FPGA. Clock skews differ, logic time delays differ and the overall timing must be redesigned.

Design strategies will differ also. For instance, one hot encoded state assignments may not be the best approach for gate arrays. Gate arrays have more flexibility than FPGAs and should not be forced to use restrictive FPGA design techniques. The same may be true for counters made with "count cells." This suggests that the best approach for retargetting is to start from the most abstract version of the design and translate it using the most efficient mappings for the final architecture. Then, the layout can proceed to meet the timing requirements using the most available freedom.

As one might suspect from the previous discussion of second sourced parts, discrepancies in the electrical characteristics will present their own set of problems. On top of this, there are packaging and pin differences to account for. To some degree, the FPGA manufacturers that offer "hard wired" versions of their parts as gate array substitutes have alleviated the pin and package problem, but not so if the designer wants another vendor's gate array solution instead.

As a summary to this complex topic, it should be noted that design tools are available for retargetting. If retargetting is a goal, best results occur if it is planned for at the outset. This means that caution should be used and here are a few hints:

1. Use a high level capture format, and make sure that the structures chosen exist on all of the final media (FPGA or gate array) used.

2. Do not restrict designs for one particular architecture by forcing the solution (that is, architecture specific tricks).

3. Use good simulation practices for the initial and final solution.

4. Do not include a feature on the FPGA solution that cannot be made on the gate array version, and vice versa for the reverse migration direction.

This last point raises an important issue, namely, reconfiguring. RAM based, reconfigurable FPGAs have their own special problem as well as this valuable benefit, and this warrants a closer look.

12.4 RECONFIGURING

ORCA™, FLEXLogic™ and the FLEX 8000™ were all announced during the writing of this book. Naturally, they are extensions of architectures discussed in this book, but they have an element in common: each is RAM based. The value of a RAM based FPGA was understood and popularized in the early 1990s. Designers now develop their prototypes in RAM based FPGAs, where the same part is reprogrammed until completion. Then they may retarget the design to a fused FPGA or a gate array, that is, unless they choose to remain RAM based forever. Some designs include permanent reconfigurable functions.

Consider a few examples where it makes sense. A designer recently developed a PLD programmer for a client. The programmer applies voltages and currents to the pins of various PLDs for very specific time periods and in particular sequences. Each PLD has a detailed specification defining just how it must be programmed, and they are all different. The chosen solution uses an LCA 2000 because the high speed is not vital and the state machines in the designs are relatively small. However, the LCA 2000 is reconfigured from an external EPROM with a different state machine for every PLD type that needs programming.

The logic analyzer example of Chapter 7, could be transformed into a digital oscilloscope, digital voltmeter, or a signature analyzer, if it were made from a RAM-based FPGA. This shows that an FPGA could be a powerful embedded diagnostic tool, capable of becoming the desired tool as needed.

Others have proposed exploiting reconfiguration by incremental in-circuit debugging. An example of this is to make scan registers using the Concurrent Logic FPGAs. The idea is simple, even though the Concurrent Logic FPGAs do not have inherent scan logic. Sections of a design are built up within the CLi cells, and surrounded by cells configured in a scan chain. The in-circuit operation of the design pieces is observed and stimulated by the "virtual scan chain" surrounding them. When the pieces are suitably debugged, the scan chain is moved or eliminated. The in-circuit debug proceeds incrementally with the design.

Reconfiguration has the overall effect of packing multiple versions of the logic into a single package. This substantially saves board space and expense, but it has its limitations. For instance, it is impossible for the RAM based FPGA to be two distinct designs simultaneously. This suggests that the class of designs for reconfiguring is that where one or more pieces of hardware are idle while only one main piece is active. There is also a time penalty for reconfiguring, so this must be accounted for as well.

Another practical reason for retargetting is that many FPGAs come in very large pinout packages. These packages have a problem because they cannot be reinserted over and over again without mutilating the pins. Because the devices are expensive, the ability to reconfigure the FPGAs while in the pc-board is important. Some designers have gone so far as to use RAM based FPGAs for design and initial system integration, with retargetting into a nonvolatile FPGA at final integration. The degree of success had here depends on solving the problems mentioned earlier in this chapter. At this writing, the author is unaware of any FPGAs from different manufacturers that have identical package and pin footprints.

12.5 AVAILABLE RETARGETTING TOOLS

As outlined earlier, key requirements of the retargetting process are netlist conversion and cell substitution. This can be done with small tools like PERC, or with more general tools designed to enhance the overall retargetting effort. Among the available tools today are CORE I and II from Exemplar Logic and ViewRetargetter from ViewLogic. At the time of this writing, Synopsis Corporation and Cadence also have retargetting software under development. These tools are provided with multiple target libraries from which to choose and additional features.

As an example, Figure 12.3 shows the sorts of flows that Exemplar's CORE supports. In particular, it permits several high-level hardware design language (HDL) input formats, and generates a host of output netlist formats. Additional inputs are the cell libraries, constraints and control files.

The translations that CORE does are optimized (according to user defined criteria) for the specific target architecture, forming a minimal intermediate netlist that the placement and routing software can directly use. Naturally, translations and optimizations for Xilinx, ACTEL and ASIC designs are all quite different. The designer specified constraints are speed or area for the final design. The software iterates attempting to translate the design within these constraints.

With knowledge of a single retargetting tool, today's designers can translate to as many end technologies as that tool handles. These tools are

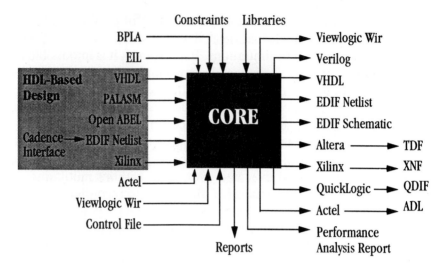

Figure 12.3 Exemplar's CORE retargetter.

available on both personal computers and engineering workstations, making them within the reach of everyone.

12.6 OTHER TOOL DIRECTIONS

As suggested earlier, future designers may not need to know specific architectural details of the FPGA chosen to form a solution. Starting from a high level hardware description language, the design could be carefully described and the design software could make all of the appropriate decisions (that is, from the list in Chapter 11) to give a best solution. That is certainly a goal. To date, it has not been met.

Similarly, there may be no single optimal architecture for all designs. As vendors perceive user needs, they will proliferate architectures to meet them as with the microprocessor world. A few architectures will dominate, but special purpose ones will also flourish. Chapter 10 suggested that design metrics could be used to evaluate the likelihood of matching a specific design to an optimal FPGA architecture. Clearly, this is also a direction for design tools to take.

The next important FPGA directions appear to be mostly in the area of design tools, and providing optimal design flexibility with maximum control is a current trend. It can be safely stated that FPGA architectures will continue to proliferate and that FPGA design tools will track the path already defined by gate arrays and other ASIC technologies.

PROBLEMS

1. Assume an FPGA design with flip flop cells that use an asynchronous reset. The design only needs to be reset when a master clear is asserted. Unfortunately, one must retarget to an FPGA that has only synchronous cells. What must be done to retarget the design for the synchronous cells?

2. The reader has been given a design that was built from commercially available PLDs. The PLDs chosen all power up with the flip flops automatically reset during the power up action. The task is to translate this design to an FPGA similar to the one described in problem 1, above. What must be done to correctly retarget for the FPGAs?

Appendix

Design for Testability

A.0 INTRODUCTION

Methods of design for testability are presented, with a quick look at fault analysis. Although the techniques for fault analysis are well understood, this tutorial focuses on basics to give the reader a fundamental understanding.

A.1 FAULTS IN DIGITAL CIRCUITS

Integrated Circuits fail for several reasons. The parts can have their bonding pads disconnected, transistors can be overloaded, or their power supply leads evaporated. It is possible that various internal electronic cells were never correctly processed (because of defects in the metal, silicon oxide, diffusions, or other causes). Because of the broad class of defects that can occur, a simple model which covers the behavior of many failures has been adopted. This model is the "stuck at" model.

In the stuck at model, the nodes of a logic function are said to be stuck at logical one or zero. The validity of this assumption is supported more from experience than from detailed analysis of exact cause. External digital logic cannot distinguish an evaporated bonding pad from an input which is tied permanently to a logical one. The input signal simply has no effect on the circuit. The electronic chip tester must view the voltage reaction of the input

247

stimulus at the output pins; it cannot distinguish failure types. This is the key to understanding fault analysis and design for testability. From the point of view of an electronic tester, which can only observe the device pins, what does it matter what the exact failure cause is?

A.2 DESIGN FOR TESTABILITY BASICS

A.2.1 Introduction

Digital ICs are tested by electronic testers. These machines are large instruments. Testers are computer controlled and very flexible in sensing voltage and current as well as defining time variables. Testers are limited to observing the operation of the device under test (DUT) by sensing pin activity. If the DUT is not working, it is rejected.

To identify broken chips, there must be a test that proves the device is correct. If the chip fails the test, the chip is rejected. To prove the device is correct, it is not enough to prove that it performs its intended function. Most intended functions are only a subset of what may be possible for the chip to do. For instance, most digital designers are aware of systems with features that were never fully debugged. These features were not thought mandatory to meet market requirements, and debug time had exceeded the project schedule. Many such systems exist. For expediency, the test of such systems is limited to testing only those primary features; the unused features go untested.

With this view of the world, many system designers are not familiar with IC design methods. In IC design, every feature must be debugged to the fullest extent possible, to eliminate field failures. Field failure of an IC is expensive because the factory must involve personnel to examine, test and verify the exact cause of failure. This may take an arbitrary amount of time. Because of economics, unused features are removed at design time. Unused features also consume chip area and limit device yield. There is a difference in philosophy between system and IC designers. It is key to have a systematic way to design digital chips for an electronic tester. This type of design is called design for testability (DFT).

A.2.2 Testability Basics

Testability design methods fall into two categories. One is a system of ad hoc rules and the other is a structured method called scan design. Underlying both of these categories are the basics of testability. Testability is based on two other ideas, controllability and observability.

Observability is simply making certain the target condition being tested is observable at the chip pins. This means it must be possible to distinguish the tested condition (usually some internal node being a one or zero) by observing the output pins. The observer knows what has occurred at the input pins. Controllability is knowing that an internal condition may be brought about, by driving the input pins.

A simple example is appropriate here. Consider a four bit counter embedded deep within an IC. When it is powered on, and clocks are applied, the counter increments. Applying twelve counts to such a device should make it traverse twelve distinct states. These state values may be gated to and observed at the pins. However, if the starting state is unknown, the results at the pins may vary from test to test. To control this test, the counter must first be initialized (controlled) to a known starting state. Then, repeated testing with twelve pulses should result in repeatable behavior. A standard ad hoc design for testability (DFT) rule, is to make sure that all counters have a reset line. Initial state setting is a simple form of controllability.

Observability is guaranteeing an internal node condition passes to the outside world. A classic observability problem is an embedded RAM. Embedded RAM occurs more with recent advent of on-chip cache memories in RISC microprocessors. If there is no path to load the RAM and read it back to the outside pins, RAM operation must be inferred. Inference means a series of indirect tests, which may be less than exhaustive. Special circuitry has to be added to the chip to address the RAM (controllability) and observe that the data may be written and read from the address (observability).

A.2.3 Ad Hoc Design for Testability

Some additional ad hoc rules include:

1. Do not use multiplexed flip flop clocks. Switching the multiplexer can glitch the flip flop into an unknown state.

2. Do not use internally derived clocks. Internally generated clocks give unreliable timing relationships which cannot be easily verified at the pins.

3. Do not use long, cascaded counters. Long counters require lengthy test sequences to cycle the counters through all the possible internal states. Techniques exist for breaking counters into smaller blocks that may be tested by shorter sequences.

4. Do not bury RAM cells. Unless special circuitry is designed to control and observe the RAM, testing is difficult.

5. Do not embed one shots. One shots are unpredictable with regard to time delay and pulse width.

6. Do not embed pulse shaping circuits. Like one shots, pulse shapers are dependent on internal gate time delays, which may be unpredictable.

7. Minimize the use of asynchronous circuits. Asynchronous circuitry is almost unavoidable. However, many of the DFT methods are less effective when asynchronous circuits are used.

The list can continue, but using these rules will enhance the testability of many designs. Remember, synchronous sequential designs often give nicely testable circuits.

A.2.4 Scan Design

As an additional concept, scan or Linear Sequential Scan Design (LSSD) stays within all of these rules. The price is extra circuitry and design discipline. Ordinary scan design uses a specially configured D flip flop with a multiplexer attached to the D input. LSSD type scan design uses a special tandem D flip flop as the storage element. The reward is automatic test pattern generation.

Scan design limits the flexibility of the designer in choosing components, and adds circuitry for test automatically. Scan makes the state variables of a design (that is, the flip flop contents) be inherently controllable and observable. This is done by providing a test mode where every flip flop is included in a shift register chain which may be set externally to any state. While in a test mode, a test state is set into the flip flops. After the test state is set, test mode is exited. At this point, the circuit is driven through a test sequence from a known starting state. After the test sequence, test mode is reentered and the new state can be observed by shifting the flip flop contents out a special output pin. The test sequence can be a large series of vectors or the application of a single clock. Many strategies exist.

Most scan design requirements include at least a serial input data pin, an output pin, a test mode pin and possibly a scan clock pin. Figure A.1 illustrates a simple scan design structure showing the shift register arrangement and all of the additional test pins needed to make it operate. The PML2552 described in Chapter 3 is an example of a FPGA type product with scan circuitry built in. FPGAs from QuickLogic also include scan circuitry. It is possible to emulate scan circuitry with other FPGAs like Concurrent Logic's CLi 6000.

Algorithms have been developed to automatically generate test vectors for scan designed circuits. This can be seen most simply by considering the generation of input vectors for a combinational circuit. A test vector is simply

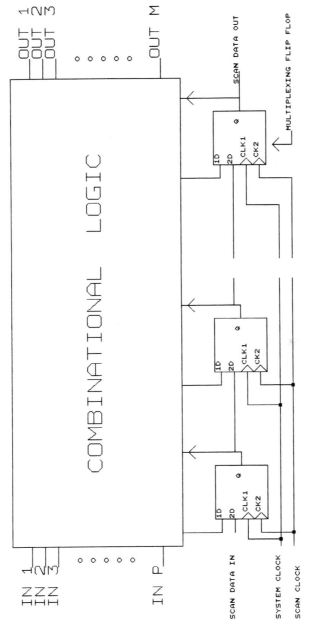

Figure A.1 LSSD scan configuration.

the binary value of the inputs taken as a group. By taking all possible combinations of input variables and applying them to a combinational circuit, an exhaustive set of vectors is derived. The problem is to reduce the number of vectors needed by eliminating redundant ones.

Redundant vectors are those which test nodes covered by other vectors. Finding the smallest set of vectors which completely test the design is the goal. This is usually done by simple bookkeeping, where the transition of each internal node from a logical one to a zero (and vice versa) is logged. For all nodes, this log shows which transitioned in response to a particular vector. Picking a subset of the total combinations is straightforward. It is possible that an internal node may never transition under all possible input combinations, suggesting a design problem.

The next step in the generation of scan design test vectors is simply to recognize that scan design reduces a sequential machine to looking like a combinational machine. In particular, the scan registers automatically have multiplexers inserted in front of the flip flops which isolate the transition logic (combinational gates) from the inputs to the flip flops. All that has to be done now is drive the transition logic of the gates through all combinations of their local input variables. This is precisely what was done for combinational logic. Of course, software bookkeeping is used to make it systematic.

An efficient intermediate form of scan design is called peripheral scan or boundary scan (Figure A.2). In boundary scan, the IC pins have the ability to be latched and shifted. The pins can be inputs, or outputs, and the set of latches forms a shift register during test mode. The idea here is that the shift register forms a ring of isolation around the chip, capable of capturing data right at the pins. If a pin is taken as an input to the chip, the latch captures data from the outside world. If the pin is an output, the latch captures data

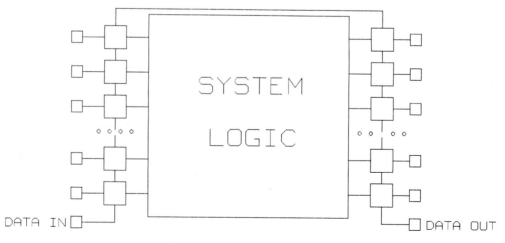

Figure A.2   Boundary scan test logic.

from the inside of the chip. Stimulation of the chip can occur by serially loading the shifter ring so input pins have the correct stimulus. Reaction to the stimulus happens on a subsequent clock and is captured at the pins that are configured as output pins. Internal flip flops are not a part of the peripheral chain, so boundary scan is currently not a candidate for exhaustive automatic test pattern generation. Testing the inside of a chip using boundary scan is of questionable value due to the large number of shifts needed per vector and the fact that buried signals are still difficult to control and observe.

Boundary scan has a fairly high payoff for efficient board level testing. The idea is that all the chips on a board can be serially cascaded and the board can be tested as a whole using very few external pins. Currently, there are very few boundary scan chips available for such systems. One leader in this area is the LCA 4000 mentioned in Chapter 4, which incorporates the I.E.E.E. boundary scan standard. Boundary scan is attractive to many because board testing with minimum additional circuitry and pins is important.

A.3 FAULT ANALYSIS IDEAS

The ability for an IC tester to distinguish a bad part from a good one depends on whether the bad part responds different than a good part does. The distinction may be only a single bit out of thousands, but one bit is all that is needed.

The goal of fault simulation is to determine an adequate set of test vectors for a design. The quality of the test vectors will be quantified by a measure called the fault grade. The basis of fault simulation is to first define a good simulation with the correct output response. The good simulation is taken as a standard for comparison.

The test approach is like experimental science. Knowing the good circuit and a comparison standard simulation, small experimental changes are introduced. In particular, internal nodes of the simulated design are artificially stuck at one or zero and the circuit is simulated. If the faulty simulation results are different from the standard, then the faulty node is detected by the simulation vectors. This procedure must be done for each node in the design, and for both conditions of stuck at one and zero. This suggests that a lot of simulations will need to be done. Much effort has been spent on speeding this process up. The result of this effort includes parallel simulations (that is, testing multiple nodes at once), hardware simulation accelerators and statistical fault simulations.

The result of all of this simulation is an assessment of how well the vectors test the circuit. If the vector set can always distinguish a good circuit from a faulty one, the fault grade is 100 percent. If the applied vectors cannot distinguish a bad circuit, the fault grade is less than 100 percent. Fault grade is calculated from the knowledge of the number of nodes in the circuit and the number of faults detected. Simply, an expression is formed with the number of faults in the numerator and the number of possible faults in the denominator. The number of possible faults is usually the number of nodes in the design multiplied by two (that is, each node can have a stuck at one or zero fault). In itself, the number is only partially useful. Of more use is a histogram relating fault grade versus applied vector. See Figure 3.15.

A.4 CONCLUSION

As system designers become more involved with the inside operation of chips, they must learn thorough testing techniques. Key to good test effectiveness are appropriate design techniques to improve testing. Neither the design techniques, nor the testing techniques, are fully automatic as yet. As FPGA products are heading to higher densities, designers must master these design and testing techniques for survival.

Glossary

Abel Trademark of the DATA I/O Corporation for PLD design software which can capture and compile designs for several commercially available PLD products.

ACT Trademark of ACTEL corporation for a family of programmable gate array products which are internally configured with a CMOS PLICE antifuse.

ACTION Trademark of ACTEL corporation for the design software used with ACT FPGAs.

AIM Acronym for Avalanche Induced Migration. It describes a vertical metallic antifuse used in Philips Semiconductor's Programmable Macro Logic product.

Antifuse Any of the programmable interconnect technologies forming an electrical connection between two circuit points rather than making an open connection.

A.P. & R. Abbreviation for automatic placement and routing.

Back annotation Process of incorporating time delay values into a design netlist reflecting the interconnect capacitance obtained from a completed design.

Benchmark In FPGAs, a test design useful for comparing products.

BLM Acronym for Behavioral Language Model. BLMs are simulation models written as modules of high level language.

Cell A logic function. It may be a gate, a flip flop, a piece of random access memory or some other structure. Usually, a cell is small compared to other circuit building blocks.

CLB Acronym for Configurable Logic Block. This element is the basic building block of the Xilinx LCA product family. CLBs currently can contain several multiplexers, one or more flip flops and a function RAM.

CMOS Acronym for Complementary Metal Oxide Semiconductor.

Congestion Effect of blockage that occurs during the interconnect of an FPGA. Congestion is a function of cell placement and interconnect architecture within the device.

Controllability An aspect of testability. Stated simply, controllability is the ease of making any correct signal appear at the IC outputs by driving the IC inputs.

CPLD Acronym for Complex Programmable Logic Device. CPLDs include an array of functionally complete or universal logic cells in an interconnection framework that has foldback connection to central programming regions.

EPLD Acronym for EPROM Programmable Logic Device. A PLD that uses EPROM cells to internally configure the logic function.

EPROM Acronym for Erasable Programmable Read Only Memory. EPROM cells are programmable connections that configure EPLDs by forming wire ANDs.

ERASIC Trademark of the EXCEL corporation for its foldback NOR CMOS programmable logic device.

Expander Section in the MAX LAB containing an array of foldback NAND functions. The Expander is used to increase the logical inputs to the LAB macrocell section or to make other logic and storage functions in the LAB. The term is also used for a logic expansion section of the Plus Logic FPGA.

Fault Condition of a circuit that results in a failure. Most failure modes, or faults, are modeled by their being stuck at a logical one or logical zero.

Fault simulation Logic simulation tailored to assess the quality of a set of test vectors. Fault simulation occurs by successively simulating with a set of vectors while changing the design netlist to have nodes forced to logical zeroes and ones during simulation. Assessment occurs by comparing results to the unaltered model results.

Fitting Software process of making a design fit into a specific architecture. Fitting involves technology mapping, placement, optimization and partitioning among other operations.

Flip flop A simple logic storage cell. A flip flop may be made as a fixed cell or from gates.

Floorplan Physical arrangement of functions within a design relative to each other.

FPGA Acronym for Field Programmable Gate Array. A regular array of cells that is either functionally complete or universal within a connection framework of signal routing channels.

Functionally complete Property of some Boolean logic functions permitting them to make any logic function by using only that function. Key properties include making the AND function with an invert or the OR function with an invert.

Fuse A metallic interconnect point that can be electrically changed from a short circuit to an open circuit by applying electrical current.

Gate An electronic structure, built from transistors, that performs a logic function. The logical NAND or NOR functions are common choices because they exhibit functional completeness.

Gate arrays Arrays of transistors interconnected to form gates. The gates in turn are configured to form larger functions.

Gate count Designation for the number of two input NAND or NOR gates needed to make a complete circuit. It is used to define the complexity of a design with a total available budget of usable gates.

Gate equivalent Gate count applied to smaller pieces of a design.

Hard macro Function larger than a single gate but made from gates. Hard macro performance is invariant from a placement point of view.

Input vectors Time-ordered binary numbers representing input voltage sequences to a simulation program.

LAB Acronym for Logic Array Block. The LAB is the basic building block of the ALTERA MAX family. Each LAB contains a macrocell array, an I/O block and an expander product term array.

LCA Trademark of the Xilinx corporation for their programmable gate array product referred to as the Logic Cell Array.

Long line Mechanism inside an LCA where a signal is passed through a repeating amplifier to drive a larger interconnect line. Long lines are less sensitive to metal delays.

Macro When used with FPGAs, a cell configuration that can be repeated as needed. See Hard macro and Soft macro.

Macrocell In FPGAs, a portion of the FPGA that is the smallest indivisible building block. A macrocell usually contains at least one flip flop and some multiplexing to permit logical configuration around the flip flop.

MAX Acronym for Multiple Array matrix, which is an Altera product family. MAX is usually considered to be a complex PLD or foldback architecture.

MAX+PLUS Development software for the MAX product line.

Model A program that behaves similarly to the operation of some digital circuit inside a simulation program. Key modeling ideas include accuracy and credibility.

Netlist A text file that describes a design. Minimal requirements are identification of function elements, inputs and outputs and connections. See Chapter 2 for examples.

Netlist optimization A means of optimizing a design by making judicious equivalent substitutions. Two indices of improvement are performance and minimum gates. The specific problem is usually to optimize the circuit for speed or gate count while keeping the original function.

Netlist synthesis Process of deriving a netlist from an abstract representation. The term has come to mean deriving a netlist from a hardware description language similar to a programming language.

NRE Acronym for Non-Recurring Engineering expense. In the gate array world, this is a one-time charge covering the use of design facilities (computer time), masks and overhead for test development. The parallel idea for FPGAs is the purchase of programming equipment, learning time for the design software and the purchase of the software.

Observability The ease of determining at the IC outputs what happened at the IC inputs.

One Hot Encoding A popular design technique used more with FPGAs than with CPLDs. It assigns a single flip flop to hold a logical one at any point in time, with the rest being held at logic zero. OHE typically uses flip flops abundantly but usually needs only a few cell inputs per bit.

PAL Trademark of Monolithic Memories Incorporated standing for programmable array logic. PAL is used to designate a common, single programming array type of fuse connectible logic devices.

Partitioning Setting boundaries within functions of a system. In particular, partitioning is used to identify the exact I/O boundaries of smaller system portions so that functions may be isolated to exist within one portion or another.

PGA Acronym for Pin Grid Array, which is a large pin count IC package type. At one point, FPGAs were called Programmable Gate Arrays.

PLA Acronym for Programmable Logic Array.

Placement Physical assignment of a logical function to a specific location within an FPGA. Usually, placement follows floorplanning. Once the logic function is placed, its interconnection is made by routing. The placement process varies from one FPGA architecture to another.

PLD Acronym for Programmable Logic Device, the general class of programmable devices comprised of PLAs, sequencers and PAL devices. It also includes FPGA and CPLD devices.

PLICE Acronym for Programmable Low Impedance Circuit Element. This programmable interconnect is based on the electrical connection of polysilicon. It is a trademark of ACTEL.

PML Acronym for Programmable Macro Logic, the foldback NAND architecture developed by Philips Semiconductors.

PROM Acronym for Programmable Read Only Memory.

Retargetting Software process of translating a design from one FPGA to another. Similarly, the design can be translated from an FPGA to a gate array, from PLDs to an FPGA and so forth. Retargetting involves technology mapping and optimization.

Routing Process of interconnecting previously placed logic functions. If success is had, the function is formed. Otherwise, congestion may block the success of a routing attempt.

Scan design Method of logic design resulting in highly testable finished designs. Scan design uses restricted logic practices incorporating D flip flops that change configuration during testing. Such flip flops cascade into a large shift register chain.

Semicustom General category of integrated circuits that can be configured directly by the purchaser of the IC. It includes gate array, standard cell, PLD, FPGA, PROM and EPROM devices.

Simulation Process of modeling a logical design and its input stimuli. Simulation involves a program that compiles a netlist description of a circuit into a model, and it applies model signals to the circuit model. The simulator calculates output signal models.

Slew rate Time rate of change of a voltage. Usually, it is applied to the output pin of an IC and is an indication of the perceived speed of a signal as it drives the outside world. Some FPGAs permit a fast or slow slew rate to be programmed for an output pin.

Soft macro A logic function made in a variable number of ways. The function will be made from cells, but its exact arrangement may be different from one version to another. This can result in performance differences.

Technology mapping Process of translating the function of a design from one technology to another. For instance, a digital design made from Xilinx LCA CLBs could be translated (technology mapped) to ACTEL logic blocks. Both versions of the design would have the same function, but the cells used would be very different. Technology mapping is a crucial step in the fitting and compiling process.

Testability Quality of a circuit that suggests there is a degree to which it may be testable. Basically, this means that any internal node may be externally controlled to a known condition and that this condition may be observed externally at the pins.

Test vectors Binary models of input stimulus signals for a circuit. They sometimes include corresponding output response signal models and are similar to simulation vectors, except that test vectors are generally restricted to being applied to the design synchronized with the strobe or selection signals used by an electronic tester.

Time delay In the logic sense, any value of additional time added to a signal. It is sometimes used to describe the added delay of a logic element, but it is also used to describe the effect of resistance and capacitance of a signal trace.

Universal cell A logic cell capable of forming any combinational logic function of the number of inputs to the cell. The standard approach is to build the function's truth table. RAM, ROM and multiplexers have been used to form universal cells. These are also called lookup tables or function generators.

Usable gates Term reflecting the fact that due to congestion, not all gates on an FPGA may be accessible.

Vectors Similar to test vectors, vectors are the set of binary stimulus and/or response signal models associated with a digital simulation.

VHDL Acronym for VHSIC hardware description language. VHDL is used to describe function, interconnect and modeling.

XACT Development software used for the LCA product. It is often referred to in the context of their placement and routing software because the overall development package includes commercially available packages for design entry and simulation.

References

Chapter 1

ANDREWS W. "Small CMOS Arrays Flourish as Channelless Types Emerge." *Computer Design* (January 1989).

CARR, W., AND J. MIZE. *MOS/LSI Design and Application*. New York: McGraw-Hill, 1971.

CAVLAN, N., AND R. CLINE. "FPLA Applications—Exploring Design Problems and Solutions." *EDN* (April 1976).

CLINE, R. "Improving Thermal Efficiency with the Help of Computer-Aided Circuit Analysis." *Semiconductor International* (October 1980).

CONNOR, D. "PLD Architectures Require Scrutiny." *EDN* (September 1989).

FLEISHER, H., AND L. I. MAISSEL. "An Introduction to Array Logic." *IBM Journal of Research and Development* (March 1975).

GAJSKI D., N. D. DUTT, AND B. PANGRLE. "Silicon Compilation (Tutorial)." I.E.E.E. Custom Integrated Circuits Conference (1986).

JENKINS, J. "PLD Solutions to Interface Problems." *1989 Microprocessor Design Guide*. Manhasset, N.Y.: High Performance Systems.

KESSLER, A. J., AND A. GANESAN. "Standard Cell VLSI Design: A Tutorial." I.E.E.E. *Circuits and Devices Magazine* (January 1985).

SMALL, C. "Programmable-Logic Devices." *EDN* (February 1987).

SMALL, C. "User Programmable Gate Arrays." *EDN* (April 1989).

Chapter 2

ARMSTRONG, J. R. "Chip-Level Modeling with VHDL." Englewood Cliffs, N.J.: Prentice Hall, 1989.

BREUER, M., AND A. FRIEDMAN. *Diagnosis and Reliable Design of Digital Systems.* New York: Computer Science Press, 1976.

D'ABREAU, M. A. "Gate-Level Simulation." I.E.E.E. *Design and Test* (December 1985).

FRANS, M. "Timing Verification Predicts Performance of Logic Arrays." *EDN* (June 1986).

GOGESCH, R. S. "Logic Simulators Exhibit Different Levels of Device Characterization." *EDN* (October 1988).

ULRICH, E., AND D. HEBERT. "Speed and Accuracy in Digital Network Simulation Based on Structural Modeling." I.E.E.E. 19th Design Automation Conference (1982).

ULRICH, E., AND I. SUETSUGU. "Techniques for Logic and Fault Simulation." *VLSI Systems Design* (October 1986).

Chapter 3

CAVLAN, N. "Third Generation PLD Architecture Breaks AND-OR Bottleneck." WESCON 1985 Conference Proceedings.

GHEISSARI, A. "Programmable Macro Logic: New Solutions for Designers." *1989 Programmable Logic Guide.* Manhasset, N.Y.: High Performance Systems.

JENKINS, J. "Bridging the Gap Between PLDs and Gate Arrays." *ESD* (January 1989).

JENKINS, J., B. LUNDEBERG, AND B. SCHONING. "Programmable Macro Logic," *1987 Semicustom Design Guide.* VLSI Systems Design.

PLD Data Manual. Signetics (1991).

TAGHVAEI, N. "Macros Aid High-Density Design Work." *1990 Programmable Logic Design Guide.* Manhasset, N.Y.: High Performance Systems.

TAGHVAEI, N. "Programmable Macro Logic—The PLD Solution for High-Density Logic Design." WESCON 1990 Conference Proceedings.

WONG, D. K. "Third Generation PLS Architecture and Applications." ELECTRO 1986 Conference Proceedings.

Chapter 4

ALFKE, P. "New Device Extends FPGA Capabilities." *1990 Programmable Logic Design Guide.* Manhasset, N.Y.: High Performance Systems.

FAWCETT, B. "User-Programmable Gate Arrays: Design Methodology and Development Systems." *Microprocessor and Microsystems* (June 1989).

FREEMAN, R. "User Programmable Gate Arrays." I.E.E.E. *Spectrum* (December 1988).

FREEMAN, R. "XC3000 Family of User-Programmable Gate Arrays." *Microprocessor and Microsystems* (June 1989).

KNAPP, S. "Optimizing Programmable Gate Array Designs." WESCON 1988 Conference Proceedings.

LAUTZENHEISER, D. P. "Replace SSI/MSI Glue Chips with a Programmable Array." *Electronic Design* (August 1988).

The Programmable Gate Array Data Book. San Jose, Calif.: Xilinx Corp. (1991).

WAUGH, T. "Programmable Array Serves as a Controller for Dynamic RAMs." *EDN* (February 1988).

Chapter 5

ALTERA Data Book, The. San Jose, Calif.: ALTERA Corporation (1991).

BEACHLER, R. K. "Design Tools for "MAX"-imizing TTL Integration." WESCON 1988 Conference Proceedings.

CREAMER, D., AND J. HONG. "MAX Architecture Addresses Both Gate Intensive and Register Intensive Applications." WESCON 1988 Conference Proceedings.

FARIA, D. "MAX EPLD Family: PAL Speed to FPGA Density." WESCON 1990 Conference Proceedings.

KOPEC, S. "Untangling Confusion in Device Specs." *1990 Programmable Logic Design Guide*. Manhasset, N.Y.: High Performance Systems.

Maximalist Handbook, The. San Jose, Calif.: ALTERA Corporation (1990).

Chapter 6

ACT 1 Data Sheet, The. Sunnyvale, Calif.: ACTEL Corporation, 1989.

ACT 2 Data Sheet, The. Sunnyvale, Calif.: ACTEL Corporation, 1991.

ACT 3 Data Sheet, The. Sunnyvale, Calif.: ACTEL Corporation, 1992.

EL-AYAT, K., ET AL. "A CMOS Electrically Configurable Gate Array." I.E.E.E. 1988 International Solid State Circuits Conference.

EL GAMEL A., ET AL. "An Architecture for Electrically Configurable Gate Arrays." I.E.E.E. *Journal of Solid State Circuits* (April 1989).

HAINES, A. "Gate Utilization Goes up with Antifuse FPGAs." *High Performance Systems* (October 1989).

HAINES, A. "Field Programmable Gate Array with Nonvolatile Configuration." *Microprocessor and Microsystems* (June 1989).

HAMDY, E., ET AL. "Dielectric Based Antifuse for Logic and Memory ICs." I.E.E.E. *IEDM88* (1988).

McCARTY, D. "Interpreting FPLD Gate-Density Data." *1990 Programmable Logic Design Guide*. Manhasset, N.Y.: High Performance Systems.

MOHSEN, A. "Desktop-Configurable Channelled Gate Arrays." *CLSI Systems Design* (August 1988).

Chapter 8

EE DATA Book. Santa Clara, Calif.: EXEL Microelectronics, Inc., 1988.

ERA60100 Data Sheet. Scotts Valley, Calif.: Plessey Semiconductors, 1989.

FPGA 2020 Data Sheet. San Jose, Calif.: PLUS Logic, 1990.

GOETTING, E. "Designing with Multi-Level EEPLDs." WESCON 1988 Conference Proceedings.

HASTIE, N., AND R. CLIFF. "The Implementation of Hardware Subroutines of Field Programmable Gate Arrays." I.E.E.E. 1990 Custom Integrated Circuits Conference Proceedings.

JIGOUR, R. "PEEL Arrays—Bridging the Gap Between PLDs and FPGAs." San Jose, Calif.: ICT, Inc. (1989).

KASSIMIDIS, S. "Use FPGAs to Match a CPU to Its Memory Subsystem." *Electronic Design* (February 1990).

1990 Data Book. San Jose, Calif.: ICT User Programmable Integrated Circuits.

1990 Design Guide. San Jose, Calif.: PLUS Logic.

PAL Conversion Guide with Xilinx EPLD Data Sheets. San Jose, Calif.: Xilinx Corporation, 1993.

SELTZER, J. "A High-Speed Predictable Field Programmable Gate Array." WESCON 1990 Conference Proceedings.

WILSON, R. "PLUS Logic Chip Reflects New PLD Focus on Usability." *Computer Design* (November 1989).

Chapter 9

CLi 6000 Series Field Programmable Gate Arrays. Sunnyvale, Calif.: Concurrent Logic, Inc., 1991.

CPZ0K 1992 Databook. Santa Clara, Calif.: Crosspoint Solutions, Inc., 1992.

FPGAS Databook. Santa Clara, Calif.: Quicklogic, 1992.

iFX780 Data Sheet. Santa Clara, Calif.: Intel Corporation, 1993.

Chapter 10

Benchmark Suite #1, Version 1.2. San Jose, Calif.: Programmable Electronics Performance Corp., 1993.

Electronic Industry Association. JEDEC Standard No. 12-2, Standard for Cell-Based Integrated Circuit Benchmark Set (1989) Washington D.C.

Appendix

ARCHAMBEAU, E. "Testability Analysis Techniques: A Critical Survey." *VLSI Systems Design* (December 1985).

BENNETTS, R. G. *Design of Testable Logic Circuits*. London: Addison-Wesley Publishers Ltd., 1984.

WILLIAMS, T., AND K. PARKER. "Design for Testability—A Survey." Proceedings of the I.E.E.E. (January 1983).

Index